# Applied Analysis of Growth, Trade, and Public Policy

Moriki Hosoe · Iltae Kim
Masahiro Yabuta · Woohyung Lee
Editors

# Applied Analysis of Growth, Trade, and Public Policy

## Ten Years of International Academic Exchanges Between JAAE and KEBA

Springer

*Editors*
Moriki Hosoe
Faculty of Economics
Kumamoto Gakuen University
Kumamoto, Japan

Masahiro Yabuta
Faculty of Economics
Chuo University
Hachioji, Tokyo, Japan

Iltae Kim
Chonnan National University
Gwangju, Korea (Republic of)

Woohyung Lee
Keimyung University
Daegu, Korea (Republic of)

ISBN 978-981-13-1875-7 ISBN 978-981-13-1876-4 (eBook)
https://doi.org/10.1007/978-981-13-1876-4

Library of Congress Control Number: 2018954044



This Springer imprint is published by the registered company Springer Nature Singapore Pte Ltd.
The registered company address is: 152 Beach Road, #21-01/04 Gateway East, Singapore 189721, Singapore

# Preface

This book is the collected papers in commemoration of the tenth anniversary of academic exchange between the Japan Association for Applied Economics (JAAE) and the Korean Economic and Business Association (KEBA). The international exchange of the two academic societies began in 2009. Several researchers from KEBA reported at the JAAE spring meeting in the spring, and several authors from JAAE reported to KEBA's conference in the fall, 10 years passed. We were able to deepen academic exchanges by mutual reporting and discussion. This book analyzes the various problems of growth, trade, and public policy on the basis of applied economics. The research applied here focuses on such areas as public policies, trade and regulation, and development economics. In Part I, the broad problems of growth and regional economy are investigated, considering the economic developments in Japan and Korea. In Part II, trade and foreign investment in Japan are studied, mainly on an empirical basis. In Part III, several public policies are examined vis-à-vis economic policy, using tools of applied analysis, and include an applied economic analysis of growth and trade in Korea and Japan. We hope that two associations will promote the further cooperation of academic exchange on the basis of this project. Lastly, we wish to express our special thanks to Prof. Tohru Naito of Doshisha University for his assistance in editing this book.

Kumamoto, Japan — Moriki Hosoe
Gwangju, Korea (Republic of) — Iltae Kim
Tokyo, Japan — Masahiro Yabuta
Daegu, Korea (Republic of) — Woohyung Lee
July 2018

# Contents

# Contributors

**Choi Chang Kon** Chonbuk National University, Jeonju, South Korea

**Jiah Choi** Bank of Korea, Seoul, South Korea

**Jihye Choi** Chonnam National University, Gwangju, South Korea

**Katsufumi Fukuda** Hiroshima University, Higashihiroshima, Japan

**Minoru Hayashida** The University of Kitakyushu, Kitakyushu, Japan

**S.-J. Hwang** Kyungpook National University, Daegu, South Korea

**Maria Ikegawa** Policy Research Institute of MAFF, Tokyo, Japan

**Kimihito Ise** Japan Electric Power Information Center, Tokyo, Japan

**Chongung Kim** Daegu Hanny University, Gyeongsan, South Korea

**Iltae Kim** Chonnam National University, Gwangju, South Korea

**Young-Jae Kim** Pusan National University, Busan, South Korea

**Keiki Kumagae** Kyushu University, Fukuoka, Japan

**Ki-Dong Lee** Keimyung University, Daegu, South Korea

**Woohyung Lee** Keimyung University, Daegu, South Korea

**X. Li** Kyungpook National University, Daegu, South Korea

**Koshi Maeda** Kyushu University, Fukuoka, Japan

**Sijin Moon** Pusan National University, Busan, South Korea

**Keisuke Morita** Kanagawa University, Yokohama, Japan

**Daisuke Nakamura** Fukuoka Women's University, Fukuoka, Japan

**Ryoichi Nanba** Cabinet Office, Government of Japan, Tokyo, Japan

**Hiroyuki Ohno** Toyo University, Tokyo, Japan

**Hitoshi Osaka** Kyoto Sangyo University, Kyoto, Japan

**Eun-Yub Park** Pusan National University, Busan, South Korea

**Kohya Takahashi** Kyushu University, Fukuoka, Japan

**Suminori Tokunaga** Reitaku University, Kashiwa, Japan

**Masahiro Yabuta** Chuo University, Tokyo, Japan

**Masaya Yasuoka** Kwansei Gakuin University, Nishinomiya, Japan

# Part I
# Growth and Regional Development

# Chapter 1
# The Middle-Income Trap Reconsidered: The Case of Asia

**Hitoshi Osaka**

## 1.1 Introduction

"Middle-income trap" is a relatively new term in economics that has, however, drawn tremendous attention in the economic development and growth field. Han and Wei (2017) emphasize the importance of the issue by introducing a paper written by Gill and Kharas (2015), the inventors of this term. Using a search of Google Scholar, Gill and Kharas (2015) identify more than 3,000 articles that include the term "middle-income trap".[1] Many of these studies have analyzed the middle-income trap issue to clarify the phenomenon and investigate the determinants. In this study, we focus on the issue more from the perspective of changes in the industrial structure during economic development and discuss early deindustrialization in middle-income countries as a key factor of this trap.

The importance of changes in the industrial structure during stages of economic development is one of the fundamental issues that has been taught in textbooks about development economics. For example, Todaro and Smith (2011) introduce the consequences by highlighting the classical works of Chenery and his colleagues.[2] In their empirical research, Chenery and his colleagues focus on structural changes associated with economic growth, which suggest particular patterns of development. In their analyses, they employ cross-country and time-series data analysis, and highlight several features of economic development. For example, they emphasize the importance of both physical and human capital accumulation, changes in consumer demands from basic agricultural foods to manufactured products, the decline in family size and population growth, and the growth of cities and urban industries.[3]

[1] Gill and Kharas (2015), p. 6.
[2] For example, see Chenery and Syrquin (1975).
[3] Todaro and Smith (2011), p. 121.

H. Osaka (✉)
Kyoto Sangyo University, Kyoto, Japan
e-mail: osaka@cc.kyoto-su.ac.jp



M. Hosoe et al. (eds.), *Applied Analysis of Growth, Trade, and Public Policy*,
https://doi.org/10.1007/978-981-13-1876-4_1

The basic concept of industrial transformation may depend on a simple assumption: every country follows a similar, if not the same, development pattern. In other words, many poor developing countries are likely to experience development patterns similar to those of rich developed countries. Moreover, the law of Petty-Clark seems to be a universal phenomenon: the importance of the industrial structure shifts from agriculture to manufacturing, and then from manufacturing to service associated with economic development. This development pattern applies to many developing countries as well as developed countries, although to different degrees. The speed of development may also differ among developing countries. Recently, it has been thought that middle-income countries are somehow trapped in the middle of industrialization, and hence at the mid-level of economic growth. Some developing countries have been faced with deindustrialization much below the level experienced by developed countries. In addition to the concept of the middle-income trap, the notion of "premature deindustrialization" in developing countries has now emerged as a research interest.

This paper is organized as follows. Following the introduction, in Sect. 1.2 we conduct a brief literature review regarding the middle-income trap, especially focusing on structural change and economic development in recent works. Section 1.3 presents the descriptive data analysis. We then introduce our regression framework and review the empirical results in Sect. 1.4, followed by concluding remarks in Sect. 1.5.

## 1.2 Literature Review

As Gill and Kharas (2015), and Han and Wei (2017) note, there is a large volume of research on the middle-income trap issue. We limit our literature review to a selection of recently written papers, and first review Gill and Kharas (2015), who initially suggested the issue in their 2007 paper. In their review paper, Gill and Kharas (2015) emphasize three points. First, they point out the lack of a suitable growth theory that could offer the policy options for middle-income countries. They suggest that endogenous growth theories consider the problem in high-income countries and the Solow growth model is useful for the development problem in low-income countries, while no satisfactory theories are available to consider the problem in middle-income countries, which are home to 5 billion people.[4] Second, their use of "trap" is based on empirical findings that indicate past growth experiences but do not suggest future growth. They warn policy makers in middle-income countries to pay more attention to their development policies to avoid a period of growth below their potential.[5] Third, they emphasize the meaning of "trap" not to deny the growth capabilities of middle-income countries but as a situation that middle-income countries can fall

[4]Gill and Kharas (2015), p. 4.
[5]Ibid.

in to.[6] They also suggest that the experiences of East Asian countries highlight an outward orientation, financial deepening, and technology and innovation as important policy issues.[7]

The existing literature might be divided into two groups: (1) those who acknowledge the issue of the middle-income trap and (2) those who do not support its existence. First, Eichengreen et al. (2013) focus on the issue of the middle-income trap in their analysis. In their regressions using cross-country data, they find possible growth slowdowns in sample countries at two different income levels: $10,000–$11,000 and $15,000– $16,000 (PPP, 2005US $).[8] Moreover, they suggest that high levels of secondary and tertiary education and higher proportions of high-technology product exports may help avoid the middle-income trap, while growth slowdowns are often found in economies with high old dependency ratios, high investment rates, and undervalued real exchange rates.[9] In addition to the importance of high quality human capital and a higher share of high-technology product exports, Eichengreen et al. (2013) also indicate that political and financial stability are consequences of sustainable growth. Ito's (2016) view is different from that of Eichengreen et al. (2013), explaining this issue by emphasizing the different convergence of income groups in Asia. According to Ito (2016), countries need innovations through policy reforms to move to a higher convergence of income groups.

On the other hand, Im and Rosenblatt (2013), Bulman et al. (2014), and Han and Wei (2017) cast doubt on the issue. Bulman et al. (2014) deny the existence of the middle-income trap by indicating the fast growing countries that do not show any growth slowdowns at the middle-income level.[10] However, they find different growth determinants at low and high income levels. In their cross-country regressions, they suggest that industrialization, openness, and equality are positively associated with economic growth at the middle-income level. However, in their analysis, education and innovation are not clearly associated with economic growth at the low and middleincome levels. Han and Wei (2017) also do not support the notion of the "middle-income trap," including the "low-income trap." In their transition matrix analysis, countries in the low and middle-income levels have a more than 50% chance of having a positive growth rate, and an average country can move to a higher income level given enough time.[11] Similar to Bulman et al. (2014), they suggest that countries have different economic fundamentals and development policies. Han and Wei (2017) summarize that a large working age population, sex ratio imbalance, macroeconomic stability, and financial development might be the key determinants for any developing countries at the middle-income level. Im and Rosenblatt (2013) also present a transition matrix analysis that does not support the middle-income trap.

---

[6]Ibid.

[7]Ibid., p. 20.

[8]Eichengreen et al. (2013), p. 10.

[9]Ibid.

[10]Bulman et al. (2014), p. 20.

[11]Han and Wei (2017), p. 26.

In relation to economic growth in middle-income countries, many researchers focus on the issue of structural change, notably industrialization (or deindustrialization). There are numerous works in development economics that investigate the relationship between industrialization and economic growth. Dasgupta and Singh (2006), for example, recall Kaldor who sees manufacturing as an engine of growth,[12] and suggest a higher income elasticity of demand for manufacturing products than for agriculture products.[13] This association between manufacturing and economic growth is now receiving new attention. "Deindustrialization" has recently emerged as a consequential issue for developing countries since they face this issue at a much lower level of income than experienced by developed countries. In this literature review, we thus highlight the issue of premature deindustrialization as one of the possible explanations for the middle-income trap.

The examinations of premature deindustrialization have two dimensions: cross-country data analysis and individual country data analysis. Recent cross-country analyses of premature deindustrialization can be found, for example, in Dasgupta and Singh (2006), Felipe et al. (2014), and Rodrik (2015). Dasgupta and Singh (2006) employ a cross-country analysis of 48 countries for the period 1990–2000. They emphasize premature deindustrialization in terms of employment. Felipe et al. (2014) utilize data from 52 countries. They find that manufacturing employment share, which was previously around 18–20%, has now declined to around 13–16%.[14] They moreover find that manufacturing employment is more important than manufacturing output for economic growth.[15] Rodrik (2015) uses data of 42 countries from the Groningen Growth and Development Center for the period of the late 1940s or early 1950s to the early 2010s. He observes the recent trend of deindustrialization, and suggests both globalization and labor-saving technology contribute to growth in manufacturing.

Moreover, single country-based analyses are found in McCaig and Pavcnik (2013) for Vietnam, McCaig et al. (2015) for Botswana, and Lawrence and Edwards (2013) for the United States. The outcomes of these studies are somewhat similar to those in the cross-country analyses.

Last, the objectives of our empirical analyses are similar to Felipe et al. (2014) in considering the issue of the middle-income trap. We reexamine their agendas[16] in the case of Asian countries as follows:

[12]Dasgupta and Singh (2006), p. 1. Moreover, in this paper, we use "industry" and "manufacturing" synonymously in most cases. This is especially important in Sect. 1.4, where we employ sector level data of industry rather than of manufacturing. Manufacturing data are simply not available at the time this paper is written.

[13]Dasgupta and Singh (2006), p. 3.

[14]Felipe et al. (2014), p. 22.

[15]Ibid., p. 5.

[16]Ibid., p. 2.

(1) The industrial sector's peak employment share has declined.
(2) The turning points of the inverted U curves for both employment and GDP have declined over time.
(3) The inverted U curve is more evident in employment than output.

Based on the above, we attempt to provide a possible explanation for the middle-income trap in view of the changes in industrial structure in the Asian region, notably deindustrialization.

## 1.3 Descriptive Data Analysis

Inspired by Ito (2016), we calculated the decade average of real GDP per capita (PPP, 2011US$) and its growth rate for the period of 1990–2014. The results are found in Table 1.1, which compare each income level of LIC (low income countries), LMIC (lower middle income countries), UMIC (upper middle income countries), and HIC (high income countries) at the global level, classified based on the World Bank.[17] It is understandable that the standard neo-classical growth model may require conditions necessary for unconditional convergence. The growth rates of each income level need to fulfill the following condition:

$$LIC > LMIC > UMIC > HIC$$

However, the worldwide growth rates of each income level for the sample period of 1990–2014 are shown in Table 1.1 as:

$$UMIC(3.769\%) > LMIC(3.171\%) > HIC(1.565\%) > LIC(1.181\%)$$

This may imply that there is no worldwide unconditional convergence over the period. Moreover, LIC could be trapped at the low income level as their growth rates are the lowest. If we only focus on the middle-income countries (LMIC and UMIC), it is very plausible that LMIC and UMIC can catch up with HIC at some point in time since their growth rates are higher than those of HIC. To escape from the middle-income trap, the following condition needs to be fulfilled.

$$LMIC \text{ or } UMIC > HIC$$

Table 1.1 demonstrates that LMIC and UMIC meet the necessary condition and their average growth rates are higher than those of HIC. This means our sample countries might be able to catch up with HIC at some time in the future if they maintain their current growth rates in the long term.

---

[17] The World Bank data for each income level are only available since the 1990s (World Bank 2017).

**Table 1.1** GDP per capita growth rates (Decade average)

| | 1990s | 2000s | 2010s | 1990–2014 |
|---|---|---|---|---|
| LIC | −0.538 | 1.915 | 2.809 | 1.181 |
| LMIC | 1.454 | 4.163 | 4.279 | 3.171 |
| UMIC | 1.493 | 5.325 | 4.752 | 3.769 |
| HIC | 1.980 | 1.256 | 1.435 | 1.565 |
| World | 1.277 | 2.437 | 2.611 | 2.038 |

Source: Author's estimation based on the World Bank (2017)
Notes: (World Bank classification for each income level, 2015): LIC (annual GNI per capita is less than US$1,025), LMIC (US$1,026–US$4,035), UMIC (US$4,036–US$12,475), HIC (more than US$12,476)

## 1.4 Regression Analysis

Our descriptive data analysis reveals that the middle-income trap can be avoided if LMIC and UMIC maintain their current levels of economic growth until they catch up with HIC. We now investigate this possibility in view of structural changes associated with economic development, notably deindustrialization, in our sample countries. As noted in the existing literature, the inverted U curve between per capita GDP and the industrial sector's share in economic development can be observed in both GDP and employment. In this section, we empirically examine those associations for our sample countries in Asia.[18] The findings of premature deindustrialization may cast doubt on the continuity of the current growth rates in our sample countries. We pay particular attention to possible growth slowdowns in the region. The following standard regression framework is used for this analysis.

$$Y = c + \alpha_x X + \alpha_o O + \varepsilon \tag{1.1}$$

The dependent variable, Y, is the share of the industry sector in either GDP or employment. The independent variables in X are both per capita GDP and its square, which examine the inverted U curve between the two variables of income level and the level of industrialization. Moreover, the independent variables in O indicate other variables of interest in the regressions, including population, trade openness, investment, and two different education variables, which are selected based on previous

[18]Our sample countries in this analysis are Australia, Bangladesh, China, Hong Kong, India, Indonesia, Japan, South Korea, Malaysia, New Zealand, Pakistan, the Philippines, Singapore, Sri Lanka and Thailand (15 countries).

studies such as Eichengreen et al. (2013), and Felipe et al. (2014). $\varepsilon$ is the error term. Our final regression is specified as follows:

$$\begin{aligned} LYIND(\text{ or } LEMPIND) = c &+ \alpha_1 LGDPH + \alpha_2 SLGDPH + \alpha_3 LPOP \\ &+ \alpha_4 SLPOP + \alpha_5 LOPEN + \alpha_6 LGFCF + \alpha_7 LSECEDU \\ &+ \alpha_8 LTEREDU + \alpha_9 YearDummy + \alpha_{10} RegionalDummy \end{aligned} \quad (1.2)$$

The necessary data are obtained from the World Bank (2015). The details for the variables are as follows: LYIND (log of the industry sector's share of GDP), LEMPIND (log of the industry sector's share of employment), LGDPH (log of per capita GDP, 2005 constant US dollars), SLGDPH (the squared value of LGDPH), LPOP (log of population), SLPOP (the squared value of LPOP), LOPEN (log of trade openness), LGFCF (log of gross fixed capital formation's share of GDP), LSECEDU (log of the secondary education enrollment ratio, gross), LTEREDU (log of the tertiary education enrollment ratio, gross). Moreover, we include two different dummy variables: a year dummy for the 1960s, 1970s, 1980s, 1990s, 2000s, and a regional dummy for South Asia and East Asia. Our sample includes 15 countries in Asia and the Pacific over the period 1960–2013. Data availability varies among the sample countries. We have examined the inverted U curve of industrialization in two dimensions in our pooled regressions, one for GDP and the other for employment.

### *1.4.1 Deindustrialization in GDP*

Appendices 1.1 and 1.2 show our regression results for the GDP data. Model 1 is the base model and the year dummy variables are included in Model 2. We also include the variables of interest in both Models 3 and 4. In particular, the variables of gross fixed capital formation (LGFCF) and trade openness (LOPEN) are included in Model 3 while the education variables of secondary education enrollment ratio (LSECEDU) and tertiary education enrollment ratio (LTEREDU) are added in Model 4. Population (LPOP) and its squared value (SLPOP) are included in both Models 3 and 4. Moreover, we include the regional dummy variables in Model 1, and at least one dummy variable is statistically significant. Therefore, we conduct a separate regression for each region: East Asia and South Asia. We find five observations.

First, the two income variables, LGDPH and SLGDPH, exhibit the expected signs and an inverted U curve at the 1% significance level in all regressions. Second, the year dummy variables generally perform very poorly. Only the dummy variable for the 1960s is statistically significant. Third, the education variables are statistically significant. The secondary education enrollment ratio, LSECEDU, contributes to industrialization. On the other hand, the tertiary education enrollment ratio, LTEREDU, promotes deindustrialization. Promotion of higher education may enhance activities in the service sector, which may reduce the portion of industrial output in GDP. Fourth, the coefficient for the regional dummy variable for South Asia is negative in the regression, which implies a lower inverted U curve for South Asia than for other countries. Moreover, separate regressions demonstrate that the estimated inverted U curves are indeed different among the sub-regions in Asia. Finally, the variables of interest, LPOP, SLPOP, LOPEN, and LGCFC, do not demonstrate robust results, as their signs and parameter values vary in the regression models.

In summary, the regression results generally indicate the expected outcomes in line with existing literature, although the variables of interest do not exhibit statistically meaningful results.

### *1.4.2 Deindustrialization in Employment*

Appendices 1.3 and 1.4 exhibit our regression results for employment data. Similar to the regressions for GDP data, Model 1 is regarded as the base model and the year dummy variables are included in Model 2. We also include the variables of interest in both Models 3 and 4. Moreover, we include the regional dummy variables in Model 1, which in fact demonstrate regional differences for East Asia and South Asia. Therefore, we also examine separate regressions for each region. We find five observations.

First, the two income variables, LGDPH and SLGDPH, exhibit the expected signs and inverted U curve at the 1% significance level in all regressions. Second, the dummy variables for the 1980s and 1990s are significant in the regressions. Third, the education variables are statistically significant, and the secondary education enrollment ratio, LSECEDU, contributes to industrialization in East Asia. On the other hand, the tertiary education enrollment ratio, LTEREDU, promotes deindustrialization in East Asia; these results are similar to the regression results for the GDP data. Fourth, the coefficients for the regional dummy variables for both East Asia and South Asia are positive in the regression, which implies a higher inverted U curve for both regions. Moreover, separate regional regressions for employment data also demonstrate that the estimated inverted U curves differ among the sub-regions in Asia. In sum, the regression results generally indicate the expected outcomes, consistent with recent literature.

### *1.4.3 Discussion*

Based on Model 1's results, we estimate the turning point for each inverted U curve as indicated in Table 1.2. Moreover, the actual data and estimated fitted lines are shown in Figs. 1.1, 1.2 and 1.3. Table 1.2 provides perplexing results in two ways. First, there is a large gap in the estimated turning points between GDP and employment. Per capita GDP at the peak income level for all sample countries is US$3,380 while

**Table 1.2** Estimated turning points

| Data | Model 1 | Estimated turning point (US$, 2005 price) |
|---|---|---|
| GDP | All countries | 3,380 |
| | East Asia | 2,347 |
| | South Asia | 1,417 |
| Employment | All countries | 14,484 |
| | East Asia | 21,881 |
| | South Asia | 1,281 |

Source: Author's estimation.

that for employment is US$14,484. Moreover, the difference in peak income levels in East Asia and South Asia is much bigger in the employment data. The turning point in East Asia is US$21,881, while it is just US$1,281 in South Asia. The large differences in peak income levels for the inverted U curve are not, however, unique to this kind of analysis as Dasgupta and Singh (2006) estimate that the turning point of the inverted U curve has been declined from per capita of about US$10,000 to US$3,00 in some countries.[19] Table 1.2 also demonstrates a higher turning point for East Asia compared with that of South Asia in both GDP and cmployment regressions. Our estimation thus supports premature deindustrialization, which is evident in the region. It should be noted, however, that our estimation is preliminary, and depends on the data availability of sample countries. This result thus needs to be treated with caution since it is based on pooled OLS regressions.

Moreover, Figs. 1.1, 1.2 and 1.3 demonstrate both actual and fitted values of the proportion of the industry sector in both GDP and employment. In particular, Fig. 1.1 shows the actual and fitted values for the industry sector share in GDP while Fig. 1.2 shows them for employment. These figures clearly indicate that deindustrialization begins at a lower income level in South Asia compared to East Asia.

Figure 1.3 shows that the estimated turning points of the inverted U curve in the regressions for employment have declined over time. Since our regression results indicate that the most of the dummy variables for the year are not statistically significant for GDP, we only show the fitted values for employment.[20] These figures are evidence that the turning points of the inverted U curve for employment have declined over time.

[19]Dasgupta and Singh (2006), p. 5.

[20]It should be noted, however, that in the regressions for GDP, Appendices 1.1 to 1.4 show the year dummy variable as statistically significant only for the 1960s, but not for other years. Moreover, the dummy variable for the 2000s in the regressions for employment is not statistically significant at the 10% level.

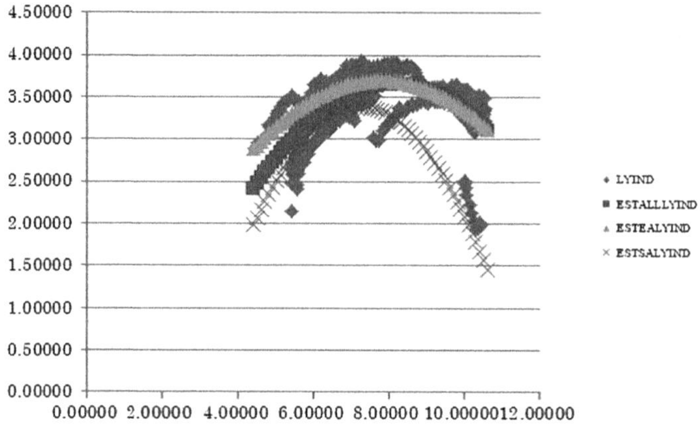


**Fig. 1.1** Actual and fitted LYIND (All sample countries, East Asia, and South Asia)

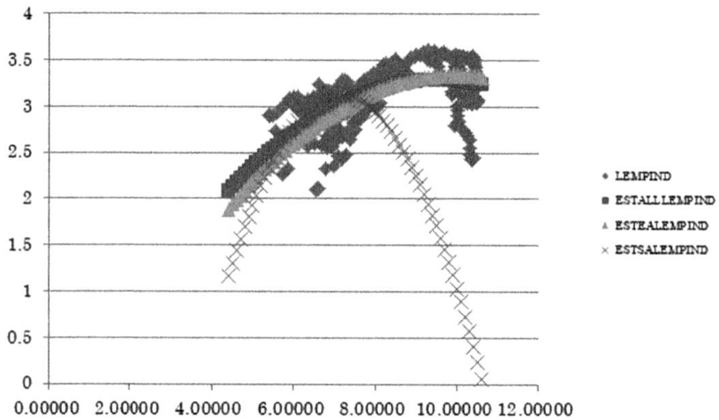


**Fig. 1.2** Actual and fitted LEMPIND (All sample countries, East Asia, and South Asia)

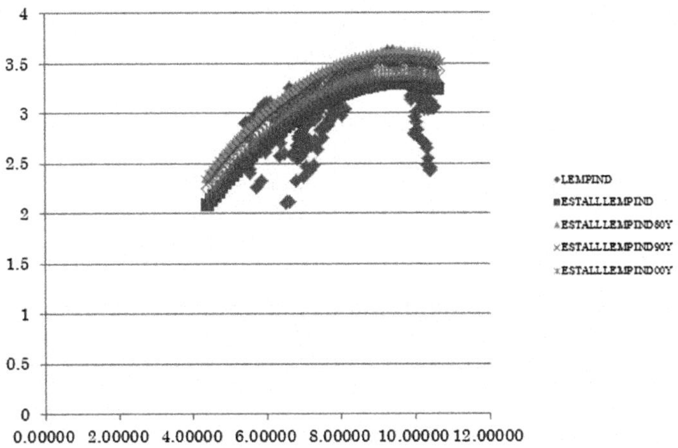


**Fig. 1.3** Actual and fitted LEMPIND (all sample countries, the data for 1980s, 1990s, and 2000s)

Notes for Figs. 1.1, 1.2, and 1.3:

LYIND (the share of industry sector output in GDP, log, actual data), ESTALL-LYIND (the estimated fitted value of LYIND, using all sample data), ESTEALYIND (the estimated fitted value of LYIND, using the data for East Asia), ESTSALYIND (the estimated fitted value of LYIND, using the data for South Asia), LEMPIND (the share of industry sector employment in total employment, log, actual data), ESTALLLEMPIND (the estimated fitted value of LEMPIND, using all sample data), ESTEALEMPIND (the estimated fitted value of LEMPIND, using the data for East Asia), ESTSALEMPIND (the estimated fitted value of LEMPIND, using the data for South Asia), ESTALLEMPIND80Y (the estimated fitted value of LEMPIND, using the data for the 1980s), ESTALLEMPIND90Y (the estimated fitted value of LEMPIND, using the data for the 1990s), ESTALLEMPIND00Y (the estimated fitted value of LEMPIND, using the data for the 2000s).

## 1.5 Concluding Remarks

In this study, we reconsider the issue of the middle-income trap. We first focus on the cross-country data and examine the growth trends of different income levels at the global level, which appear to be generally free from such a trap. However, when we focus on the issue of premature deindustrialization, our empirical analysis suggests it is a possibility, as well as a plausible explanation for regional growth slowdowns in Asia in the future. In particular, we revisit three agendas suggested by Felipe et al. (2014). Our empirical results provide evidence to support them. First, the peak employment share for the industry sector has declined, and is evident from the different turning points for employment share in East Asia and South Asia. Second, the turning points of the inverted U curve for both employment and GDP have declined over time. In this study, our estimation provides evidence for employment but not for GDP. Third, the inverted U curve is more evident in employment than in output. These results may also provide evidence for the importance of educational attainment in avoiding the middle-income trap suggested by Eichengreen et al. (2013).

Finally, we note that our empirical analysis is preliminary since most of the analysis is based on pooled data regressions. The analysis needs to be reexamined using other econometric methods when relevant data becomes more available.

**Acknowledgements** We gratefully acknowledge the financial support of the Japan Society for the Promotion of Science (JSPS) "Grants-in-Aid for Scientific Research" on this research (Kakenhi (c): No.15K03480). This is a modified version of "The effect of premature deindustrialization on labor productivity and economic growth in Asia," which was initially presented at the 74th Conference of the Japan Society of International Economics (JSIE), Senshu University, November 8, 2015. This is moreover the second version of the paper presented at the JAAE Spring Session, Kurume University, June 17–18, 2017.

## Appendix 1.1: Regression Result 1 (Dependent Variable: LYIND)

| | All Countries | | East Asia | | South Asia | |
|---|---|---|---|---|---|---|
| | Model 1 | Model 2 | Model 1 | Model 2 | Model 1 | Model 2 |
| Constant | -2.255 | -0.452 | -0.628 | 0.213 | -5.698 | -4.944 |
| | ***(0.337) | (0.297) | **(0.282) | (0.357) | ***(1.396) | ***(1.493) |
| LGDPH | 1.454 | 1.081 | 1.114 | 0.916 | 2.503 | 2.311 |
| | ***(0.088) | ***(0.082) | ***(0.080) | ***(0.087) | ***(0.437) | ***(0.466) |
| SLGDPH | -0.089 | -0.070 | -0.072 | -0.061 | -0.172 | -0.160 |
| | ***(0.006) | ***(0.005) | ***(0.005) | ***(0.006) | ***(0.034) | ***(0.036) |
| Year60s | | -0.155 | | -0.217 | | -0.079 |
| | | ***(0.054) | | ***(0.083) | | (0.049) |
| Year70s | | -0.055 | | -0.037 | | -0.061 |
| | | (0.050) | | (0.080) | | (0.044) |
| Year80s | | -0.008 | | 0.022 | | -0.052 |
| | | (0.045) | | (0.075) | | (0.037) |
| Year90s | | 0.047 | | 0.100 | | -0.016 |
| | | (0.045) | | (0.075) | | (0.034) |
| Year00s | | -0.002 | | 0.005 | | -0.015 |
| | | (0.053) | | (0.088) | | (0.032) |
| RegionEA | | 0.012 | | | | |
| | | (0.042) | | | | |
| RegionSA | | -0.366 | | | | |
| | | ***(0.045) | | | | |
| Obs | 687 | 687 | 395 | 395 | 216 | 216 |
| F-test | 145.49 | 158.66 | 140.34 | 78.88 | 166.37 | 53.79 |
| Prob > F | 0.000 | 0.000 | 0.000 | 0.000 | 0.000 | 0.000 |
| $R^2$ | 0.394 | 0.559 | 0.314 | 0.353 | 0.605 | 0.612 |

## Appendix 1.2: Regression Result 2 (Dependent Variable: LYIND)

| | All Countries | | East Asia | | South Asia | |
|---|---|---|---|---|---|---|
| | Model 3 | Model 4 | Model 3 | Model 4 | Model 3 | Model 4 |
| Constant | -0.732 | -14.636 | -1.200 | -47.774 | 15.214 | -12.528 |
| | (0.989) | ***(2.144) | (2.158) | ***(4.269) | ***(1.585) | ***(3.292) |
| LGDPH | 1.472 | 1.874 | 1.755 | 2.070 | 1.674 | 1.593 |
| | ***(0.110) | ***(0.191) | ***(0.162) | ***(0.205) | ***(0.296) | ***(0.316) |
| SLGDPH | -0.092 | -0.117 | -0.107 | -0.122 | -0.124 | -0.112 |
| | ***(0.007) | ***(0.012) | ***(0.010) | ***(0.012) | ***(0.023) | ***(0.025) |
| LPOP | -0.312 | 1.162 | -0.310 | 4.259 | -1.710 | 1.043 |
| | ***(0.086) | ***(0.194) | (0.190) | ***(0.416) | ***(0.159) | ***(0.336) |
| SLPOP | 0.009 | -0.029 | 0.011 | -0.108 | 0.043 | -0.029 |
| | ***(0.002) | **(0.005) | **(0.004) | ***(0.011) | ***(0.004) | ***(0.009) |
| LOPEN | -0.073 | -0.065 | 0.012 | 0.234 | -0.344 | -0.234 |
| | (0.048) | (0.049) | (0.074) | ***(0.051) | ***(0.029) | ***(0.037) |
| LGFCF | -0.021 | -0.081 | -0.141 | -0.078 | 0.236 | 0.194 |
| | (0.055) | *(0.048) | **(0.061) | (0.079) | ***(0.043) | ***(0.055) |
| LSECEDU | | 0.111 | | 0.227 | | 0.246 |
| | | **(0.046) | | ***(0.083) | | ***(0.048) |
| LTEREDU | | -0.055 | | -0.192 | | 0.036 |
| | | **(0.025) | | ***(0.043) | | (0.034) |
| Year60s | -0.113 | | 0.076 | | -0.494 | |
| | *(0.068) | | (0.140) | | ***(0.053) | |
| Year70s | -0.087 | -0.088 | 0.083 | 0.191 | -0.410 | -0.004 |
| | (0.061) | (0.072) | (0.123) | *(0.103) | ***(0.047) | (0.071) |
| Year80s | -0.015 | 0.035 | 0.145 | 0.245 | -0.372 | -0.020 |
| | (0.055) | (0.064) | (0.104) | ***(0.081) | ***(0.041) | (0.054) |
| Year90s | 0.040 | 0.035 | 0.173 | 0.161 | -0.224 | 0.002 |
| | (0.046) | (0.052) | **(0.082) | **(0.069) | ***(0.037) | (0.046) |
| Year00s | 0.001 | 0.007 | 0.023 | 0.056 | -0.083 | 0.011 |
| | (0.051) | (0.047) | (0.085) | (0.055) | ***(0.028) | (0.027) |
| RegionEA | 0.058 | -0.428 | | | | |
| | (0.037) | ***(0.085) | | | | |
| RegionSA | -0.283 | -0.755 | | | | |
| | ***(0.037) | ***(0.084) | | | | |
| Obs | 605 | 389 | 357 | 250 | 172 | 84 |
| F-test | 251.08 | 133.30 | 47.29 | 62.91 | 166.98 | 118.36 |
| Prob > F | 0.000 | 0.000 | 0.000 | 0.000 | 0.000 | 0.000 |
| $R^2$ | 0.577 | 0.682 | 0.393 | 0.734 | 0.869 | 0.941 |

## Appendix 1.3: Regression Result 3 (Dependent Variable: LEMPIND)

| | All Countries | | East Asia | | South Asia | |
|---|---|---|---|---|---|---|
| | Model 1 | Model 2 | Model 1 | Model 2 | Model 1 | Model 2 |
| Constant | -0.850 | -2.765 | -1.286 | -2.060 | -10.121 | -11.895 |
| | *(0.512) | ***(0.803) | (0.994) | **(0.967) | ***(2.779) | ***(2.879) |
| LGDPH | 0.864 | 1.180 | 0.926 | 1.050 | 3.704 | 4.098 |
| | ***(0.126) | ***(0.188) | ***(0.237) | ***(0.226) | ***(0.858) | ***(0.871) |
| SLGDPH | -0.045 | -0.061 | -0.046 | -0.053 | -0.259 | -0.280 |
| | ***(0.008) | ***(0.011) | ***(0.014) | ***(0.013) | ***(0.066) | ***(0.066) |
| Year80s | | 0.304 | | 0.312 | | 0.275 |
| | | ***(0.068) | | ***(0.087) | | ***(0.071) |
| Year90s | | 0.235 | | 0.273 | | 0.094 |
| | | ***(0.066) | | ***(0.084) | | *(0.055) |
| Year00s | | 0.109 | | 0.107 | | 0.081 |
| | | (0.067) | | (0.086) | | (0.053) |
| RegionEA | | 0.181 | | | | |
| | | ***(0.027) | | | | |
| RegionSA | | 0.446 | | | | |
| | | ***(0.051) | | | | |
| Obs | 403 | 403 | 282 | 282 | 67 | 67 |
| F-test | 104.90 | 70.69 | 53.42 | 69.25 | 41.86 | 24.66 |
| Prob > F | 0.000 | 0.000 | 0.000 | 0.000 | 0.000 | 0.000 |
| $R^2$ | 0.370 | 0.504 | 0.386 | 0.465 | 0.673 | 0.774 |

## Appendix 1.4: Regression Result 4 (Dependent Variable: LEMPIND)

Notes for Appendices 1.1, 1.2, 1.3, and 1.4: the pooled OLS regressions.

LYIND: the share of industry sector output in GDP (%, log).

LEMPIND: the share of industry sector employment in total employment (%, log).

LGDPH, and SLGDPH: per capita GDP (constant international dollar, 2005 price, log), and its squared value, respectively.

LPOP, and SLPOP: population (log), and its squared value, respectively.

LOPEN: trade openness in GDP (%, log).

LGFCF: the share of gross fixed capital formation in GDP (%, log).

LSECEDU, LTEREDU: the secondary education enrollment ratio, and the tertiary education enrollment ratio, respectively (%, log).

Year60s, Year70s, Year80s, Year90s, and Year00s: the dummy variables for 1960s, 1970s, 1980s, 1990s, and 2000s, respectively.

RegionEA, and RegionSA: the regional dummy variables for East Asia, and South Asia, respectively.

Obs: the number of observations.

***, **, and *: statistical significance at 1, 5, 10%, respectively.

| | All Countries | | East Asia | | South Asia | |
|---|---|---|---|---|---|---|
| | Model 3 | Model 4 | Model 3 | Model 4 | Model 3 | Model 4 |
| Constant | 6.868 | -2.045 | 14.431 | -10.510 | -17.706 | -6.902 |
| | ***(1.482) | ***(1.857) | ***(1.960) | *(5.363) | ***(4.511) | (7.691) |
| LGDPH | 1.667 | 2.015 | 1.914 | 1.807 | 3.666 | 3.733 |
| | ***(0.185) | ***(0.232) | ***(0.271) | ***(0.325) | ***(1.127) | **(1.669) |
| SLGDPH | -0.089 | -0.107 | -0.106 | -0.096 | -0.240 | -0.258 |
| | ***(0.011) | ***(0.013) | ***(0.016) | ***(0.019) | ***(0.087) | *(0.132) |
| LPOP | -1.262 | -0.361 | -2.018 | 0.447 | 0.685 | -0.344 |
| | ***(0.122) | **(0.160) | ***(0.171) | (0.542) | (0.552) | (0.910) |
| SLPOP | 0.035 | 0.011 | 0.055 | -0.011 | -0.017 | 0.010 |
| | ***(0.003) | **(0.004) | ***(0.004) | (0.014) | (0.014) | (0.022) |
| LOPEN | -0.169 | -0.192 | -0.281 | -0.125 | 0.145 | 0.229 |
| | ***(0.031) | ***(0.036) | ***(0.042) | *(0.069) | (0.157) | *(0.111) |
| LGFCF | 0.044 | 0.024 | -0.059 | 0.210 | -0.162 | -0.078 |
| | (0.061) | (0.063) | (0.069) | **(0.096) | (0.128) | (0.172) |
| LSECEDU | | 0.020 | | 0.386 | | -0.280 |
| | | (0.072) | | ***(0.120) | | (0.183) |
| LTEREDU | | -0.170 | | -0.285 | | 0.002 |
| | | ***(0.027) | | ***(0.045) | | (0.145) |
| Year80s | 0.203 | -0.019 | 0.010 | -0.056 | 0.407 | 0.008 |
| | ***(0.066) | (0.072) | (0.080) | (0.103) | ***(0.119) | (0.152) |
| Year90s | 0.204 | 0.048 | 0.140 | 0.008 | 0.187 | -0.029 |
| | ***(0.059) | (0.061) | **(0.067) | (0.075) | *(0.098) | (0.107) |
| Year00s | 0.125 | 0.056 | 0.071 | 0.059 | 0.125 | -0.095 |
| | **(0.055) | (0.052) | (0.063) | (0.057) | *(0.068) | (0.059) |
| RegionEA | 0.324 | 0.120 | | | | |
| | ***(0.033) | **(0.055) | | | | |
| RegionSA | 0.605 | 0.231 | | | | |
| | ***(0.044) | **(0.085) | | | | |
| Obs | 392 | 271 | 272 | 201 | 66 | 29 |
| F-test | 161.71 | 128.32 | 121.75 | 163.18 | 16.93 | 17.15 |
| Prob > F | 0.000 | 0.000 | 0.000 | 0.000 | 0.000 | 0.000 |
| $R^2$ | 0.660 | 0.693 | 0.688 | 0.720 | 0.795 | 0.880 |

## References

Bulman, D., M. Eden, and H. Nguyen. 2014. Transitioning from low-income growth to high-income growth: Is there a middle income trap? *World Bank Policy Research Working Paper 7104*. Washington, D.C.: World Bank.

Chenery, H.B., and M. Syrquin. 1975. *Patterns of Development 1950–1970*. London: Oxford University Press.

Dasgupta, S., and A. Singh. 2006. Manufacturing, services and premature deindustrialization in developing countries. United Nations University, *World Institute for Development Economics Research (UNU-WIDER), Research Paper No. 2006/49*, May.

Eichengreen, B., D. Park, and K. Shin. 2013. Growth slowdowns redux: new evidence on the middle-income trap. *NBER Working Paper Series 18673*. Mass, Cambridge: National Bureau of Economic Research.

Felipe, J., A. Mehta, and C. Rhee. 2014. Manufacturing matters... but it's the jobs that count. *ADB Economics Working Paper Series No. 420*, November.

Gill, I.S., and H. Kharas. 2015. The middle-income trap turns ten. *World Bank Policy Research Working Paper 7403*. Washington, D.C.: World Bank

Han, X., and S.J. Wei. 2017. Re-examining the middle-income trap hypothesis (MITH) what to reject and what to revive? *NBER Working Paper Series 23126*. Mass, Cambridge: National Bureau of Economic Research.

Im, F.G., and D. Rosenblatt. 2013. Middle-income traps: A conceptual and empirical survey. *World Bank Policy Research Working Paper 76594*. Washington, D.C.: World Bank

Ito, T. 2016. Growth convergence and the middle income trap. Columbia Business School, *Center on Japanese Economy and Business, Working Paper Series No. 349*, June.

Lawrence, R.Z., and L. Edwards. 2013. US employment deindustrialization: Insights from history and the international experience. *Peterson Institute for International Economics, Policy Brief Number PB13-27*, October.

McCaig, B., M.S. McMillan, I. Verduzco-Gallo, and K. Jefferis. 2015. Stuck in the middle? structural change and productivity growth in Botswana. *NBER Working Paper Series, 21029*, Mass, Cambridge: National Bureau of Economic Research.

McCaig, B., and N. Pavcnik. 2013. Moving out of agriculture: Structural change in Vietnam. *NBER Working Paper Series, 19616*, Mass, Cambridge: National Bureau of Economic Research.

Rodrik, D. 2015. Premature deindustrialization. *School of Social Science Economics Working Papers, Paper Number 107*, January.

Todaro, M.P., and S.C. Smith. 2011. *Economic Development*, 11th ed. Harlow: Addison Wesley.

World Bank. 2015. *World Development Indicators*. Washington, D.C.: World Bank. Accessed (homepage).

World Bank. 2017. *World Development Indicators*. Washington, D.C.: World Bank. Accessed March (homepage).

# Chapter 2
# Identifying the Determinants of Employment Elasticity of Economic Growth

**Choi Chang Kon**

## 2.1 Introduction

The issue addressed in this chapter is about the relationship between job creation and economic growth. Job shortage has become a central economic issue in many countries and been lasting for a long time, becoming a persistent problem. Looking persistent and apparently permanent, this problem appears to start challenging the sustainability of market economy.[1] Many job seekers, specially including college graduates are spending substantial amount of money and time in searching for and getting a job. Getting a job has become a kind of serious musical chair game. Based on the widely accepted but not fully identified observation that the employment does not increase enough even in the growing economy, the phenomenon has been often named "Jobless growth". The frequently quoted observation is that the employment growth accompanied by economic growth looks having been decreasing.[2] This paper addresses that issue, aiming to identify the structural reasons why recently, employment has not been growing as fast as in the past.

There have been several studies about that issue. Most studies look at empirical data of output and employment, and estimate the empirical elasticity which is defined to be ratio of percentage change in employment to that in output.[3] Empirical studies appear to confirm the hypothesis that employment effect of economic growth has

[1]For example, people begin to question the meaning and effectiveness of college education in getting a job. It turns out that the traditional and social goal of raising critical citizens cannot be supported and may face a difficulty in allocating resources to the college.
[2]It is measured as employment growth with respect to output growth, which is called 'employment elasticity' or 'employment intensity' of growth. In this paper, unless specified otherwise, the former is mainly used.
[3]While it is defined in this way, empirically, it is often estimated by regression method because the calculated elasticity is subject to some reliability problem. See Kapos (2005).

C. Chang Kon (✉)
Chonbuk National University, Jeonju, South Korea
e-mail: ckchoi@jbnu.ac.kr



M. Hosoe et al. (eds.), *Applied Analysis of Growth, Trade, and Public Policy*,
https://doi.org/10.1007/978-981-13-1876-4_2

been declining.[4] For example, Kapos (2005) estimates employment elasticity in several countries, and finds that the elasticity has indeed decreased in some countries. Piacentini and Pini (2000) also estimate the employment elasticity for the G-6 + Sweden over the period 1960–97, show that during '90s, the estimated elasticity was found to be negative in Italy, Germany, UK and Sweden. Unlike other countries, however, it is reported that Japan did not experience a decrease in the employment elasticity.[5] Seyfried (2006) shows that employment elasticity is in the range from 0.31 to 0.61 in several states and an average estimate is 0.47 for the whole U.S economy. Looking at data of the G-7 economies over the period 1960–1994, Padalino and Vivarelli (1997) find that employment elasticity estimated in U.S.A is different from that in Europe. They find that job creation in North America has been much greater than in Europe.[6]

One problem in this line of research, however, is that no paper has identified structural determinants of employment elasticity with respect to economic growth. That is, there exists no theoretical model answering to the question of what structural characteristic of the economy determines the size of the employment elasticity. With no identification of structural determinants about the relationship, we cannot answer to the question why employment elasticity has declined recently. We cannot also get any policy suggestion to deal with this problem, even if there is any one.

Related to the above problem, another drawback arises in the empirical studies. While looking at empirical data of output and employment and estimating the elasticity, the underlying premise in the previous studies is that declining employment effect of growth is caused by technological factor (so, labor demand), not giving attention to other side of market (so, labor supply). That is, most studies are based on an implicit presumption that labor-saving technology might have reduced job creation effect of economic growth. One problem in those studies is, however, that the role of labor demand and labor supply is not identified. That is, the most basic fact that employment is determined in the labor market as intersection of both labor demand and supply is not being counted.[7] This paper attempts to address the missing discussion about recent job issue.

In sum, there are two problems in this line of research. One is that there has been no theoretical model of identifying the structural determinants of employment elasticity, and the other is that they do not look at both sides of labor market jointly. Not

[4]While the estimated values of employment elasticity depend on country or industry, it would be fair to say that most of them are in the range of (0.2, 0.5).

[5]They also compare elasticity in manufacturing and services industries. See also Choi (2010, 2011).

[6]Importantly, they argue that long run evolution has to be distinguished by short run correlation; while North America and Europe structurally differ in their job creation capacity in the long run, both of them keep on showing a strong and statistically significant short run correlation between growth and employment.

[7]Choi (2006) are studies of dealing with the identification problem of labor supply and demand in understanding labor market structure.

surprisingly, the empirical studies only estimating the employment elasticity cannot explain what has changed it and why. This paper aims to look into these shortcomings. Like other elasticity in the economics, the employment elasticity of output growth should be defined and affected by structural characteristics of the economy, the preference and technology structure. Since we are talking about employment, it should be determined by the structure of labor market which is labor demand and supply. In identifying its determinant, therefore, we need to look at the structure of labor market. A promising model should allow us to distinguish labor demand and supply effects in determining employment elasticity of output growth.

Concerning the methodology and approach taken in this paper, following points need to be mentioned here. First, we focus on the aggregate side of economy in the long run since this paper aims to look at employment effect of growth. So, we attempt to look at what happens to the employment in the labor market when the economy is growing.[8] One typical way to look at employment in the growing economy is to measure 'capital intensity', or 'capital deepening' which is ratio of capital to labor. The employment elasticity estimated in the literatures mentioned above, however, is to look at growth rate of employment and output. So, output instead of capital is used. The usage of output may be more preferred for some reasons. First, output data is more available than capital stock data in most countries since GDP data are published periodically. Secondly, growth is typically defined on the GDP rather than capital stock.[9]

The results of this paper are following. First, in Sect. 1.2, we shows theoretically that employment elasticity is determined by the structure of labor market and others such as tax system and nonlabor income. More specifically, the employment elasticity with respect to output growth gets larger as the wage elasticity of labor supply and output elasticity of labor demand get larger, and wage elasticity of labor demand gets smaller. And it has a negative relationship with respect to asset (or non-labor income) elasticity of labor supply and the growth rate of asset. Extending this result to the economy with tax, it is shown that the employment elasticity gets smaller with taxes on wage income of worker and payroll tax on labor demand, but increases with tax on asset (or nonlabor income).

Based on this result, this paper suggests hypotheses about the declining employment elasticity observed in most countries recently. First, there are three possible factors coming from labor market, which are inelastic labor supply and elastic labor demand with respect to wage, and smaller output elasticity of labor demand. Secondly, coming from others than labor market, high labor tax and the growing asset due to accumulation of capital over time may be responsible for declining employment

[8]So, this employment elasticity is conceptually different from the Okun's law which is about relationship between short run fluctuations of unemployment and GDP.

[9]Technically, since growth of output should be proportional to that of capital, the choice of capital or output would not make a difference in looking at the employment effect of growth Theoretically, however, one may want to distinguish two methods in the sense that employment elasticity of output is defined on flow variable, but employment elasticity of capital (like the inverse of capital intensity) is on stock variable of capital.

elasticity during last decades. Finally, government policies to increase the employment elasticity are suggested. A useful policy direction is to reduce labor taxes and increase the tax on asset or non-labor income.

## 2.2 A Model of Labor Market in a Growing Economy

Here, we introduce the model economy with one good, two inputs and a large number of household-workers and firms. It is assumed that there are many numbers of workers with different reservation wages. Output is subject to a random technology shock. To focus on employment effect of output growth, we look at the labor supply and demand on which the shocks to the economy have been already counted. As can be seen in the below, since asset and income from it is an important determinant of employment elasticity, we distinguish the labor market in terms of its existence.

### *2.2.1 Preferences and Technology*

Each agent is assumed to have a preference structure over a composite consumption good and leisure, which is described by a timeinvariant utility function: $U[C,\ L]$; $R_2 -> R_1$ where $R_i$ is $\boldsymbol{i}$ dimensional nonnegative real space, and $C$ and $L$ denote consumption and leisure. Supply of working hours is limited by the maximum hours available to an agent, say, $\bar{H}$ : so $L = \bar{H} - H$, where $H$ is working hours. The utility function is strictly concave, $U_C$ and $U_L$ are nonnegative, and $U_{CC}$, $U_{LL}$ are negative.[10] Counting the fact the asset ( $=$ $A\ (t)$) is accumulated by the worker over time, the individual worker's budget can be written as:

$$A\ (t+1) = A\ (t)\ (1 + r\ (t)) + W\ (t)\ H\ (t) - C\ (t) \tag{2.1}$$

Worker's labor supply decision is summarized by the choice of reservation wage

$$U\left(W^R H\right) = U(I, \bar{H}) \tag{2.2}$$

Here, $I$ is a non-labor income including income from asset holding of $A$ and $W^R$ is reservation wage which is affected by preference and non-labor income.

This economy has access to an instantaneous production technology subject to a random shock: $Y(t) = Z(t)F[N(t),\ K(t)]$, where $Y(t)$ is the flow of output produced at time $t$ requiring input services of labor $N(t)$ and capital stock $K(t)$. $Z(t)$is the technology shock. The production function $F[N(t),\ K(t)]$ is assumed to satisfy the marginal productivity and strict concavity conditions. Technology is assumed to be of constant returns to scale and stationary over time.

---

[10]Hereafter, subscripts denote the derivative of a function.

### 2.2.2 Market Equilibrium and Growth

The economy is closed with a budget constraint and law of transition for capital stock: $\leq C(t) + K(t+1)[1\delta L] = C(t) + I(t)\ Y(t)$ where $\delta$ denotes the constant capital depreciation rate. This economy keeps growing through the accumulation of capital stock and technology growth. Driven by technology shocks and accompanying accumulation of capital stock, output, $Y(t)$ and other major variables including employment $N(t)$ are growing on growth paths of this model, for which detailed argument is not necessary here since this paper aims to look at relationship between them, but not how they are growing.[11]

### 2.2.3 Labor Market Without Asset

First, let's examine a simple case without asset. As explained above, labor supply decision of individual worker is the choice of reservation wage. Assuming a set of workers with different reservation wages, therefore, the aggregate labor supply becomes a distribution function of reservation wages as specified below.[12]

$$N^S(t) = N^S(W(t)), \quad or \quad W = W^S(N(t)) \tag{2.3}$$

Here, $N^S$ = labor supply, $W$ = real wages, $t$ = time. The latter is an inverse labor supply function. And labor demand function is given as following. While there are many other variables affecting labor demand in the short run, in looking at the employment effect of growth in the long run, it is enough to define a labor demand as a function of real wage, conditional on output.

$$N^D(t) = N^D(W(t), R(t), Y(t)) \tag{2.4}$$

Here, $N^D$ = labor demand, $Y(t)$ = output at time $t$. Since labor demand and supply are equal in equilibrium, the equilibrium employment would be determined by the above two equations: $N^S = N^D$.

To see how employment is determined in more details, it is convenient to use an inverse labor supply function.[13] The equilibrium employment equation can be obtained by putting the inverse labor supply function into the labor demand function.

$$N(t) = N^D[W^S(N(t), R(t), Y(t))] \tag{2.5}$$

[11] It should be emphasized that what we want to see is ex post relationship between output and employment, but not any causality.

[12] It is explained well in many other labor economics literatures For example, see Cahuc and Zylberberg (2004).

[13] Superscript 's' denotes labor supply.

By differentiating this equilibrium condition, one can get a formula of employment elasticity showing how employment is growing as output is growing over time in the long run.[14]

$$\frac{\dot{N}/N}{\dot{Y}/Y} = \frac{\varepsilon_w^S \varepsilon_Y^d}{\varepsilon_w^S \varepsilon_W^d} \tag{2.6}$$

Here, for example, $\dot{N}$ denotes time derivative of $\frac{dN}{dt}$, and $\varepsilon_i^j$ is the elasticity of labor supply and demand ($\mathbf{j} = \mathbf{S}, \mathbf{D}$) with respect to $i(i = W \ or \ K)$. Superscripts $d$ and $S$ denote demand and supply respectively, and $W$ and $K$ wage and capital respectively. So, defining each elasticity,

$\varepsilon_w^S$ =wage elasticity of labor supply, $\varepsilon_W^d$ = wage elasticity of labor demand, $\varepsilon_Y^d$ = elasticity of labor demand with respect to output, which is supposed to be positive.

This result is showing that employment growth due to economic growth is determined by the structure of labor market, which is captured by the wage elasticity of labor supply and labor demand, and the elasticity of labor demand with respect to output. Put differently, one can see how the employment elasticity with respect to output is related to the labor demand and supply elasticity with respect to wage, and by the output elasticity of labor demand. The latter is positive since labor demand should be in positive relationship with respect to output. In sum, it is easy to see that employment effect for output growth gets bigger as wage elasticity of labor supply increases and that of labor demand decreases. And it also increases with the labor demand elasticity with respect to output.

**Proposition 2.1** *In a growing economy without asset, the employment elasticity with respect to output growth is in a positive relationship with wage elasticity of labor supply and output elasticity of labor demand, but in a negative relationship with wage elasticity of labor demand.*

### 2.2.4 Labor Market with Asset

In the above with no asset, any income effect for asset holding on labor supply has been assumed away. But it is not realistic to ignore that kind of income effect in the analysis about long run employment effect of economic growth since one key characteristic of long run growth is the wealth accumulation by households. So, we should take into account the fact that wealth owned by household is also increasing over time following economic growth. The wealth generates nonlabor income to the household, which certainly affects worker's labor supply decision through the income effect. In the following, a labor supply function including asset holding is specified.

[14]Based on the fact that typically, interest rate $R(t)$ does not show a trend, it is assumed that $\frac{\dot{R}}{R} = 0$.

Following the standard optimization result in the labor supply,[15] the asset holding by worker generates an income effect which is supposed to decrease work incentive, so, labor supply. Counting this point, the aggregate labor supply function is presumed to be a decreasing function of asset holding as following. And a standard labor demand function is specified as following.

$$N^S(t) = N^S(W(t), R(t), A(t)) \tag{2.7}$$

$$N^D(t) = N^D(W(t), R(t), Y(t)) \tag{2.8}$$

Since labor demand and supply are equal in equilibrium, the equilibrium employment would be determined by the above two equations: $N^S = N^D$. By taking growth rate of labor supply and demand functions, one can have

$$\frac{\dot{N}}{N} = \varepsilon_w^S \frac{\dot{W}}{W} + \varepsilon_R^S \frac{\dot{R}}{R} + \varepsilon_A^S \frac{\dot{A}}{A} \tag{2.9}$$

$$\frac{\dot{N}}{N} = \varepsilon_w^d \frac{\dot{W}}{W} + \varepsilon_R^d \frac{\dot{R}}{R} + \varepsilon_Y^d \frac{\dot{Y}}{Y} \tag{2.10}$$

Here, we use two conditions. First, for the same reason in the previous section without asset, it is assumed that $\frac{\dot{R}}{R} = 0$. And we can substitute $\frac{\dot{W}}{W}$ from (12.8) into (14.7) since $N^S = N^D$ in equilibrium. In doing this algebra, a convenient assumption is that the growth rate of asset is proportional to that of output[16]: $\frac{\dot{A}}{A} = \phi \frac{\dot{Y}}{Y}$. Here, $\phi$ measure the relative growth rate of asset to output. By exercising a modest algebra under this assumption, one can show that

$$\frac{\dot{N}/N}{\dot{Y}/Y} = \frac{\varepsilon_w^S \varepsilon_Y^d - \varepsilon_w^d \varepsilon_A^S \phi}{\varepsilon_w^S - \varepsilon_W^d} \tag{2.11}$$

where $\varepsilon_w^S$ = wage elasticity of labor supply, $\varepsilon_w^d$ = wage elasticity of labor demand, $\varepsilon_Y^d$ elasticity of labor demand with respect to output which is supposed to be non-negative and $\varepsilon_A^S$ = elasticity of labor supply with respect to asset which would be negative for a typical worker due to the income effect of asset on labor supply decision.

Comparing this result to the above one with no asset effect in labor supply function, one can see a remarkable difference. First, it is easy to see that denominator is positive. And in the numerator, the first term is positive since both elasticities in it are positive, and the second term itself is positive. So the sign and size of employment elasticity depend on the difference between the first and second terms in numerator. The elasticity becomes positive if the first term is greater than the second one. In determining the difference, one interesting role is assigned to the size of $\phi$, the ratio

[15]Reservation wage of individual worker is determined by his (her) preference and budget, more specifically by the non-labor income.

[16]This assumption is innocuous from the fact that capital-output ratio does not show any trend.

of asset growth rate to output growth rate. It is saying that as the growth rate of asset gets larger than that of output, the employment elasticity gets smaller. It makes intuitively right point since as asset grows faster than output, it reduces work incentive of workers, so decreasing labor supply.

Since the amount of asset is closely related to that of capital stock in the economy,[17] this result is just confirming a fact. As accumulated over economic growth, it is obvious that capital stock may increase or decrease employment through output or substitution effect. From the fact that empirically output growth is accompanied by employment increase in the long run, it must be the case that output effect dominates the substitution effect. The above derivation, however, points out that there is another force reducing employment elasticity. That is, besides substitution effect of replacing labor, capital accumulation has another negative effect on employment effect of output growth. The effect could get smaller because of wealth effect from asset holding. As the latter effect gets larger, employment increase from economic growth may be weakened, reducing the employment elasticity.[18] The negative effect is accelerated if ratio $\phi$ gets bigger. Including this capital or asset effect on employment elasticity, we have following summary.

**Proposition 2.2** *In the growing economy with capital accumulation, the employment elasticity with respect to output growth gets larger as the wage elasticity of labor supply and output elasticity of labor demand get larger, and as wage elasticity of labor demand get smaller. The growth of asset caused by the accumulated capital stock may have a negative effect on employment growth by influencing labor supply negatively.*

### 2.2.5 Employment Elasticity with Taxes

The above discussion identifies how a mapping structure from output growth to employment is affected by the structure of labor market. We can extend this result to see the effect of tax policy on the employment elasticity: taxes on wage income and asset holding for worker's side and taxes on labor input for firm's side. These taxes change the above labor supply and demand functions as following.

$$N^S(t) = N^S[W(t)(1 - t_W), A(t)(1 - t_A)] \tag{2.12}$$

$$N^D(t) = N^D[W(t)(1 + t_N), R(t), Y(t)] \tag{2.13}$$

[17] They should be equal in a closed economy.

[18] Theoretically, it is possible to have the case the second term is greater than the first term, making the employment elasticity negative, which is ignored since so far no country has ever experienced it.

Here, $t_W$ and $t_A$ are taxes on wage income and nonlabor income, $t_N$ is the tax on hiring workers, called payroll tax most of which is social security contributions. These taxes modify the employment elasticity as in the below.

$$\frac{\dot{N}/N}{\dot{Y}/Y} = \frac{\varepsilon_w^S(1-t_W)\varepsilon_Y^d\varepsilon_w^d\varepsilon_A^S\,(1-t_A)\,(1+t_N)]\phi}{\varepsilon_w^S - \varepsilon_W^d} \tag{2.14}$$

This result is just confirming what we expect about the effect of taxes on employment. First, the labor income tax ($= t_W$) has a negative effect on employment elasticity and the payroll tax ($= t_N$) does the same. It is not new, but we are familiar with the argument that labor tax has a negative effect on employment by increasing the price of labor and decreasing the work incentive.[19] What is more interesting is the second outcome that the tax on the nonlabor income (mostly, asset income) has a positive effect on employment elasticity. This second outcome is intuitively right since what the non-labor income for workers produces income effect in labor supply decision. It is obvious that the tax on income reduces the income effect, increasing labor supply.

Since the taxes on labor income and on hiring workers have other purposes, not just about job creation or something, it is not simple to say a tax policy suggestion based on the above discussion. What we can say moderately is that higher labor tax on both sides of labor market may be detrimental to job creation, which is widely acknowledged. We may focus on the other type of tax on non-labor income which is mostly generated from assets owned by workers. That is, assets accumulated over economic growth by workers generate non-labor income to worker, which is supposed to reduce work incentive and labor force participation.

**Proposition 2.3** *In the growing economy with asset on worker's side, the employment elasticity gets smaller with taxes on wage income of worker and payroll tax on labor demand, but increases with tax on asset holding.*

## 2.3 A Simulation Experiment and Some Suggestions

In this section, first, a simple simulation experiment is performed to make a clear understanding about determinants of employment elasticity. Secondly, some suggestions are provided for future researches and policy issues.

### *2.3.1 A Simulation Experiment*

To make it simple, the experiment is performed for two cases of with taxes and without taxes. Several determinants may be classified in two different kinds, one of

[19] While labor taxes affect both extensive and intensive margins of labor supply, it is known that the response along the former is much stronger than along the latter. See Eisa et al. (2006).

which is about labor market structure and the other about tax structure. So, simulation exercise is performed to see each effect. By doing so, one can understand better the effect of each determinant on employment elasticity, especially the effect of labor market structure and tax system. First, the effect of labor market structure is presented in Table 1.1. In Table 1.1, taxes are assumed away and some parameters are calibrated as following: $\varepsilon_Y^d = 0.7,\ \ \varepsilon_Z^S = -0.1,\ \phi = 0.1$. While there is no universally-agreed point estimates for these elasticity, Hamermesh (1993) is a good reference on the estimated structure of labor demand function. Based on many studies about labor demand function, Hamermesh (1993) suggests that the good estimates of output elasticity of labor demand is 0.7, and the range of wage elasticity of labor demand is $[-1.54, -0.12]$. In Table 2.1, its range is given to be $[-1.2, -0.2]$. Since there is no widely-accepted empirical estimate for non-labor income elasticity of labor supply and growth rate of non-labor income relative to output, the values are calibrated. The result in Table 2.1 is confirming the Proposition 2.2. The employment elasticity gets smaller as labor supply becomes wage-elastic and labor demand wage-inelastic. Other interesting point is that several combinations of wage elasticity of labor supply and demand can result in the same employment elasticity. For example, one can see three possible cases of $\varepsilon_w^S$ and $\varepsilon_w^d$ for the employment elasticity of 0.34, which is typed in bold.

In Table 2.2, other simulation experiment is summarized to see the effect of tax structure. Among taxes, tax rate on wage income is specified to be 0.1 a priori and calculate the employment elasticity for varying rates of tax on non-labor income and payroll tax. Partly supporting the selection of these values, based on Hamermesh (1993), the value of $-0.5$ is picked for wage elasticity of labor demand. Other parameter values are given as following: $\varepsilon_Y^d = 0.9,\ \ \varepsilon_Z^S = -0.1,\ \ \phi = 0.3,$ $\varepsilon_w^S = 0.4, \varepsilon_w^d = -0.5, t_W = 0.1$. Wage elasticity of extensive labor supply in the long run is assumed to be greater than that of intensive margin. Without any empirical estimates for other parameters, they are given values so that the calculated employment elasticity is more or less consistent with the empirically estimated ones. Simulation results are confirming the Proposition 2.3. It is shown that for a given value of tax on asset holding ($=\mathbf{t_A}$), employment elasticity decreases as payroll tax ($=\mathbf{t_N}$) increases. And one can also see that for a given value of payroll tax, employment elasticity gets

**Table 2.1** Labor market structure and employment elasticity (with no taxes and $\varepsilon_Y^d = 0.7, \varepsilon_Z^S = -0.1, \phi = 0.3$)

| | $\varepsilon_w^S$ = wage elasticity of labor supply | | | | |
|---|---|---|---|---|---|
| $\varepsilon_w^d$ = wage elasticity of labor demand | | ***0.1*** | ***0.3*** | ***0.6*** | ***0.9*** |
| | ***−0.3*** | **0.203** | **0.435** | 0.590 | 0.668 |
| | ***−0.6*** | 0.103 | **0.280** | **0.435** | 0.528 |
| | ***−0.9*** | 0.063 | **0.203** | 0.342 | **0.435** |
| | ***−1.2*** | 0.042 | 0.156 | **0.280** | 0.369 |

**Table 2.2** Tax structure and employment elasticity ($\varepsilon_Y^d = 0.7, \varepsilon_Z^S = -0.1, \phi = 0.3, \varepsilon_w^S = 0.4, \varepsilon_w^d = -0.5, t_W = 0.1$)

| | Tax on nonlabor income = $t_A$ | | | | | |
|---|---|---|---|---|---|---|
| Tax on labor input = $t_N$ | | *0.1* | *0.3* | *0.5* | *0.7* | *0.9* |
| | *0.1* | **0.340** | 0.343 | 0.347 | 0.351 | **0.354** |
| | *0.3* | 0.303 | 0.307 | 0.311 | 0.315 | 0.319 |
| | *0.5* | 0.274 | 0.278 | 0.282 | 0.286 | 0.290 |
| | *0.7* | 0.249 | 0.253 | 0.257 | 0.261 | 0.266 |
| | *0.9* | 0.228 | 0.232 | 0.236 | 0.241 | 0.245 |

smaller as tax on non-labor income gets smaller. In the experiment, we get the value of employment elasticity is maximized with $\mathbf{t_N} = 0.1$ and $\mathbf{t_A} = 0.9$.

### 2.3.2 *Some Suggestions for More Works*

Several determinants of employment elasticity have been identified in the above discussion, which may be classified into two categories of labor market and non-labor market ones. Identifying the reasons empirically for declining employment elasticity, a substantial empirical work is needed, which is beyond the range of this paper.[20] Here, we briefly mention which of them might have leaded to the declining of employment elasticity.

**(1) Labor Market Structure**

**(a) Change in labor supply elasticity**: First, it is shown that employment elasticity increases with the wage elasticity of labor supply. It means that more employment could be made with output growth when labor supply is more wage-elastic. So, if labor supply has become less elastic over time, meaning that the aggregate labor supply is more sluggish for rising wages due to economic growth, the employment elasticity can get smaller. Several points should be kept in mind in this discussion. First, the labor supply here is about extensive margin in the aggregate labor market.[21] And secondly, wage elasticity of labor supply here is about long run, so we are talking about long run or permanent change in wages. First of all, it is well-known among labor economists that labor supply elasticity with respect to the permanent wage growth is small.[22] Talking about the possibility for it to have decreased over long-run economic growth, one possible factor reducing the response of aggregate labor

[20] Note that discussion in this section is for suggestion of future study.

[21] It looks better to see this labor supply as one faced by all firms in the economy, explaining an increase in number of total workers for an increase in average wage in the aggregate labor market.

[22] See Basu and Kimball (2002).

supply for rising wages may be related to mobility of workers between the booming sectors and the declining ones. The rapid change in technology requires workers to move quickly to new technology. But adjusting to new technology is not simple, but takes time because of education and training. If workers have difficulty in moving from the former to the latter, the aggregate labor supply would responds more slowly than necessary, making the wage elasticity of labor supply in the aggregate labor market smaller.[23]

**(b) Change in wage elasticity of labor demand**: The above employment elasticity means that employment elasticity has an inverse relationship with labor demand elasticity. To check the possibility that an increase in wage elasticity of labor demand may cause a decrease in employment elasticity, the Hicks-Marshall law of labor demand may be used. Based on the law of derived demand, there are several reasons for increasing wage elasticity of labor demand. First, as the portion of service sector gets bigger relative to that of manufacturing, the labor demand structure may be more wage-elastic.[24] Second, in the service industry, the ratio of labor costs out of total costs tends to increase and increase wage elasticity of labor demand. One can see that the blooming of service industry and declining manufacturing is deeply related to the declining employment elasticity. Thirdly, product market tends to be more competitive over economic growth, the price elasticity of product demand has increased, which made the labor demand more wage elastic.

**(c) Change in output elasticity of labor demand**: The above derivation of elasticity shows that employment elasticity gets larger if the labor demand becomes more output-elastic. If this argument is plausible, it must be the case that other production factors have been employed more than worker. It has been pointed out that the continuously invented IT technology has replaced the labor or reduced the demand for labor. While it sounds convincing, it needs a rigorous empirical investigation in the future study since labor is needed to produce IT devices. If it has taken place overall for the aggregate economy, it should be accompanied by increase in the productivity of labor.

**Hypothesis 2.1** Based on the changes in the structure of labor market over time, one can think of three possible reasons for the declining employment elasticity, which are inelastic labor supply and more wage-elastic, but less output-elastic labor demand.

### (2) Determinants Other Than Labor Market

**(a) Asset accumulation**: As mentioned above, one key characteristics of economic growth is the continuing growth of asset over time, which is closely related to capital

[23]The so called active labor policies aim to increase the labor mobility, increasing the elasticity of aggregate labor supply. Employment service, provision of job training and subsidizing labor mobility are a few examples.

[24]One can check the explanation in the labor demand literatures that labor demand tends to be more elastic in service industry than in manufacturing. For example, as well-summarized in most labor economics textbooks, the ratio of labor costs out of total costs tends to be higher, so making wage-elastic labor demand in the service industry.

accumulation following economic growth. The asset accumulated generates nonlabor income, like dividend, interest, rent and capital gain, basic source of which is the accumulated capital.[25] As shown and explained in the above, the nonlabor income reduces employment elasticity due to its negative effect on labor supply. More specifically, what matters in the employment elasticity is the growth rate of nonlabor income relative to that of GDP. Without any empirical data, while it is not possible to pin down how much the growing nonlabor income has affected job growth over time, it is clear to see that the continuously increasing capital stock has been a factor for declining employment elasticity.
**(b) Tax Structure**: There are two kinds of taxes in the above derivation of employment elasticity: labor tax and tax on asset. As well known in labor economics literature, first, labor taxes have negative effect on job creation.[26] This fact is also confirmed in this paper. It is shown that taxes on labor income and payroll tax reduce employment elasticity. The labor taxes are main sources for government revenue and the social security expense in most countries, which are considered inevitable in modern market economy. Taking granted its necessity, this paper is pointing out that the taxes have another price of less job growth. The relevant question, therefore, is to choose the optimal structure of labor tax in the sense of maximizing job growth, subject to the other goal of tax.[27] Secondly, we can look at the tax on asset (equivalently on non-labor income). The tax on asset may reduce the negative effect of non-labor income on employment elasticity, so job creation.[28] Based on this result, while left for future work, it would be useful to check a possibility that more tax revenue is generated from asset market rather than labor market.

**Hypothesis 2.2** The growing nonlabor income due to accumulation of capital over time and increasing labor tax could be responsible for declining employment elasticity.

## 2.4 Conclusion

In this chapter we identifies the structural determinants of employment elasticity with respect to output growth. It is shown that the elasticity is primarily determined by the structure of labor supply and demand. Next, it is also shown that tax structure and nonlabor income affect the size of employment elasticity. More specifically, the employment elasticity with respect to output growth gets larger as the wage elasticity of labor supply and output elasticity of labor demand get larger, and as wage elasticity of labor demand gets smaller. It also decreases as nonlabor income elasticity of labor supply gets smaller and the growth rate of nonlabor income gets larger. Extending

[25] The so-called "NEET" may be related to this effect.

[26] This issue has been well summarized in Agell and Sorensen (2006).

[27] So, the discussion about optimal tax structure needs to include its job effect.

[28] Since tax rates are different for different types of assets. It is not easy to get any evidence of increasing or decreasing trend in it.

this result to the economy with tax, it is shown that the employment elasticity gets smaller with taxes on wage income of worker and payroll tax on labor demand, but increases with tax on nonlabor income.

Above all, this paper simply reminds us the basic fact that employment is determined by labor supply and demand in the labor market, which should be examined to understand the why employment elasticity has been decreasing. So, this paper point out that we should be careful to blame the labor-saving technology for the slow increase in employment for GDP growth. Based on this result, this paper suggests several hypotheses to identify the possible reasons for the declining employment elasticity observed in many countries recently. First, there are three reasons coming from the structural change in labor market, which are inelastic labor supply and elastic labor demand with respect to wage, and decrease in output elasticity of labor demand. Secondly, coming from others than labor market, labor tax and its increase, and the growing nonlabor income due to accumulation of capital over time may be responsible for declining employment elasticity. This paper also suggests research topics to increase the employment elasticity. From the above discussion, a policy direction is clear: reduce labor tax and increase the tax on nonlabor income.

## References


Agell, J. and P.B. Sorensen. 2006. *Tax Policy and Labor Market Performance*. Cambridge: The MIT Press.

Basu, S., and M.S. Kimball. 2002. Long-run Labor Supply and the Elasticity of Intertemporal Substitution for Consumption. In *NBER*.

Cahuc, P., and A. Zylberberg. 2004. *Labor Economics*. Cambridge: The MIT Press.

Choi, C.K. 2006. Building an identified Equilibrium Model of Aggregate Labor Market. *Journal of Korean Econometric Association* 17 (4): 25–44.

Choi, C.K. 2010. The Structure of Labor Market and Employment Elasticity: Growth and Employment. *The Journal of Korean Associations of Applied Economics* (in Korean) 12 (3): 83–105.

Choi, C.K. 2011. Industrial Difference in Employment Effect of Economic Growth. *Journal of Economic Studies* 29 (4): 175–187.

Eisa, N., H.J. Kleven, C.T. Kreiner. 2006. Welfare Effects of Tax Reform and Labor Supply at the Intensive and Extensive Margins. In *Tax Policy and Labor Market Performance*. CESifo Seminar Series, ed. Jonas Agell and Peter Birch Sorensen.

Hamermesh, D. 1993. *Labor Demand*. Princeton: Princeton University Press.

Kapos, Stepen. 2005. The Employment Intensity of Growth: Trends and Macroeconomic Determinants. ILO, 1–50

Padalino, S., and M. Vivarelli. 1997. The Employment Intensity of Economic Growth in the G-7 Countries. *International Labour Review* 136 (2): 191–214.

Piacentini, P., and P. Pini. 2000. Growth and Employment. In *The Employment Impact of Innovation: Evidence and Policy*, ed. Vivarelli, M., and M. Pianta, 44–76. London: Routledge.

Seyfried, William. 2006. Examining the Relationship Between Employment and Economic Growth in the Ten Largest States. *Southwestern Economic Review* 32: 13–24.

# Chapter 3
# The Relationship Between Local Employment Growth and Regional Economic Growth: Evidence from Korea

**Jihye Choi and Iltae Kim**

## 3.1 Introduction

Job creation and economic growth are considered as main issues in economic policies around the world. Specifically Korea has experienced low and jobless economic growth in the recent past. Employment problem is one of the sensitive issues framing national and regional economic policies in Korea. In this context, it is important to capture the relationship between the employment and economic growth in any Korean regional economy.

In aggregate demand policy, government spending based on fiscal policy increases the gross domestic product (GDP). However, in recent years it has been found that most of the increase in GDP is due to the capital factor of production and that the share of the labor factor in GDP growth has been low. This led to the "jobless growth". On the other hand, job creation involves the use of income policy to increase the share of labor income. The rising share of income increases purchasing power, boosts consumption, and induces investment. An increase in employment and the accompanying income leads to an increase in economic growth.

Numerous previous studies on the relationship between employment and economic growth suggested a validation of Okun's law. According to the law, GDP growth is faster than employment growth during the period of economic recovery, and GDP reduction is faster than unemployment growth in a recession. For example, Freeman (2000), Cuaresma (2003), and Ball et al. (2013) have identified the role of Okun's law on the negative relationship between unemployment and real GDP.

In recent years, several studies have conducted the relationship between employment and growth to verify "jobless growth" in the economy where capital input has

J. Choi · I. Kim (✉)
Chonnam National University, Gwangju, South Korea
e-mail: kit2603@jnu.ac.kr

J. Choi
e-mail: iamwise7@jnu.ac.kr



M. Hosoe et al. (eds.), *Applied Analysis of Growth, Trade, and Public Policy*,
https://doi.org/10.1007/978-981-13-1876-4_3

been saturated. The United States has already experienced this phenomenon in the early 1990s. Since the early 2000s, employment rates have been stagnated in Asian countries including Korea, and the analysis has focused on the clarification of causes.

In general, previous studies examined that the technological progress is the cause of "growthless employment". On the macroscopic level, a number of researchers have identified changes in labor time or labor productivity due to technology shocks (Gali 1999; Chang and Hong 2006; Fisher 2006; Kim 2012). On a microeconomic level, researchers indirectly identify the effects of technological advances, which are the source of economic growth, on employment. They used panel data from companies or countries to show that the impact of productivity improvements on employment can depend on the type of technological progress (Van Reenen 1997; Blien et al. 2006; Lachenmaier and Rottmann 2011; Bogliacino et al. 2012; Choi and Kim 2017). However, since 2010, when the shock of the global financial crisis has eased somewhat, "growthless employment", where employment growth is greater than economic growth, has emerged in some countries. Kim (2017) confirmed that the phenomenon of "growthless employment" appears in seven countries.

This paper differs from the existing literatures in that examining the causality between employment growth and economic growth before the analysis of cointergration and showing the existence of long-run equilibrium using panel error correction model (ECM) analysis. This paper estimates the mutual elasticity between regional economic growth and local employment growth and suggests policies to keep a stable growth base in the long term.

In this paper we examine the long-run relationship between the economic growth and employment growth using the panel data of 16 regions in Korea[1] from 1995 to 2013 by Fully Modified Ordinary Least Squares (FMOLS) method. We also identify the causality between regional economic growth and local employment growth and show the existence of long-run equilibrium by the panel cointegration relationships between the local employment and regional economic growth variables, which have a unit root.

This paper is organized in the following way. Section 3.2 presents the model and data. Section 3.3 contains the empirical results and interpretations. Finally, Sect. 3.4 provides the concluding remarks.

## 3.2 The Model and Data

Most of economic timeseries variables are known to be difference-stationary. In general, an Ordinary Least Square (OLS) estimation of non-stationary timeseries data which has a unit root, will produce spurious regression results. This means that the relationship between unrelated variables is shown to be significant. Engle and Granger (1987) note that a linear combination of two or more **I(1)** series may be

[1]The data of Ulsan ranges from 1998 to 2013 because it was raised to the status of metropolitan city in 1998.

stationary, or $\mathbf{I(0)}$, in this case, we call the series are cointegrated. Such a linear combination defines a cointegrating equation with a cointegration vector of weights that characterizes the long-run relationship between the variables.[2]

This cointegration relationship is applicable to panel data. The basic concept of the cointegraion test is that the unit root test applies to the residual of the estimated equation of the panel cointegration regression model. The cointegration test is generally considered a prerequisite for causality that is tested in the vector error correction (VEC) model framework and it enables to estimate short- and long-run causal relationship. The Johansen cointegration test is used in most investigations of cointegration relationships. However, it is unlike to relatively obtain reliable results in short timeseries. To solve this problem, the FMOLS technique was introduced by Phillips and Hansen (1990). The FMOLS estimator has advantages of robustness to endogeneity bias, serial correlation, and short timeseries.[3] The FMOLS for panel data is suggested by Pedroni (2001), and its advantage is that researcher can selectively pool the long-term information contained in the panel data, while allowing for the presence of short dynamic characteristics and fixed effects across the panels.[4]

This fully modified panel OLS estimator is asymptotically unbiased for both the standard case intercepts as well as the fixed effects model with heterogeneous intercepts. In addition, the corresponding asymptotic distribution will be free of the nuisance parameters.

The panel regression model should include the error correction term when there is a cointegration relationship between panel variables. For example, ECM with $Y_{i,t}$ can be modelled as autoregression of order k, which is denoted by[5] $VAR(k)$. The equation can be written as follows[6]:

$$\Delta \mathbf{Y}_{\mathbf{i,t}} = \Pi \mathbf{Y}_{\mathbf{i,t-1}} + \psi_1 \Delta \mathbf{Y}_{\mathbf{i,t-1}} + \ldots + \psi_{\mathbf{k-1}} \Delta \mathbf{Y}_{\mathbf{i,t-k+1}} + \epsilon_{\mathbf{i,t}},\ \ \epsilon_{\mathbf{i,t}} \sim \mathbf{iid(0)}.$$

If this equation is integrated of order one, then the left-hand side is $\mathbf{I(1)}$, and the right-hand side is also $\mathbf{I(1)}$ except for $\Pi \mathbf{Y}_{\mathbf{i,t-1}}$. Therefore, if $\mathbf{Y}_{\mathbf{i,t}}$ has (p-r) unit roots, then the number of $\mathbf{rank}(\Pi)$ should be $\mathbf{r}$ because the number of linearly independent cointegrating vectors is $\mathbf{r}$, therefore, if matrix $\mathbf{B}_{(\mathbf{r}\times\mathbf{p})}$ is a set satisfying $\mathbf{BY}_{\mathbf{i,t-1}} \sim \mathbf{I(0)}$, there exist $\mathbf{A}'\mathbf{B} = \Pi$, and $\mathbf{A}_{(\mathbf{r}\times\mathbf{p})}$.

In general, a cointegration relationship is called to be the long-run equilibrium; therefore, $\mathbf{BY}_{\mathbf{i,t-1}}$ is an error deviating from the long-run equilibrium. $\mathbf{A}$ is an error correction matrix which shows how the error move affecting the VAR system. $\mathbf{A}'\mathbf{BY}_{\mathbf{i,t-1}}$ (i.e., $\Pi \mathbf{Y}_{\mathbf{i,t-1}}$) of the cointegration system is an error correction term (ECT). If the ECT has a minus sign, then the relationship among the variables returns

---

[2]See StataCorp (2005, pp.231).

[3]See Stolbov (2015, pp.15).

[4]See Pedroni (2001, pp.93–94).

[5]Vector Autoregressive (VAR) model is used a lot for forecasting of economic time series. In the vector system, two or more variables are handled as endogenous variables, and the dynamic change of these variables is found by their lag value.

[6]See Choi and Kim (2015, pp7–8).

to the long-run equilibrium relationship, and the ECT tends toward zero in the long-run equilibrium. Thus, the ECM is one of the representations of a cointegration system.

Assuming that the variables of this paper have trends and are non-stationary, the panel ECM equations for the analysis are given as follows[7]:

$$\Delta \mathbf{lnGRDP}_{i,t} = \mu_i + \alpha_i \left(\mathbf{ln\,GRDP}_{i,t-1} - \theta_i - \beta_i \mathbf{ln\,EMP}_{i,t-1}\right) + \sum_{j=1}^{2} \gamma_i \Delta \mathbf{ln\,GRDP}_{i,t-j} + \sum_{j=1}^{2} \lambda_i \Delta \mathbf{ln\,EMP}_{i,t-j} + \epsilon_{i,t} \tag{3.1}$$

$$\Delta \mathbf{lnEMP}_{i,t} = \delta_i + \varphi_i \left(\mathbf{lnEMP}_{i,t-1} - \tau_i - \rho_i \mathbf{lnGRDP}_{i,t-1}\right) + \sum_{j=1}^{2} \omega_i \Delta \mathbf{lnEMP}_{i,t-j} + \sum_{j=1}^{2} \sigma_i \Delta \mathbf{lnGRDP}_{i,t-j} + \varepsilon_{i,t} \tag{3.2}$$

$\mathbf{i = 1, 2, \ldots, 16; \; t = 1995, 1996, \ldots, 2013,}$

where **GRDP** denotes real gross regional domestic product per capita and **EMP** is the number of employees. $\alpha_i \left(\ln GRDP_{i,t-1} - \theta_i - \beta_i \ln EMP_{i,t-1}\right)$ and $\varphi_i \left(\ln EMP_{i,t-1} - \tau_i - \rho_i \ln GRDP_{i,t-1}\right)$ are the ECTs. In Eqs. (3.1) and (3.2), $\mu_i$ and $\delta_i$ represent the deterministic factors and are constant. When coefficients of ECTs, $\alpha_i$ and $\varphi_i$ have minus signs, there are cointegration relationships. The ECT tends to zero at the long-run equilibrium, adjusting at the rate $\alpha_i$ and $\varphi_i$. The **GRDP** generally has a trend, and this paper assumes that the **EMP** also has a trend. Thus, these variables are considered integrated.

This paper uses Korean regional panel data from the Korean Statistical Information Service (KOSIS). The number of panels are 16 (7 metropolitan councils, 9 provinces) and the annual data range is from 1995 to 2013.[8] All data values are transformed into their natural logarithmic forms. Table 3.1 shows the common sample statistics of the data.

The changes between GRDP per capita and the number of employees in Korea used in this paper is represented in Fig. 3.1. As shown in Fig. 3.1, Korea's regional economic growth has been slow since the 2000s, but it has steadily grown, while the employment growth rate left between 0 and 1%. In addition, this trend shows similar movements of two economic variables.

The panel unit root test is classified into the common unit root process and individual unit root process tests. In the common unit root process, it is assumed that the each panel member's unit roots are the same. In contrast, the individual unit root process assumes that the unit roots are different. The representative common unit root process test is the Levin-Lin-Chu statistic, and the representative individual unit

[7]The lag length is chosen 2, as per the Akaike information criterion (AIC).

[8]Ulsan Metropolitan City has been promoted to metropolitan city since 1998, so the data for 3 years are missing.

**Table 3.1** The common sample statistics (Unit: KRW, person)

| | GRDP | lnGRDP | EMP | lnEMP |
|---|---|---|---|---|
| Mean | 20,767,894 | 17.607 | 1,417,642 | 13.859 |
| Median | 18,131,871 | 17.544 | 931,000 | 13.744 |
| Maximum | 59,347,996 | 19.547 | 5,988,000 | 15.605 |
| Minimum | 10,365,154 | 15.698 | 243,000 | 12.401 |
| Std. Dev. | 9,388,633 | 0.808 | 1,357,505 | 0.729 |
| Observations | 301 | 301 | 301 | 301 |

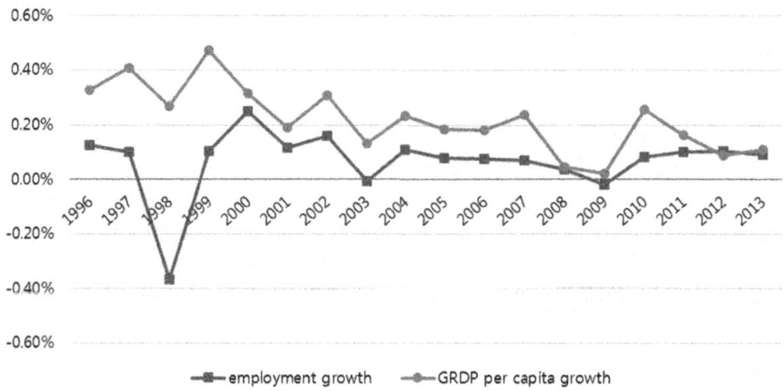


**Fig. 3.1** Trend of employment growth and GRDP growth

**Table 3.2** Trend of employment growth and GRDP growth

| | lnGRDP | | lnEMP | |
|---|---|---|---|---|
| | Level | 1st difference | Level | 1st difference |
| Common unit root process | | | | |
| Levin, Lin and Chu | −1.829** | 14.119*** | −2.943*** | −11.668*** |
| Individual unit root process | | | | |
| Im, Pesaran and Shin | 3.504 | −12.242 * ** | 0.944 | −10.108 * ** |
| ADF-Fisher | 13.706 | 189.627*** | 30.854 | 152.342*** |
| PP-Fisher | 42.691* | 536.013*** | 37.584 | 187.399*** |

*, **, and *** are statistically significant at the 10, 5, and 1% levels

root processes are the Im–Pesaran–Shin statistic, the ADF-Fisher statistic, and the PP-Fisher statistic. Table 3.2 shows the panel unit root test results. In the individual unit root process test, this paper finds that all variables have unit roots.

## 3.3 Empirical Results and Interpretations

In this section we employ the panel cointegration test. As mentioned previously, the OLS estimator could be biased and heterogeneity could exist in the panel variables. Therefore, this paper attempts to find the relationship between regional economic growth and local employment growth. From the panel unit root test results, we expect that all variables are **I**(**1**). Therefore, this paper tests whether the error term of the linear combination of **lnGRDP** and **lnEMP** is **I**(**0**).

If the error term is **I(0),** then the relationship between **lnGRDP** and **lnEMP** can be stationary and has a long-run equilibrium. The traditional panel cointegration test results are represented in Table 3.3. This paper expects that there is a cointergraion relationship between **lnGRDP** and **lnEMP** except the rho-statistic results.

This paper tests the Granger causality between two variables before estimating the long-run relationship. The Granger causality investigates whether the lag independent variables have power of explanation for the current dependent variable. Table 3.4 shows Granger causality test results using W-statistics. The null hypothesis (**lnGRDP** does not cause **lnEMP**) is rejected. The reverse null hypothesis (**lnEMP** does not cause **lnGRDP**) is also rejected. Therefore, **lnEMP** can be an explanatory variable for **lnGRDP**, and **lnGRDP** can be an independent variable for **lnEMP**.

**Table 3.3** Panel unit root test results

| $H_0$: No cointegration | Statistic | | |
|---|---|---|---|
| Pedroni Residual Cointegration test | $H_1$: Common AR coefs | Panel v-Statistic | 21.040*** |
| | | Panel rho-Statistic | −0.402 |
| | | Panel PP-Statistic | −3.009 * ** |
| | | Panel ADF-Statistic | −3.898 * ** |
| | $H_1$: Individaul AR coefs | Group rho-Statistic | 1.196 |
| | | Group PP-Statistic | −5.159 * ** |
| | | Group ADF-Statistic | −5.767 * ** |
| Kao Residual Cointegration test | | ADF-Statistic | −2.386 * ** |

***is statistically significant at the 1% level

**Table 3.4** Panel cointegration test results

| Null Hypothesis | W-statistics (Zbar-statistics) | p-value |
|---|---|---|
| **lnGRDP does not cause lnEMP** | 4.101 (2.274) | 0.023*** |
| **lnEMP does not cause lnGRDP** | 4.627 (2.982) | 0.003*** |

***is statistically significant at the 1% level

**Table 3.5** Granger causality test results

| Explanatory variable | Dependent variable: **lnGRDP** | Dependent variable: **lnEMP** |
|---|---|---|
| **lnEMP** | 1.086*** (0.060) | – |
| **lnGRDP** | – | 0.448*** (0.072) |
| Adjusted R-squared | 0.99 | 0.99 |
| Durbin–Watson stat | 1.15 | 0.87 |

( )means standard error
***is statistically significant at the 1% level

Next we estimate the cointegrating equation using the panel FMOLS after standardization.[9] Table 3.5 shows panel FMOLS estimation results. The value of second column is the coefficient of the effect of employment growth on economic growth at the local level. The effect of economic growth on employment growth are also shown in the third column. The cointegrating relationship implies that the causal and reverse causation relationships between **lnGRDP** and **lnEMP** are stationary in the long-run and the relationships can be the long-run equilibrium. We find that the effect of **lnGRDP** on **lnEMP** is more than that found in the reverse relationship. A 1% increase in employment causes economic growth to rise by 1.086%, when the economic growth increases by 1%, the employment increases by 0.448%.

The panel ECM equations based on the cointegration relationship are given as follows:

$$\mathbf{\Delta lnGRDP = 1.678 - 0.065\left(lnGRDP_{i,t-1} - \theta_i - \beta_i lnEMP_{i,t-1}\right) + \sum_{j=1}^{2} \gamma_i \Delta lnGRDP_{i,t-j} + \sum_{j=1}^{2} \lambda_i \Delta lnEMP_{i,t-j}} \tag{3.1}$$

$$(\mathbf{-4.55 * **})$$

$$\mathbf{\Delta lnEMP = 1.673 - 0.159\left(lnEMP_{i,t-1} - \tau_i - \rho_i lnGRDP_{i,t-1}\right) + \sum_{j=1}^{2} \omega_i \Delta lnEMP_{i,t-j} + \sum_{j=1}^{2} \sigma_i \Delta lnGRDP_{i,t-j}} \tag{3.2}$$

$$(\mathbf{-5.67 * **})$$

As mentioned earlier, **ECTs** are $\alpha_i\left(\ln GRDP_{i,t-1} - \theta_i - \beta_i \ln EMP_{i,t-1}\right)$ and $\varphi_i\left(\ln EMP_{i,t-1} - \tau_i - \rho_i \ln GRDP_{i,t-1}\right)$. The numbers in the parentheses indicate these t-statistics on coefficients of ECT, $\alpha_i$ and $\varphi_i$. From Eqs. (3.1) and (3.2), $\alpha_i$ and $\varphi_i$ are **−0.065** and **−0.159,** respectively, and thus coefficients of ECTs have minus signs. The ECM estimation result implies that the relationship between regional

[9]Elimination of the dependence on nuisance parameter and the heterogeneity problem.

economic growth and local employment growth can be restored to the long-run equilibrium after unexpected shocks cause the disruption.

## 3.4 Concluding Remarks

In this chapter we examine the long-run equilibrium relationship between local employment growth and regional economic growth using Korean panel data from 1995 to 2013 at the local level. This paper employs the panel FMOLS estimation, which is useful in dealing with heterogeneous panel data. We also estimate the panel ECM to measure the speed of convergence of the variables toward long-run equilibrium by the cointegrating equations.

We show that the employment growth elasticity of economic growth is greater than the economic growth elasticity of employment growth. This implies that employment expansion leads to long-run stable economic growth. This paper suggests that the regional employment policy for job creation or reemployment opportunities involves industrial restructuring or job training for various skill levels, to enhance regional economic growth.

## References

Ball, L. M., Leigh, D., and Loungani, P. 2013.Okun's law: Fit at fifty?, NBER working paper Series No. 18668, *National Bureau of Economic Research.*

Blien, U., J. Suedekum, and K. Wolf. 2006. Local employment growth in West Germany: A dynamic panel approach. *Labour Economics* 13 (4): 445–458.

Bogliacino, F., M. Piva, and M. Vivarelli. 2012. R&D and employment: An application of the LSDVC estimator using European microdata. *Economics Letters* 116 (1): 56–59.

Chang, Y., and J.H. Hong. 2006. Do technological improvements in the manufacturing sector raise or lower employment? *American Economic Review* 96 (1): 352–368.

Choi, J., and I. Kim. 2015. The relationship between regional economic variables and local employment growth. *The Korea Spatial Planning Review* 86: 3–15. (in Korean).

Choi, J., and I. Kim. 2017. Regional total factor productivity and local employment growth: evidence from Korea. *Asia-Pacific Journal of Regional Science* 1 (2): 511–518.

Cuaresma, J.C. 2003. Okun's law revisited. *Oxford Bulletin of Economics and Statistics* 65 (4): 439–451.

Engle, R.F., and C.W.J. Granger. 1987. Co-integration and error correction: Representation. *Estimation, and Testing, Econometrica* 55 (2): 251–276.

Gali, J. 1999. Technology, employment, and the business cycle: Do technology shocks explain aggregate fluctuations? *American Economic Review* 89 (1): 249–271.

Fisher, J.D. 2006. The dynamic effects of neutral and investment-specific technology shocks. *Journal of Political Economy* 114 (3): 413–451.

Freeman, D.G. 2000. Regional tests of Okun's law. *International Advances in Economic Research* 6 (3): 557–570.

Kim, B. 2012. Do technological innovations cause jobless growth? *The Korean Economic Review* 60 (3): 5–54.

Kim, J. 2017. Growthless jobs: A comparative analysis of seven countries. *Ordo Economics Journal* 20 (2): 131–154. (in Korean).

Lachenmaier, S., and H. Rottmann. 2011. Effects of innovation on employment: A dynamic panel analysis. *International Journal of Industrial Organization* 29 (2): 210–220.

Pedroni, P. 2001. Fully modified OLS for heterogeneous cointegrated panels, In Nonstationary panels, panel cointegration, and dynamic panels. *Emerald Group Publishing Limited* 15: 93–130.

Phillips, P.C., and B.E. Hansen. 1990. Statistical inference in instrumental variables regression with I (1) processes. *The Review of Economic Studies* 57 (1): 99–125.

StataCorp, L. P. 2005. *Stata base reference manual* (Vol. 2).

Stolbov, M. 2015. Causality between credit depth and economic growth: Evidence from 24 OECD countries, *BOFIT Discussion Paper*, No.15, 1-32.

Van Reenen, J. 1997. Employment and technological innovation: evidence from UK manufacturing firms. *Journal of Labor Economics* 2: 255–284.

# Chapter 4
# Identification of Demand Factors for Life Insurance and Savings Deposits Using Nonlinear ARDL Framework: Korea and Japan

**Eun-Yub Park and Young-Jae Kim**

## 4.1 Introduction

In recent years, the global economy has been faced with high volatility since the 2008 global financial crisis. For this reason, it is difficult to predict the prospects of each specific industry especially in the area of financial sector. In particular, the global insurance industry responds sensitively to the highly volatile global economy coupled with low economic growth and low inflation rates, and near-zero interest rates. These factors have reduced the growth rate of life insurance industry, by making an adverse transition from the real sector to the financial sector.

Life insurance industry bears potential risks that individuals and corporate cannot properly manage by themselves, and it enables each stakeholder to freely engage in economic activities. In the case of property insurance industry, it has marked a quite stable growth rate despite low growth of the global economy. However, life insurance industry has encountered rapid declines in investment revenues due to low interest rates.

In addition, the low interest rate has been pointed out as the most significant factor that threatens the insurance industry. The interest rate risks would not have a positive impact on future momentum of interest rate rises. The difference between the current and the future interest rates of insurance firms is referred to as secondary losses of interest rates, and it originates from unexpected low future interest rates. In fact, this phenomenon comes out from intrinsic characteristics of insurance firms. For insurance holders, they are more likely to cancel their insurance contracts if it is expected not to guarantee a desired return, which would lead to liquidity risks for insurers.

---

E.-Y. Park (✉) · Y.-J. Kim
Pusan National University, Busan, South Korea
e-mail: rarara3028@pusan.ac.kr

Y.-J. Kim
e-mail: kimyj@pusan.ac.kr



M. Hosoe et al. (eds.), *Applied Analysis of Growth, Trade, and Public Policy*,
https://doi.org/10.1007/978-981-13-1876-4_4

Increasing interest rate volatility influences duration of both assets and liabilities, and that is also directly linked with bank's profits. Therefore, unexpected low interest rates severely deteriorate banks' business environments, which is closely related to increasing mergers and acquisitions of insurance firms and banks in recent days.

Due to relatively easy access to insurance companies and banks, public individuals rely much on those institutions for their present and future economic activities. Since they have a direct connection with the public, instability of those institutions would bring about significant social problems in addition to economic difficulties. To ensure the stability of those sectors, each insurer and bank should embark on internal financial management. Then, it will ensure them minimum revenues despite the volatility risks.

This paper attempts to identify demand factors of life insurance and savings deposits in Korea and Japan, where the two countries share similar socio-cultural characteristics. Furthermore, each industry makes a large effort on conducting a stable and sustainable management. Figuring out the relationship between performance of each industry and macro-economic variables would help make the best business strategy.

Briefly comparing the similarities of insurance inclination in Korea and Japan, the main purpose of Korea's insurance purchase is investigated, which is assumed to prepare for a retired life due to rapidly aging population. Likewise, retirement funds that aim to prepare for entering aging society has constantly increased in Japan, despite declining generation subscription rate since 1994. In addition, two countries have similarly undergone diversification of sales channels, which results in increased young consumers, and leads to change in population composition arising from low birth rates.

Japan's insurance market is much larger than that of Korea, but both marked similar number of insurance policy holders per household, which is about 'four'. And average annual insurance premium expenditure in Japan was 3,554 dollars per capita and ranked 14th in the world insurance market. In case of Korea, it was 3,034 dollars per capital and ranked 18th. Insurance preference referred to as insurance premium to GDP ratio was 11.42% in Korea, ranked 6th, and 10.82% in Japan, ranked 8th. These figures stem from not only high affinity to insurance, but also aging population and economic recession. By comparing the life insurance industry in each country, then we can provide meaningful implications for insurance firms' good decision-making in Korea.

Short-run demand elasticities of both life insurance and savings deposits are predicted to be low because those are perceived as long-run products. However, we need to perform both the short-run and the long-run relationships as well as forecast in order to secure the stability of each corresponding industry.

Therefore, the aim of our research is to identify the demand factors of life insurance and savings deposits in association with macro-economic variables. Specifically, we first analyze the short-run and the long-run relationships between each industry and macro-economic variables by using NARDL model incorporating a time difference. NARDL model helps to determine whether macroeconomic variables have a symmetrical or asymmetrical effect on both demands.

An overall structure of this chapter takes the form of five sections, beginning with this introduction. Section 4.2 presents the previous research associated with insurance demand factors. Section 4.3 explains the methodology used for this study. In Sect. 4.4, empirical results are described. And finally, the conclusion gives a brief summary and critiques of the findings together with some implications.

## 4.2 Literature Review

The importance of insurance regarding its risk-transferring role, has been recently emphasized in financial sectors. However, the insurance sector has still received less attention than the sectors of banks and stocks. Also, there are few previous researches that cover demand factors of insurance and savings deposits, which are greatly influenced by cultural aspects of each individual country such as unique traditions, religions and customs. Therefore, when we attempt to compare the demand factors, we should consider the above-mentioned cultural aspects, in addition to the levels of economic and financial developments.

The demand factors of life insurance and savings deposits can be divided into several categories; economic factors, socio-cultural factors, demographic factors and insurance factors that cover risks. Economic factors include the size of GDP, inflation and unemployment rates, the level of income, stock price and interest rates. Hammond et al. (1996) investigated a correlation between life insurance premium and various variables through regression analysis, and figured out that income was statistically significant. Beenstock et al. (1988) again revealed that there was a positive correlation between non-life insurance premiums and income. Also, Browne and Kim (1993) claimed that economic growth and life insurance premium were closely related focusing on the rapid growth of insurance market in the post-World War II era. In short, most of the previous studies point out that the demand for life insurance is positively related with income, and it grows with the economic growth.

Haiss and Sümegi (2008) showed how insurance investment and insurance premium were related with GDP growth rate. That is, the growth rate of life insurance has a positive impact on GDP growth, and actual interest rate and the level of economic development are deeply interrelated with the insurance industry. S. Nam (2013) revealed that China's economic growth and insurance industries are in a positive relationship, and however, the long-term relationship between total savings in the nation and insurance premiums turns out to be negative. China is emerging as a superpower in the sector of insurance.

S. Nam (2006) investigated the insurance industry's economic contribution to the overall economy using GMM and Pane-VAR model with 16 advanced countries. That is, the development of a country's insurance industry serves to increase economic growth. Also the insurance industry plays an important role in determining major economic variables, such as GDP per capital. Therefore this paper asserts the insurance industry leads to economic growth by helping increase GDP per capita.

The insurance industry contributes to price stability, which in turn servers to stabilize the overall economy.

After East Asian financial crisis, personal views on finance have been changed considerably. Kim and Park (2014) researched the linkage between demands for life insurance and savings deposits, and macro-economic fluctuations. This paper proved that demand elasticity of life insurance is greater than that of savings deposits.

Following the economic factors, socio-cultural factors may include religion, ethnicity, social security and educational backgrounds. Beck and Webb (2003) noted that life insurance has become an increasingly important part in the financial sector and a major source of investment in the capital market. But what drives a large variation in the life insurance market across countries remains unclear yet. In this article, we assume that developments in a banking sector, religious and institutional indicators can be good predictors for demand factors of life insurance. However, education, life expectancy, young dependency ratio, and level of social security system do not have a great significance with demands for life insurance.

Nevertheless, Browne and Kim (1993) insists that countries with Islamic cultures have a negative impact on demands for life insurance. Similarly, in Korea, market sellers of insurance, associated with school connections and kinships, take an important role in affecting demands for insurance. In case of Japan, unlike Korea demands for insurance highly depend on the sales agent's level of education. Besides, social security and political stability also contribute to lowering dependence on private insurance. The higher the level of education, especially the education level of the wife, the higher demand in the life insurance. These socio-cultural factors provide useful information for analyzing insurance demand factors by country.

The demographic and insurance-specific factors may include the size of family members, life expectancy, age structure, the proportion of economically active population, sex, and variables related to human services in the insurance business. Demand for insurance is expected to increase with higher anticipated life expectancy and the number of families increases. Truett and Truett (1990) estimated the life insurance demands for both of United States and Mexico. It is shown that the age, education and income levels affect the demands for life insurance. Particularly, the level of income showed a positive relationship in Mexico, while the age of the household showed a positive relationship in the United States. Donghui Li et al. (2007) investigated the determinants of life insurance consumption in OECD countries and showed that demand increases with education level, but life expectancy and expenditures on social security reduce a life insurance demand. The higher level of financial development and the higher degree of competition in the insurance market stimulate the sale of life insurance. Ichiro et al. (2012) argues that aging populations has a negative impact on GNP, because of reduced proportion of labor force and less savings. Considering the aging population in small open economies, a decline in the domestic capital return encourages investment in foreign capital, mitigating the adverse effects of aging population on GNP. Joung et al. (2000) analyzed a causality between GNP, savings and insurance. This research identifies that growth of both GNP and total savings lead to more life insurance.

In this chapter we analyze and compare the demand elasticities of household life insurance and savings deposits in Korea and Japan. Both countries are considered to face similar economic and socio-cultural environments. In recent years, Korea has been experiencing a low economic growth, rapid aging and population decline as Japan had in the past.

## 4.3 Methodology and Model

Nonlinear model is typically applied to the error correction mechanism associated with long-run relationships with threshold ECM by Balke and Fomby (1997), Markov-Switching ECM of Psaradakis et al. (2004). The long-run relationship has been noted with the properties of asymmetry or non-linearity in the framework of nonlinear model. Recently, nonlinear modelling framework based on the ARDL approach is developed considering both long-run and short-run asymmetries by Shin et al. (2014). Shin et al. (2014) also extends the ARDL-based dynamic corrections model incorporating the works of Phillips and Hansen (1990), and Pesaran and Shin (1998) in a dynamically parametric framework. It is called NARDL- based ECM.

We assume that the lag order of macroeconomic variables and any change of them will have an asymmetric effect on demands for life insurance and savings deposits. In particular, the demand for life insurance and savings deposits occur in order to prepare for after the retirement period.

To represent NARDL model, asymmetric long-run regression Eq. (4.1) is presented, following Shin et al. (2014).

$$y_t = \beta^+ x_t^+ + \beta^- x_t^- + u_t$$

$$\Delta x_t = v_t \tag{4.1}$$

Where $\beta^+$ and $\beta^-$ are respective long-run parameters. $y_t$ and $x_t$ are scalar I(1) variables, and $x_t$ is decomposed as $x_0 + x_t^+ + x_t^-$, where $x^+$ and $x^-$ are partial sum processes of positive or negative changes in $x_t$ defined as follows.

$$x_t^+ = \sum_{j=1}^{t} \Delta x_j^+ = \sum_{j=1}^{t} \max(\Delta x_j, 0)$$

$$x_t^- = \sum_{j=1}^{t} \Delta x_j^- = \sum_{j=1}^{t} \min(\Delta x_j, 0) \tag{4.2}$$

OLS estimator of Eq. (4.1), remains consistent, but its asymptotic distribution is non-Gaussian. The estimator (4.1) may also possess endogeneity of the regressors or serially correlated error. To solve this problem, the NARDL(p, q) is developed by Pesaran et al. (2001). Estimator (4.2) dealt with a dynamically parametric framework with flexible, in which it represents relationships that exhibit combined long-run and short-run asymmetries.

$$y_t = \sum_{j=1}^{p} \phi_j y_{t-j} + \sum_{j=0}^{q} (\theta_j^{+'} x_{t-j}^{+} + \theta_j^{-'} x_{t-j}^{-}) + \varepsilon_t \tag{4.3}$$

where $x_t$ is a k $\times$ 1 vector of multiple regressors in the form of s $x_t = x_0 + x_t^{+} + x_t^{-}$. $\phi_j$ is an autoregressive parameter, $\theta_j^{+}$ and $\theta_j^{-}$ are the asymmetric distributed-lag parameters, and the error term, $\varepsilon_t$ has an iid process, $\varepsilon_t \sim iid(0, \sigma_\varepsilon^2)$. Shin et al. (2014) focuses on the case in which $x_t$ is decomposed into $x_t^{+}$ and $x_t^{-}$ around a threshold of zero. Thus, the partial sum processes$(x_t^{+} x_t^{-})$ may offer an economically meaningful interpretation.

For NARDL model equation (4.3) is rewritten in a form of error correction form(ECM), as shown in Eq. (4.4).

$$\Delta y_t = \rho y_{t-1} + \theta^{+'} x_{t-1}^{+} + \theta^{-'} x_{t-1}^{-} + \sum_{j=1}^{p-1} \gamma_j \Delta y_{t-j} + \sum_{j=0}^{q-1} (\pi_j^{+'} \Delta x_{t-j}^{+} + \pi_j^{-'} \Delta x_{t-j}^{-}) + e_t \tag{4.4}$$

where j $= 1, \ldots,$ q $- 1$, and $\beta^{+} = -\theta^{+}/\rho$, and $\beta^{-} = -\theta^{-}/\rho$ are asymmetric long-run coefficients. The NARDL model admits three general forms of asymmetry. (i) long-run or reaction asymmetry associated with $\beta^{+} \neq \beta^{-}$, (ii) impact asymmetry associated with the inequality of the coefficients on the contemporaneous first differences $\Delta x_t^{+}$ and $\Delta x_t^{-}$, (iii) adjustment asymmetry captured by the patterns of adjustment from initial equilibrium to new equilibrium following an economic perturbation. Adjustment asymmetry derives from the interaction of impact and reaction asymmetries in conjunction with the error correction coefficient, $\rho$.[1]

Shin et al. (2014) suggested two operational testing procedures for the existence of long-run relationship based on Eq. (4.4). If $\rho = 0$, it becomes to the regression involving only first differences, implying that there is no long-run relationship between the levels of $y_t$, $x_t^{+}$ and $x_t^{-}$. This is a t-statistic test for $H_0 : \rho = 0$ by Banerjee et al. (1998). It is denoted by $t_{BDM}$ in Table 4.2, while the other F-test by Pesaran et al. (2001). The F-test of joint null hypothesis is $H_0 : \rho = \theta^{+} = \theta^{-} = 0$ in Eq. (4.4). Likewise, we denote this test by $F_{PSS}$ in Table 4.2.

Following the previous literature, we decompose the movements of the FX into its two patterns as FX $= FX_0 + FX_t^{+} + FX_t^{-}$ where $FX_t^{+}$ and $FX_t^{-}$ are the partial sum process of positive(depreciation), and negative(appreciation) changes in FX. More precisely

[1]Shin et al. (2014), pp.7 – 15.

$$POS = FX_t^+ = \sum_{j=1}^{t} \Delta FX_j^+ = \sum_{j=1}^{t} \max(\Delta FX_j, 0)$$

$$NEG = FX_t^- = \sum_{j=1}^{t} \Delta FX_j^- = \sum_{j=1}^{t} \min(\Delta FX_j, 0) \quad (4.5)$$

Within NARDL-based ECM framework, we depict the model by the following equation.

$$\Delta K\_DEPO_t = \rho K\_DEPO_{t-1} + \theta^{+'} X_{t-1}^+ + \theta^{-'} X_{t-1}^- + \sum_{j=1}^{p-1} \gamma_j \Delta K\_DEPO_{t-j} + \sum_{j=0}^{q-1} (\pi_j^{+'} \Delta X_{t-j}^+ + \pi_j^{-'} \Delta X_{t-j}^-) + e_t \quad (4.6)$$

where $X_t$ is a k $\times$ 1 vector of I(1) regressors which include interest rate(R), IPI(IPI), exchange rate(FX), and stock index(ST) variables. Then we use Eq. (4.6) for the estimates of demands for deposits and life insurance in two counties, Korea and Japan.

In general, people in both countries purchase most of life insurance and/or savings deposits in preparation for the after-retirement period. According to the recent survey, the growth rates of pension and insurance assets in household sectors have increased by entering the aged society in both Korea and Japan, in particular, since the global financial crisis in Korea and the real estate bubble burst in Japan. Therefore we assume that both countries are faced with the similar social and economic environments since the 2000s. For this reason, life insurance and savings deposits seem to compete with each other as alternative long-term products. Therefore, we assume that the demands for life insurance and savings deposits may react differently to macroeconomic variables. For example, while an increase in interest rate might have a positive effect on savings deposits, it might have a negative effect on the demand for life insurance. In addition, we assume that the increase of IPI is expected to raise savings deposits. Depreciation of exchange rate also increases the savings deposits in the long run. On the other hand, stocks and deposits are predicted to have a negative relationship because they are considered to be substitutes.

## 4.4 The Empirical Results

To identify the demand factors of domestic life insurance and savings deposits, life insurance firms' new premium(NP), bank's 3 year household savings deposits-(DEPO), interest rate(R) based on CD yield (91 days), index of industrial production(IPI), exchange rate(FX), and the composite price index of stocks(ST) are used as the variables in both Korea and Japan. Each variable appropriately manipulated

**Table 4.1** Definition of variables

| Variable | | Definition | Measurement |
|---|---|---|---|
| Korea | K_DEPO | Savings deposits | Total household savings on bank(unit : KRW, 1 million), natural logarithm, BOK |
| | K_NP | Premiums of new polices(business) | New policy premium of the private life insurance company (unit : KRW 1 million), Natural logarithm, KIDI |
| | K_R | Interest rate | 3 months rate (CD) BOK |
| | K_IPI | Index of industrial production | All the industrial production index, Seasonally adjusted, Natural logarithm, BOK (2010 = 100) |
| | K_FX | Exchange rate | Korean Won to One U.S. Dollar, Natural logarithm, BOK |
| | K_ST | Korea composite stock Price index | KOSPI index, Natural logarithm, BOK |
| Japan | J_DEPO | Savings deposits | Total household savings on bank(unit : JPY, 1 million), Natural logarithm, BOJ |
| | J_NP | Premiums of new polices(business) | New policy premium of the private life insurance company(excluded post office life insurance, unit : JPY, 1 million), Natural logarithm, LIAJ |
| | J_R | Interest rate | 3month-Market interest rates BOJ |
| | J_IPI | Index of industrial production | All the industrial production index, Seasonally adjusted, Natural logarithm, BOJ |
| | J_FX | Exchange rate | Japanese Yen to One U.S. Dollar, Natural logarithm |
| | J_ST | Nikkei stock Price index | Nikkei(225), Natural logarithm, BOJ, |

Notes: BOK is the central in Korea and KIDI is Korea Insurance Development Institute, while BOJ is Japan's central bank and LIAJ is The Life Insurance Association of Japan

to verify and secure its stability and to measure the coefficient of elasticity. The variables except interest rate are denoted by taking natural logarithms. The samples are from January 2002 to December 2017, using monthly data.[2]

We construct two separate empirical models of demands for life insurance and banks deposits in Korea by denoting K_NP and K_DEPO, respectively. Just like, we put J as the first letter for the corresponding equation in case of Japan. Table 4.1 shows the summary of the variables.

[2]The NP series for Japan were used from April 2011 to September 2017. Therefore, this model represents the estimating unbalanced data set.

### 4.4.1 Unit Root Test

Statistically, most of time series data have the features of non-stationary stochastic trend and random walk with a drift. If these non-stationary data are included in regression, the outcomes can be driven by unrelated variables. Although, it does not matter whether the regressors are stationary processes I(0) or non-stationary processes I(1), in the specification of NARDL error correction model, but model does not allow I(2) noted by Pesaran et al. (2001) in an NARDL error correction model.

In considering the tendency of the time and constant term of each variable, both ADF(Augmented Dickey-Fuller) and PP(Phillips-Perron) tests were performed to check the existence of unit root.

Table 4.2 shows the results of ADF and PP tests which are based on MacKinnon (1996). ADF test results are presented that all variables are integrated of order one, I(1) at the 5% significance level. Since we need to consider the variable of K_DEPO as partial sum of positive(K_$DEPO^{+}$) and negative(K_$DEPO^{-}$) change, we should check the order of integration in the form of partial sum of positive and negative associated with all variables whether they represent I(2). The unit root test of all corresponding variables shows stationary processes at integration of order one.

**Table 4.2** The results of unit root test

| Variable | | ADF | | PP | |
|---|---|---|---|---|---|
| | | Level | First difference | Level | First difference |
| Korea | K_DEPOSIT | 0.302 | −11.273*** | −0.052 | −11.747*** |
| | K_NP | −1.500 | −3.601*** | −4.634*** | |
| | K_R | −1.479 | −7.763*** | −1.349 | −6.948*** |
| | K_IPI | −2.076 | −14.303*** | −2.052 | −14.366*** |
| | K_FX | −2.588 | −9.861*** | −2.594 | −8.974*** |
| | K_ST | −1.404 | −10.043*** | −2.255 | −9.911*** |
| Japan | J_DEPOSIT | 0.988 | −3.444*** | 0.012836 | −45.009*** |
| | J_NP | 1.247 | −3.249** | −9.2051*** | |
| | J_R | −1.139 | −6.370*** | −1.21115 | −10.055*** |
| | J_IPI | −2.643 | −11.916*** | −2.74933 | −11.978*** |
| | J_FX | −1.997 | −10.806*** | −1.920 | −10.901*** |
| | J_ST | −0.919 | −11.081*** | −0.958 | −11.251*** |

Notes: 1. K_DEPOSIT, K_R, and K_IPI variables include both intercept and time trend
Other variables only include intercept
2. ** implies significant at 5%, *** implies significant at 1%

**Table 4.3** Bounds test: overall models

| Division | Korea | | Japan | |
|---|---|---|---|---|
| | K_DEPO | K_NP | J_DEPO | J_NP |
| F-value | 9.964 | 6.369 | 7.400 | 40.083 |
| Critical values | Lower bounds critical values I(0) | | Upper bounds critical values I(1) | |
| 5% | 3.47 | | 4.57 | |
| 10% | 3.03 | | 4.06 | |

Notes: The critical value is applied with unrestricted intercept and unrestricted trend following Pesaran et al. (2001, p.301) table C1(v) case V.

### *4.4.2 Bounds–Test*

Before implementing the NARDL model, we need to check if the variables are co-integrated, and the coefficients are significant. Shin et al. (2014) suggests that testing procedures for existence of a cointegrated(asymmetric) long-run relationship based on the NARDL-ECM using the F-test done by Pesaran et al. (2001). More specifically, if $\rho = 0$ implying that there is no long-run relationship between the levels of $y_t$, $x_t^+$ and $x_t^-$ in Eq. (4.4), then null hypothesis becomes $H_0 : \rho = \theta^+ = \theta^- = 0$.

We now apply the combined null hypothesis of all variables at levels to secure the stability of each model following the above procedure. The outcomes are presented in Table 4.3. Bounds tests figuring out the asymmetric long-run relationship between related variables are shown in Table 4.8 with brief interpretation. The null hypothesis is 'no cointegration'. If the value of the test F-statistics exceeds the upper critical bounds value, then the null hypothesis is rejected. While the statics is lower than the lower bounds value, then the null hypothesis cannot be rejected. Thus, the models of K_DEPO, K_NP, J_DEPO and J_NP show the existence of cointegration significantly at 5% of critical values, higher than upper bounds. Then models are secured NARDL.

### *4.4.3 Estimation Results*

More than 200 models should be assumed, to get the efficient empirical results using an optimized model, the optimal lag order was selected using AIC(Akaike Information Criterion) and SBC(Schwartz Bayesian Criterion). In this paper, we refer to these estimators as NARDL-AIC. K_NP equation which is the demand for life insurance in Korea was selected as NARDL(2,2,0,0,0,1,1,3,0), K_DEPOSIT equation which is the demand for household savings deposits as NARDL(2,0,0,2,0,1,0,1,1), J_NP which is the demand for life insurance in Japan as NARDL(3,2,2,2,2,2,1,2,2) and demand for household savings deposits, J_DEPO equation are selected as NARDL(2,0,1,0,0,2,2,0,1).

The results of estimating the long-run and short-run coefficients using optimal NARDL equations are presented in Tables 4.4, 4.5, 4.6 and 4.7.

**Table 4.4** Estimation Results for K_DEPO

| Lags | 0 | 1 | 2 | 3 | 4 |
|---|---|---|---|---|---|
| Panel A: short-run coefficient estimates | | | | | |
| ΔK_DEPO | | −0.150*<br>[−1.754] | −0.207**<br>[−2.353] | | |
| $\Delta FX^{+}$ | 0.200***<br>[4.454] | | | | |
| $\Delta FX^{-}$ | −0.081<br>[−1.546] | | | | |
| $\Delta R^{+}$ | 0.022**<br>[2.295] | 0.019<br>[1.628] | 0.023**<br>[2.391] | | |
| $\Delta R^{-}$ | −0.007<br>[−0.977] | | | | |
| $\Delta IPI^{+}$ | −0.069<br>[−1.325] | −0.097**<br>[−2.429] | | | |
| $\Delta IPI^{-}$ | −0.083<br>[−1.447] | | | | |
| $\Delta ST^{+}$ | −0.003**<br>[−2.256] | −0.075***<br>[−2.736] | | | |
| $\Delta ST^{-}$ | 0.054**<br>[2.181] | 0.059**<br>[2.387] | | | |
| Panel B: long-run coefficient | | | | | |
| $FX^{+}$ | 1.045**<br>[2.001] | $IPI^{+}$ | −0.901<br>[−1.385] | | |
| $FX^{-}$ | −0.796<br>[−1.223] | $IPI^{-}$ | −0.439<br>[−0.735] | | |
| $R^{+}$ | 0.147**<br>[2.463] | $ST^{+}$ | −0.622*<br>[−1.807] | | |
| $R^{-}$ | 0.005<br>[0.086] | $ST^{-}$ | 0.497**<br>[2.027] | | |
| | | constant | 0.543**<br>[2.173] | | |
| Panel C: diagnostic statistics | | | | | |
| | Adj.$R^2$ | D-W | $F_{SC}$ | $F_{HET}$ | $x^2_{NORM}$ |
| | 0.555 | 2.007 | 1.601<br>(0.176) | 0.901<br>(0.651) | 0.108<br>(0.955) |

Notes : Parentheses, [ ], ( ) are respectively t-statistics and p-value; *, **, *** indicates significant levels at 10% 5%,1%, respectively; superscripts(+) and (-) indicate positive and negative partial sums

Tables 4.4, 4.5, 4.6, 4.7 and 4.8 report the empirical results of demands for saving deposit and life insurance each Korea and Japan. Each table is consisted of three panels. Panel A reveals the estimates of short-run coefficients. Panel B shows the long-run coefficients, and diagnostic statistics are reported in Panel C. Long-run coefficient is captured by $-\theta_i^+/\rho$ and $-\theta_i^-/\rho$ respectively for positive and negative effect of each variable on both demands.

Diagnostic statistics imply the fitness of the overall model. Several tests such as serial correlation($F_{SC}$), heteroskedasticity ($F_{HET}$), and normality($x^2_{NORM}$) were conducted to assess the fitness of the NARDL model. As Tables from 4.4, 4.5, 4.6 suggest, it is confirmed that there is no serious problem in the validity and inference of the models of the K_DEPO, J_DEPO and J_NP models based on the results of the tests mentioned in the above. Even though there is one thing to note that normality in K_NP model is rejected.

Table 4.4 shows that in the long-run the effect of interest rate on saving deposit for Korea(K_DEPO) have asymmetric results. That are negative interest rate effect on K_DEPO is different from that of positive interest rate effect. The long-run coefficient for the lagged positive interest rate effect is positive as 0.113. This implies that in long-run, in increasing interest rate leads to an increase in K_DEPO. Especially, a 1% increase in interest rate causes a 0.113% increase in K_DEPO. According to Table 4.4, 1% point increase in stock price(ST) decreases Korea's demand for savings deposits(K_DEPO) by 0.622% point, while the demand rises by 0.479% point in response to 1% decrease in stock price. This outcome is compatible with our expectation, resulted from household's rearrangement of assets portfolio depending on stock prices.

Depreciation (fall in domestic currency) results in a positive effect on demand for life insurance in Korea as shown in Table 4.5. The long-run coefficient, 0.145, implies that demand for Korea's life insurance would rise by 0.145% point due to 1% depreciation in Korean currency. Unlikely, the demand falls by 0.064% point when Korean currency appreciates by 1 % point, which is more than the previous case. Thus, the responses of demands for life insurance turn out to be asymmetrical depending on the direction.

In case of Japan, demands for savings deposits are affected by the foreign exchange rate, interest rate, index of industrial production and stock price at 5% significance level as shown in Table 4.6 More specifically, demands for Japan's savings deposits rise due to JPY depreciation, increase in both interest rate and index of industrial production, but increase in stock price rather decreases those demands. These results are consistent with those in Korea.

Table 4.7, showing the estimation results of long-run relationship, asserts that JYP depreciation leads the demand for Japan's life insurance with a high coefficient of 8.203. Rather, the demand falls significantly due to the fall in IPI and the rise in stock price.

As discussed in the above, it is worthwhile to point out the similarities and differences between Korea and Japan when we analyze the responses of demands for savings deposits and life insurance to the changes in macroeconomic variables.

**Table 4.5** Estimation Results for K_NP

| Lags | 0 | 1 | 2 | 3 | 4 |
|---|---|---|---|---|---|
| Panel A: short-run coefficient estimates | | | | | |
| ΔK_NP | | −0.399*** [−4.354] | −0.285*** [−3.710] | | |
| $\Delta FX^{+}$ | 0.771 [0.846] | 0.271 [0.232] | 1.568*** [2.324] | | |
| $\Delta FX^{-}$ | 0.886 [0.809] | | | | |
| $\Delta R^{+}$ | 0.158 [0.813] | | | | |
| $\Delta R^{-}$ | 0.097 [0.740] | | | | |
| $\Delta IPI^{+}$ | 0.351 [0.335] | 0.839*** [2.851] | | | |
| $\Delta IPI^{-}$ | −0.310 [−0.301] | −0.527 [−0.438] | | | |
| $\Delta ST^{+}$ | −0.245 [−0.456] | −0.543 [−1.307] | −0.125 [−0.228] | −0.820* [−1.903] | |
| $\Delta ST^{-}$ | 0.594* [1.869] | | | | |
| Panel B: long-run coefficient | | | | | |
| $FX^{+}$ | 0.145** [2.193] | $IPI^{+}$ | 0.418 [0.459] | | |
| $FX^{-}$ | −0.604 [−0.689] | $IPI^{-}$ | 0.362 [0.571] | | |
| $R^{+}$ | −0.246* [−1.756] | $ST^{+}$ | −0.584 [−1.215] | | |
| $R^{-}$ | −0.015 [−0.164] | $ST^{-}$ | 0.341 [0.857] | | |
| | | | 8.380*** [4.287] | | |
| Panel C: diagnostic statistics | | | | | |
| | Adj.$R^2$ | D-W | $F_{SC}$ | $F_{HET}$ | $x^2_{NORM}$ |
| | 0.560 | 2.098 | 1.565 (0.186) | 1.707 (0.093) | 358.1 (0.00) |

Notes: Parentheses, [ ], ( ) are respectively t-statistics and p-value; *, **, *** indicates significant levels at 10% 5%,1%, respectively; superscripts(+) and (−) indicate positive and negative partial sums

**Table 4.6** Estimation Results for J_DEPO

| Lags | 0 | 1 | 2 | 3 | 4 |
|---|---|---|---|---|---|
| Panel A: short-run coefficient estimates | | | | | |
| ΔJ_DEPO | | −0.423***<br>[−7.311] | −0.249***<br>[−5.002] | | |
| $\Delta FX^{+}$ | 0.034<br>[0.908] | | | | |
| $\Delta FX^{-}$ | 0.003<br>[0.071] | −0.001<br>[−0.036] | | | |
| $\Delta R^{+}$ | −0.088***<br>[−3.722] | | | | |
| $\Delta R^{-}$ | −0.011<br>[−0.300] | | | | |
| $\Delta IPI^{+}$ | 0.014<br>[0.231] | 0.003<br>[0.586] | 0.006*<br>[1.802] | | |
| $\Delta IPI^{-}$ | −0.037*<br>[−1.719] | −0.058**<br>[−2.539] | −0.060*<br>[−1.689] | | |
| $\Delta ST^{+}$ | 0.001<br>[0.058] | | | | |
| $\Delta ST^{-}$ | 0.028**<br>[2.546] | 0.030**<br>[2.352] | | | |
| Panel B: long-run coefficient | | | | | |
| $FX^{+}$ | 0.158***<br>[4.932] | $IPI^{+}$ | 0.158***<br>[4.362] | | |
| $FX^{-}$ | 0.001<br>[0.024] | $IPI^{-}$ | −0.033<br>[−1.274] | | |
| $R^{+}$ | 0.055***<br>[6.570] | $ST^{+}$ | −0.033*<br>[−1.794] | | |
| $R^{-}$ | 0.026<br>[0.789] | $ST^{-}$ | 0.012<br>[0.0658] | | |
| | | constant | 6.563***<br>[5.917] | | |
| Panel C: diagnostic statistics | | | | | |
| | Adj.$R^2$ | D-W | $F_{SC}$ | $F_{HET}$ | $x^2_{NORM}$ |
| | 0.788 | 2.064 | 2.286<br>(0.121) | 1.272<br>(0.127) | 0.286<br>(0.866) |

Notes: Parentheses, [ ], ( ) are respectively t-statistics and p-value; *, **, *** indicates significant levels at 10% 5%,1%, respectively; superscripts(+) and (−) indicate positive and negative partial sums

**Table 4.7** Estimation Results for J_NP

| Lags | 0 | 1 | 2 | 3 | 4 |
|---|---|---|---|---|---|
| Panel A: short-run coefficient estimates | | | | | |
| ΔJ_NP | | 0.922*** [9.780] | −0.255*** [−4.338] | −0.179** [−2.769] | |
| $\Delta FX^+$ | 5.789*** [3.074] | −12.629*** [−5.341] | −10.104*** [2.515] | | |
| $\Delta FX^-$ | −4.561 [−1.756] | −14.118*** [−5.761] | | | |
| $\Delta R^+$ | −32.059*** [−3.783] | −0.179** [−2.304] | | | |
| $\Delta R^-$ | −3.013 [−1.680] | −11.005*** [−6.699] | −7.190*** [−4.038] | | |
| $\Delta IPI^+$ | −14.50*** [−4.721] | −21.29*** [−6.339] | −20.968*** [−5.934] | | |
| $\Delta IPI^-$ | 8.712*** [4.022] | 7.707*** [2.879] | | | |
| $\Delta ST^+$ | −1.534 [−1.46] | 3.127*** [3.153] | 2.278** [2.215] | | |
| $\Delta ST^-$ | 2.331** [2.893] | 4.779*** [4.487] | 2.275** [2.437] | | |
| Panel B: long-run coefficient | | | | | |
| $FX^+$ | 8.203*** [6.330] | $IPI^+$ | 0.556 [0.432] | | |
| $FX^-$ | −0.052 [−0.073] | $IPI^-$ | −1.639** [−2.523] | | |
| $R^+$ | 0.612 [0.0679] | $ST^+$ | −3.531*** [−6.607] | | |
| $R^-$ | −0.177 [−0.233] | $ST^-$ | 0.523 [1.178] | | |
| | | | 32.021 [1.210] | | |
| Panel C: diagnostic statistics | | | | | |
| | Adj.$R^2$ | D-W | $F_{SC}$ | $F_{HET}$ | $x^2_{NORM}$ |
| | 0.967 | 1.625 | 1.108 (0.451) | 0.727 (0.795) | 2.325 (0.312) |

Notes: Parentheses, [ ], ( ) are respectively t-statistics and p-value; *, **, *** indicates significant levels at 10, 5, 1%, respectively; superscripts (+) and (−) indicate positive and negative partial sums

**Table 4.8** Bounds Test: Asymmetric Long-run Relationship

| Variable | $F_{PSS}$ | $t_{BDM}$ |
|---|---|---|
| | $H_0: \rho = \theta^+ = \theta^- = 0$ | $H_0: -(\theta_i^+)/\rho = -(\theta_i^-)/\rho$ |
| Panel A: K_DEPO equation | | |
| FX | 3.637** | 2.012** |
| R | 2.720** | 1.067 |
| IPI | 3.162** | −1.591 |
| ST | 2.112 | −2.502** |
| Panel B: K_NP equation | | |
| FX | 6.277*** | 2.674** |
| R | 9.366*** | −1.160 |
| IPI | 6.722*** | 0.068 |
| ST | 6.566*** | 3.461*** |
| Panel C: J_DEPO equation | | |
| FX | 12.601*** | 3.581*** |
| R | 21.536*** | 0.778 |
| IPI | 13.476*** | 5.649*** |
| ST | 12.185*** | −0.731 |
| Panel D: J_NP equation | | |
| FX | 139.964*** | 5.297*** |
| R | 126.242*** | 0.082 |
| IPI | 137.642*** | 1.642 |
| ST | 143.321*** | −6.321*** |

Notes: *, **, *** indicates respectively for significant at 10% 5%,1%; Testing to $F_{PSS}$, the 5% upper and lower bound critical values are [3.47, 4.57] for k = 4

An increase in interest rate gives a positive effect on the demand for savings deposits in both countries, but ambiguous effects on the demand for life insurance. It is also shown that depreciation in both countries results in the increase in demands for both savings deposits and life insurance.

Since appreciation decreases demands for both products in a less magnitudes, there exists a strong asymmetry in association with foreign exchange rate. As expected, demands for both savings deposits and life insurance fall in response to the rise in stock price.

Table 4.8, describes the results of bounds test for asymmetric co-integration using the F-test of Pesaran et al. (2001) and t-test of Banerjee et al. (1998). Banerjee et al. (1998) proposed the t-statistic test $\rho = 0$ against $\rho > 0$ in Eq. (4.4). We then test the asymmetric long-run coefficients using t-statistic.

The null hypothesis was rejected as shown in Table 4.8. Table 4.8 shows that there is one asymmetric long-run cointegration relationship in all variables except for the stock variable. Furthermore, the null hypothesis that positive long-run coefficient and negative long-run coefficient are equal was not accepted because FX does not meet the critical value of 5% significance level. FX and IPI in the J_DEPO model and FX, ST variables in the J_NP model are all rejected. Therefore, we can interpret that exchange rate in Korea results in a long-run asymmetric relation in savings deposits. It means that depreciation of the KRW leads to a smaller effect on savings deposits than appreciation.

On the other hand, in Japan depreciation has a greater effect on savings deposits than appreciation. This means that when JPY depreciates, the demand for savings deposits increases. Positive change in IPI variable increases savings deposits in Japan. A positive change is more significant than a negative change in IPI. Life insurance in Japan is more sensitive to depreciation of JPY than appreciation, which implies that demand for life insurance increased when JPY depreciated. In Japan, positive changes in stock index have a greater effect on life insurance than negative changes.

It is known that the demands show asymmetric responses to the changes in macroeconomic variables depending on a positive or negative change. This implies that the increase in demands to a positive change in stock index is greater than the decrease to a negative change. The other variables such as foreign exchange and the interest rate show similar responses, which can be interpreted that the households accelerate demand thus expecting an optimistic outlook on future economy.

Unlike the other variables, the interest rate results in different responses of the demands for life insurance between Korea and Japan, where in Japan the demands have continuously increased due to the fact that the majority of households asset belongs to the aged people over 60's. They hold higher percentage of life insurance and bank deposits as they are getting older. Korea is expected to follow the same trend in the aftermath of the 2008 global financial crisis, we assert. As unexpected, Korea's demand for bank deposits rather falls in response to the increase in IPI, which may be interpreted that people has less incentives for bank deposits due to lower interest rates. The lower interest rate also reduces the cost of borrowing, which improves borrowing environments and thus leads to high household debts.

## 4.5 Summary and Conclusions

In this chapter we identify demand factors of savings deposits and life insurance in Korea and Japan where we assume the two countries share social and cultural similarities, based on the fact that peoples depend on private financial institutions for their wealth managements in order for their long life expectancy in addition to public pension systems and/or social securities revealed in a recent survey.

The followings are main empirical results; first, an increase in interest rate leads to the rise in demand for savings deposits in both countries, but it rather decreases demand for life insurance in Korea. In case of Korea, demand deposits are more sensitive than life insurance to the change in interest rate when the two products are competing for their after-retirement life. Second, favorable stock prices reduce demands for both savings deposits and life insurance, which implies that profitability is more pursued than stability unlike the trend in the past. Third, depreciation in domestic currencies raises demands for both savings and life insurance, but appreciation reduces both demands, where the responses of demands are asymmetric depending on depreciation or appreciation. Besides, depreciation results in improvements in balance of payments, and thus helps achieve sustainable economic growth in the long-run. This reminds us that the aggressive expansionary monetary policy after 2008 global financial crisis may help the recovery of depressed economy by increasing aggregate demand.

As mentioned in the above, the paper investigates the effects of macroeconomic variables on savings deposits and life insurance which directly influence the profits of banks and insurance companies. We found that the demands for two alternative products are affected by both foreign exchange rate and stock prices. This finding suggests that banks and insurance companies both need to develop new financial products with high profitability and stability to attract more consumers.

## References

Balke, N.S., and T.B. Fomby. 1997. Threshold Cointegration. *International Economic Review* 38 (3): 627–645.

Banerjee, A., J. Dolado, and R. Mestre. 1998. Error-correction Mechanism Tests for Cointegration in a Single-Equation Framework. *Journal of Time Series Analysis* 19 (3): 267–283.

Beck, T., and I. Webb. 2003. Economic, Demographic, and Institutional Determinants of Life Insurance Consumption across Countries. *The World Bank Economic Review* 17 (1): 51–88.

Beenstock, M., G. Dickinson, and S. Khajuria. 1988. The Relationship Between Property-Liability Insurance Premiums and Income: An International Analysis. *Journal of Risk and Insurance* 55: 259–272.

Browne, M.J., and K. Kim. 1993. An International Analysis of Life Insurance Demand. *The Journal of Risk and Insurance* 60: 616–634.

Donghui, L. 2007. The Demand for Life Insurance in OECD Countries. *The Journal of Risk and Insurance* 74 (3): 637–652.

Haiss, P., and K. Sümegi. 2008. The Relationship Between Insurance and Economic Growth in Europe: A Theoretical and Empirical Analysis. *Empirica* 35 (4): 405–431.

Hammond, D.J., D.B. Houston, E.F. Melander. 1996. Determinants of Household Life Insurance Premium Expenditure: An Empirical Investigation. *Journal of Risk and Insurance*. 34–3: 397–408.

Ichiro M., T. Oda, N. Sudo. 2012. Macroeconomic Impact of Population Aging in Japan: A Perspective from an Overlapping Generations Model, NPRA Paper No. 42550, Posted 12.

Joung, H., H. Jeong, and M. Chi. 2000. The Study of Empirical Studies of the Relationship Between Insurance, Savings and GNP. *Journal of Insurance* 56: 91–116.

Kim, H., and E. Park. 2014. An Empirical Study on Demand Factors for Life Insurance and Bank Deposits using ARDL-Bounds Test. *Korea Insurance Institute* 97: 133–157.

MacKinnon, J. 1996. Numerical Distribution Function for Unit Root and Cointegration Tests. Journal of Applied Econometrics 11 (6): 601–618.

Nam, S. 2006. A Study on the Causality Between the Insurance Industry and Economic Growth. *Korean Insurance Journal* 74: 169–197.

Nam, S. 2013. The Long-Run Relationship between Insurance Development and Economic Growth in China. *The Journal of Philippine & Southeast Asian Studies* 16 (1): 105–129.

Pesaran, M.H., Y. Shin. 1998. *An Autoregressive Distributed-Lag Modelling Approach to Co-regration Analysis, Econometrics and Economic Theory in the 20th Century: The Ragnar Fisch Centennial Symposium*, ed. Steinar Strom, 371–413. Cambridge: Cambridge University Press.

Pesaran, M., Y. Shin, and R.J. Smith. 2001. Bounds Testing Approaches to the Analysis of Level Relationships. *Journal of Applied Econometrics* 16: 289–326.

Phillips, P.C.B., and B. Hansen. 1990. Statistical Inference in Instrumental Variables Regression with I(1) Processes. *Review of Economic Studies* 57: 99–125.

Psaradakis, Z., M. Sola, and F. Spagnolo. 2004. On Markov Error-Correction Models, with an Application to Stock Prices and Dividends. *Journal of Applied Economics* 19 (1): 69–88.

Shin, Y. et al. 2014. Modelling Asymmetric Cointegration and Dynamic Multipliers in a Nonlinear ARDL Framework. *Festschrift in Honor of Peter Schmidt*, ed. Sickles, R.C., William C. Horrace. Berlin: Springer.

Truett, B.D., and L.J. Truett. 1990. The Demand for Life Insurance in Mexico and The United States: A Comparative Study. *The Journal of Risk and Insurance* 57: 321–328.

# Chapter 5
# Analysis on Firm Behavior and Individual's Utility Maximization Through Regional Agglomeration Economies

**Daisuke Nakamura**

## 5.1 Introduction

In conventional economic theory, an individual's utility maximization behavior is measured based on his or her consumption of goods and services under a given budget constraint. Based on this idea, the argument here also includes the element of job environment. Here, the job environment can be interpreted to mean that every laborer faces time consumption for work, which requires them to purchase outsourcing services to complete private tasks. The quantity of such external services demanded will be much higher if the individual is responsible for the care of his or her family. In addition, working individuals who are categorized as highly skilled labors may have less time for spare time, as the organization's dependence on them is not lower.

This chapter also explains the relationship between those services and the level of regional welfare. The study shows that as the level of regional welfare improves, the quantity of external services demanded could be smaller. The level of regional welfare may depend on the extent of local community cooperative arrangements. In other words, a region where advanced regional welfare is achieved may have more opportunities for cooperation among local individuals. Hence, the examination expands to include a self-sustaining regional system under limited local resources. The self-sustaining regional system under limited local resources has already been analyzed by Nakamura (2016) in terms of rural transportation network and by Nakamura (2018) with respect to the optimal spatial economic organization in rural areas. However, local firm behavior and individual's utility maximization through regional agglomeration economies have not been sufficiently investigated in the relevant studies on this subject.

The following section reveals that the availabilities of local resources and the job environment of each individual are indirectly relevant to each other via firm behavior.

D. Nakamura (✉)
Fukuoka Women's University, Fukuoka, Japan
e-mail: dnakamura@fwu.ac.jp



M. Hosoe et al. (eds.), *Applied Analysis of Growth, Trade, and Public Policy*,
https://doi.org/10.1007/978-981-13-1876-4_5

There, we demonstrate that firm behavior may affect the job environment of individuals as well as the availability of local resources. It is also shown that the regional welfare level can be enhanced through regional agglomeration economies. Here, regional agglomeration economies are slightly different from established agglomeration economies based on external terms such as localization economies and urbanization economies. Localization economies were initially addressed by Marshall (1892), and applied to location analysis by Weber (1909 [1928]); these economies are closely related to the manufacturing industry. Urbanization economies were introduced by Hoover (1937) and examined in more detail by Isard (1956), Evans (1972), Glaeser (2001), and Parr (2002); these economies have the advantages of administrative accessibility, well-organized infrastructure, a variety of labor supply, and an advanced transportation system and communication network. In addition to these two representative types, activity-complex economies were also introduced by Parr (2002); these economies can be seen at processes involving upstream and downstream linkages with other firms.

While localization, urbanization, and activity-complex economies are engaged within the industry, regional agglomeration economies are units among different types of economic agents within the region. The notion may be similar to urbanization economies, but regional agglomeration economies are also applicable in rural areas. In this sense, they have certain similarities with the "regional externalities" in Parr (2015), while our analysis of "regional agglomeration economies" involves household economics in addition to the location decision-making of firms. The conceptual framework of our analysis can be directly relevant to externality in economic activity. Using a theoretical approach, Hanley et al. (2007) added natural environmental quality as an external element of the individual's utility level, and this is included in the form of the household's utility function. They addressed how the natural environmental quality such as clean air and clean water, or polluted air and polluted water may positively or negatively affect an individual's satisfaction through household's utility maximization behavior.

Under this background, the next section introduces a simple economic model for households and firms, connected with the job environment of the individual. Section 5.3 introduces a hypothetical analysis using the household economic model. Also, regional policy is discussed to detect the condition of utilizing regional agglomeration economies, and further avenues are explored in Sect. 5.4.

## 5.2 Economic Model on Households and Firms

This section presents a simple model for the decision-making behavior of households and firms, which begins with the utility maximization of a representative local household as a consumer and as a working individual under the given budget constraint:

$$\max U = U\ (x, b) \tag{5.1}$$

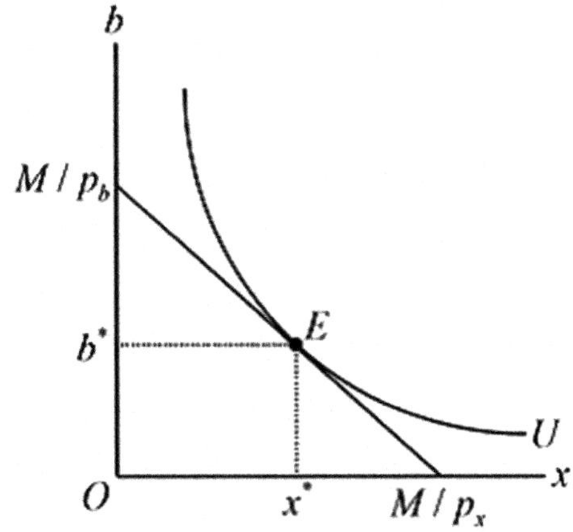


**Fig. 5.1** Individual's utility maximization behavior with given budget constraint

$$s.t.\quad M = p_x x + p_b b \tag{5.2}$$

where $U$ = this household's utility level, determined by the quantity demanded of a composite commodity, $x$ ($x > 0$), and services, $b$ ($b > 0$). Here, supplemental services are needed when the individual faces a limitation of time allocation due to his or her job in Eq. (5.1). This individual's budget, ($M > 0$), is used to purchase the composite commodity, $x$, that has price $p_x$ ($p_x > 0$), and to obtain a service, $b$, that has a unit pecuniary charge, $p_b$ ($p_b > 0$), as stated in Eq. (5.2).

The optimal choice of $x$ and $b$ in this situation can be illustrated in Fig. 5.1 as the combination $(x^*, b^*)$ at point $E$. In the figure, the horizontal axis plots the quantity demanded of the composite commodity, $x$, and the vertical axis is the quantity demanded of services, $b$.

In this analysis, the argument assumes that excess time is required for work, for instance, due to an inefficient office environment under a fixed-salary-based contract, stated as $M = \bar{M}$. Here, the individual may face the situation illustrated in Fig. 5.2. In the figure, the actual utility level is $U^A$, which has the combination $\left(x^A, b^A\right)$, since the excess time for work requires the individual to consume the extra amount of $b$ as the volume $b^A$ $\left(b^A > b^*\right)$. In that case, it is apparent that the individual's utility level is worse-off from $U^*$ to $U^A$ unless the firm attempts to make an effort to improve this specific problem.

When the firm attempts to make an effort to improve the job environment, the following argument can be made. The effect of the firm's effort on the utility level of individuals who work at this firm is illustrated in Fig. 5.3. For instance, the firm may improve by limiting the quantity of labor demanded from the individual (i.e., working hours per week in the office) to the level $b^B$. Such shift, which may not exceed this level, can be partly due to the resource constraints of the firm. In this case, the individual obtains more $x$, $\left(x^C - x^A\right)$ where $x^A < x^C < x^B$, and the utility level recovers, but less than $U^*$. In addition, the time release of the individual, $b^A - b^B$, partly enables this person to use his or her spare time to contribute to the

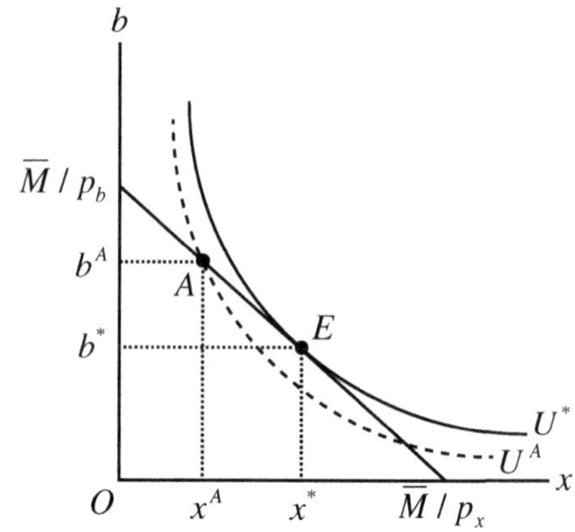


**Fig. 5.2** Actual and optimal levels

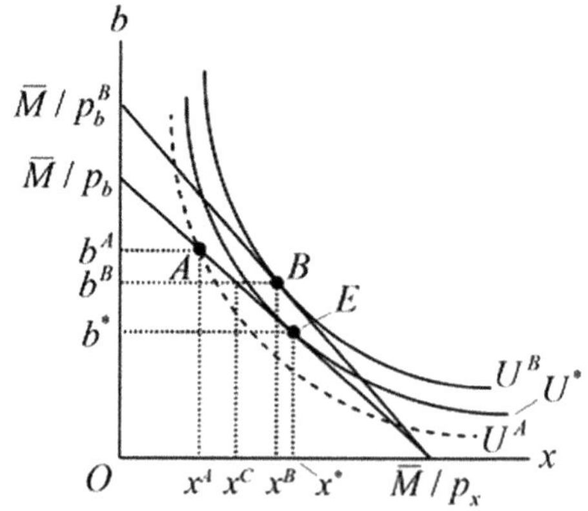


**Fig. 5.3** Individual behavior with the local community arrangement

local community or do other activities. If such a system works sufficiently within the region, each individual's $p_b$ declines, for instance, to $p_b^B$. In this case, the quantity demanded of $x$ becomes $x^B$ $(x^A < x^C < x^B < x^*)$ and the utility level is $U^B$. Hence, the agreement condition for the individual to participate in the local community is

$$U^B \geq U^*. \tag{5.3}$$

This will be feasible as long as there is no remarkable increase in $p_x$.

The next concern should be given to the impact of changes in regional agglomeration economies on the optimal decision-making of the firm, using the following expressions.

$$\max \pi = qy - \alpha wL - \beta rK \tag{5.4}$$

$$s.t.\ y = f(L, K) \tag{5.5}$$

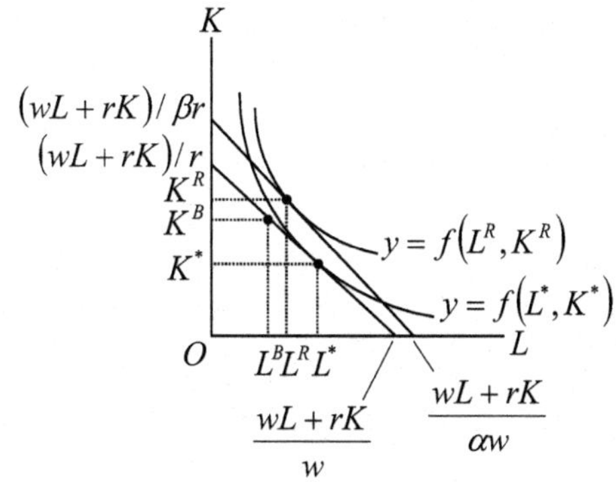


**Fig. 5.4** Regional agglomeration effect

where $q\,(q > 0) =$ the price of this firm's product; the quantity of the product, $y\ (y > 0)$, is processed using two types of input $L(L > 0)$ and $K(K > 0)$, which are labor and capital, respectively, as commonly assumed. Hence, $w(w > 0) =$ wage rate and $r\ (r > 0) =$ unit price of capital. Other parameters, namely, $\alpha\ (\alpha > 0)$ and $(\beta > 0)$, will be set as $\alpha = 1$ and $\beta = 1$ at the moment, and changed in later analysis of this chapter.

For the firm, the effort to reduce the working time of the laborer requires giving up $L^*$ to $L^B$ in Fig. 5.4. In order to recover the same output level, $K$ should increase, but it is not possible for it to do so without a cost increase beyond the original isocost curve, illustrated as the downward-sloping inward line. Here, the role of regional agglomeration economies may enable the firm to offer a discounted wage level in the long run, which will be shown in the following section.

## 5.3 Hypothetical Analysis

As introduced earlier, regional agglomeration economies are slightly different from established localization economies and urbanization economies. While localization economies are basically a cost-saving opportunity for the manufacturing industry and urbanization economies are exclusively available in large metropolitan areas, regional agglomeration economies involve all local economic agents in the observing region. Once such a system is able to work, regional agglomeration economies may enable the firm to offer a discounted wage level, $\alpha w\ (0 < \alpha < 1)$, and discounted unit price of capital, $\beta r\ (0 < \beta < 1)$ in Eq. (5.4).

The discounted wage level can be achieved by location proximity to accessible labor and labor information or by detailed and flexible arrangements for work contracts through less formal negotiations. Further, the discounted unit price of capital is available by receiving outsourcing services across local firms through informal and flexible negotiations with other local business partners. Here, parameters $\alpha$ and $\beta$ approach zero as regional agglomeration economies work sufficiently. The firm

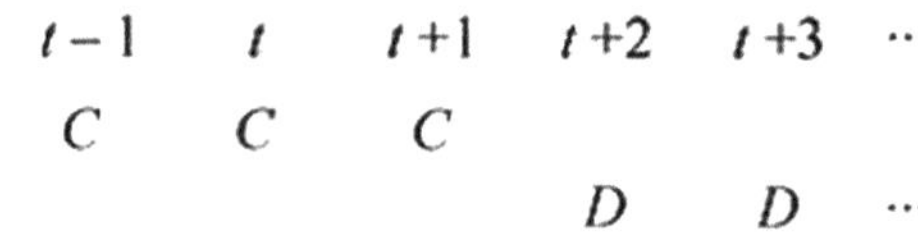


**Fig. 5.5** Trigger strategy

can now achieve a much higher output level owing to the more relaxed condition of the isocost curve, illustrated as the downward-sloping outward line in Fig. 5.4. The example in the figure shows that the firm has a combination $(L^R, K^R)$ that enables the firm to use more labor and capital so that the firm achieves a much higher output level $y(L^R, K^R)$. As a result, the condition that the firm accepts would be

$$y(L^R, K^R) > y(L^*, K^*). \tag{5.6}$$

The following argument shows that regional agglomeration economies may make it possible to satisfy these criteria. Since reductions of parameters $\alpha$ and $\beta$ are exclusively available under a special coordination of regional agglomeration economies, these may be more feasible in rural regions than in large metropolitan areas. The coordination can include an enhancement of local community participation of individuals that depends on firm behavior, as examined in previous sections. In addition, expansions of the local social network and of informal negotiation opportunities would release several constraints of economic behavior on each regional economic agent. Isard (1975) also indicated this point in his social welfare analysis.

While urbanization economies are available without any coordination, it is only possible to establish regional agglomeration economies under a special human-made arrangement. The special arrangement may include social network formation. The social network can be more securely formed as long as the atmosphere of the community has been effectively established. This is illustrated as a trigger strategy of cooperative behavior in Fig. 5.5.

In the figure, the symbols $C$ and $D$ respectively show "cooperative" and"not cooperative" behavior. When a resident (or player) deviates from $C$ at period $t+2$, the succeeding plays continue to be $D$. Even though the involved players know that choice $C$ is much better than $D$, $C$ cannot be chosen again unless a specific system is applied to the community. Regional agglomeration economies for the local firm could include one such system, as denoted by parameters $\alpha$ and $\beta$, which affect condition (5.6) as well as expression (5.3).

## 5.4 Further Avenues

This chapter further needs to reveal the relationship between regional agglomeration economies and national economic growth. These economies are particularly important for countries in which growth of the total population and of real gross domestic product are limited. Since those countries cannot expect international competitiveness on cost and price reductions of products, a high quality of firm management is required, particularly in basic industries. To achieve more efficient and productive environments, it may be important to enhance regional agglomeration economies, which can involve strategies completely different from the conventional economic growth and development policies but that help to reduce expenditures on public finance.

There are also remaining arguments that have not investigated in this analysis. First, labor can be categorized into several types. For instance, working individuals who are categorized as highly skilled labors may have less time for leisure, since the organization's dependence on them is much higher. This would relate to the topic of worklife balance. In order to conduct this type of study, it would be necessary to relax the condition of the fixed salary contract of the individual in Eq. (5.2). Second, the organizer of regional agglomeration economies has not been addressed in this paper; it could be the local government, local developers, or other public-sector actors. This would be another dimension of the argument for cooperative behavior among different regional agents who have the same general objective but commonly engage in independent activities unless there is a well-organized arrangement.

Third, firms maximize their profit, and they can choose the locations of their head office, research units, factories, and so on according to the availability of advantageous factors for revenue and cost for their activities. In this paper, local firms are assumed to situate at fixed locations, and further examinations should be done to include more dynamic location decision-making behavior by firms. The optimal location-decision making for firms depends either on revenue maximization or cost minimization. These can be partly maximizing the opportunities of agglomeration economies, and minimizing spatial cost factors such as transportation costs. From the standpoint of social optimum, the excess spatial concentration at a particular region may present several issues such as problems with diminishing rural regional economic growth. The study of central place system is a part of central place theory and its detail should see Mulligan (2012), and Parr (2017).

Further, industrial types or attributes of the observing region should be specified to conduct a more detailed investigation. For instance, explorations can be done for planning regional economic policies according to specialized industries (i.e., primary, secondary, or tertiary industry) at the observing region. Such examinations may involve the analysis of hierarchical central place system referring to Lösch (1954 [1944]).

## 5.5 Concluding Comments

This chapter has demonstrated how an individual's utility can be better-off under given constraints such as the job environment and the regional welfare level in addition to the individual's budget constraint. The study also addressed the relationship between the availability of local resources and the job environment of each individual. Furthermore, in this paper we introduced the notion of regional agglomeration economies from the standpoint of regional development, which can contribute to improving individual's utility and firm operation. Here, it was shown that the availability of regional agglomeration economies depends on the extent of a local community arrangement that can be partly determined by the human resource management of the firm. Finally, the relationship between regional agglomeration economies and national economic growth has been explored for countries in which there are certain limitations on growth of the total population and real gross domestic product under a severe condition of accelerating international market competition.

**Acknowledgements** A preliminary version of the paper is presented at the Annual Autumn Meeting of the Japan Association for Applied Economics in October 2017 at Tokyo. This research was partly supported by Japan Society for the Promotion of Science (JSPS) KAKENHI, Grant Number 16K03643.

## References

Evans, A.W. 1972. The Pure Theory of City Size in an Industrial Economy. *Urban Studies* 9: 49–77.

Glaeser, E.L., J. Kolko, and A. Saiz. 2001. Consumer City. *Journal of Economic Geography* 1: 27–50.

Hanley, N., J. Shogren, and B. White. 2007. Environmental Economics. In *Theory and Practice*, 2nd ed, 1–5. Hampshire: Palgrave Macmillan.

Hoover, E.M. 1937. *Location Theory and the Shoe and Leather Industries*. Cambridge: Harvard University Press.

Isard, W. 1956. *Location and Space-Economy*. Cambridge: MIT Press.

Isard, W. 1975. *Introduction to Regional Science*. Englewood Cliffs: Prentice-Hall.

Lösch, A. 1954[1944]. *Die Raümliche Ordnung der Wirtschaft,* Fischer, Jena. English edition: Lösch, A. 1954. *The Economics of Location (trans: Woglom WH, Stolper WF)*. New Haven: Yale Uni-versity Press.

Marshall, A. 1892. *Economics of Industry*, 3rd ed. London: Macmillan and Co Limited.

Mulligan, G.F., M.D. Partridge, and J.I. Carruthers. 2012. Central Place Theory and Its Reemergence in Regional Science. *Annals of Regional Science* 48: 405–431.

Nakamura, D. 2016. Alternative Spatial Structure for Sustainable Rural Economy: A Note on Socially Optimal Firm Location. *International Regional Science Review* 41: 86–102.

Nakamura D. 2018. Location Economics Analysis on Attractiveness of a Region. *Studies in Regional Science* 48 in printing

Parr, J.B. 2002. Agglomeration Economies: Ambiguities and Confusions. *Environment and Planning* 34: 717–731.

Parr, J.B. 2015. The City and the Region as Contrasts In Spatial Organization. *Annals of Regional Science* 54: 797–817.

Parr, J.B. 2017. Central Place Theory: An evaluation. *Review of Urban and Regional Development Studies* 29: 151–164.

Weber, A. 1909[1928]. Über den Standort der Industrien. Mohr, Tübingen. English edition: Weber A, 1928. *Alfred Weber's Theory of the Location of Industries (trans: Friedrich CJ)*. Chicago: University of Chicago Press.

# Chapter 6
# Structural Changes of the Electricity Market in Japan: Theoretical Analysis of Consumers' Eco-Friendly Behavior

**Kimihito Ise and Masahiro Yabuta**

## 6.1 Introduction

This study analyzes the consumer welfare factors in selecting energy sources in Japan's electricity market. After the Fukushima Daiichi atomic power plant accident in 2011, Japan has witnessed drastic changes in its electricity market: a tendency toward the promotion of renewable energies such as solar and wind power, and structural changes in its electricity market from regional monopoly to competitiveness. Not only has the market structure transformed toward competitiveness, but the energy development has turned toward renewable power sources as well, among which consumers can choose. This study theoretically examines the effects of the structural changes in Japan's electricity market on the price and percentage of various power sources, and on consumer welfare. Regional monopolies such as Tokyo Electric Power Company (TEPCO) had dominated Japan's integrated power generation and transmission system until the retail electricity market opening in April 2016. Therefore, TEPCO had the ability to choose its preferred power source as a mix of hydro, thermal, nuclear, and renewable power; however, its consumers had no such choice. Eco-friendly consumers today are aware of the environmental impacts of non-renewable power source usage and are particular whether their power source is an eco-friendly renewable energy. Debates on the electricity market reform in Japan have been centered on the consumer choice between green and traditional fossil energy, resulting in market structure reform and future drastic change. As a result, the study analyzes the consumer welfare factors corresponding to the development of Japan's electricity market.

K. Ise (✉)
Japan Electric Power Information Center, Tokyo, Japan
e-mail: ise-kimihito@jepic.or.jp

M. Yabuta
Chuo University, Tokyo, Japan
e-mail: yabuta@tamacc.chuo-u.ac.jp



M. Hosoe et al. (eds.), *Applied Analysis of Growth, Trade, and Public Policy*,
https://doi.org/10.1007/978-981-13-1876-4_6

The study models Japan's changing electricity market pattern into three segments: (1) a competitive market where consumers can freely choose between traditional thermal power and renewable power, (2) a market where consumers can partially choose power sources through a retail electricity market liberalization, and (3) a monopoly where consumers have no choice but to accept the power generation company's energy sources. Currently, the Japanese electricity market development pattern is witnessing a transition from the third type to the first. We incorporate policy measures for each segment in a vertical differentiation model in which environmentally friendly consumer behavior expresses their willingness to pay (WTP) for the renewable energy sources. In these segments, the study analyzes how the aforementioned changes affect the electricity market, power source share, consumer surplus, and environmental damage. We first evaluate the equilibrium in a competitive electricity market where consumers can freely choose a power source. Second, we compare the competitive equilibrium and the equilibrium incorporating various regulatory frameworks. We also investigate the regulatory measures on the electricity market such as feed-in tariffs, renewable portfolio standards, and the retail electricity market liberalization. To simplify the model analysis of the market structure development pattern, we use a model of product differentiation where electricity consumers exercise varied WTP.

The investigation proceeds as follows. Section 6.2 briefly outlines the history of recent developments in the Japanese electricity market, focusing particularly on changes in its supply structure and power-source components. We classify the development of the Japanese electricity market into three segments: a monopolistic environment in which green consumers have no power source options to choose from, a semi-competitive environment between duopolistic firms with different power sources such as traditional fossil-energy and solar-energy, and a competitive environment between firms enabling green consumers to choose a green power source depending upon their WTP for it. Section 6.3 reviews the preceding research on vertical product differentiation, largely from theoretical perspectives. Shaked and Sutton (1982) and Moorthy (1988), for example, developed a theoretical game vertical differentiation model to examine firms' strategic decisionmaking behavior concerning product quality. Cremer and Thisse (1999), Lombardini-Riipinen (2005), André et al. (2009), Toshimitsu (2010), and Lambertini and Tampieri (2011) analyzed vertical differentiation models to examine the characteristics of the equilibrium in Cournot or Bertrand competition, and investigated the effectiveness of taxes or subsidies to improve social welfare. Heterogeneity assumptions of consumer choices between high (green) and low (brown) production technology or products resulted in varied conclusions depending on both the market conditions and consumer behavior choices. Applying these theoretical aspects of vertical differentiation, duopolistic competition, and consumer choice to Japanese electricity market development, Sect. 6.4 examines how changes in the institutional design in Japan's electricity market result in different social welfare outcomes. In this context, we investigate the policy implications of promoting renewable power sources in Japan. Section 6.5 summarizes the conclusion and provides further remarks.

## 6.2 Japan's Electricity Market

Since the end of World War II, ten privately-owned electric power companies including Okinawa Electric Power have been established. Until April 2016, they had controlled regional power supply services, generated electricity, and distributed it to the consumers from their respective government-allocated service areas. Although maintaining their regional monopolies, Japan's electric power market became somewhat liberalized in 1995 when the government permitted independent power producers (IPPs) to participate in the wholesale electricity market. The electric power companies' transmission/distribution network permitted open access in March 2000, partially liberalizing the retail electricity market by permitting power producers and suppliers (PPS) to sell electricity to extra-high voltage users requiring more than 2 MW. This liberalization further expanded in April 2004 to users requiring more than 500 kW, and in April 2005 to users requiring more than 50 kW. By 2011, the scope of liberalization covered approximately 60% of Japan's total electricity demand. In April 2016, the retail electricity market was fully opened, and each consumer has been able to choose her or his own supplier since then. Despite such liberalization, the retail electricity market share by newcomers was under 10% in March 2017.

In an effort to create a competitive market, the Japanese government has introduced measures to increase renewable energy use in the electricity sector. In April 2003, a Renewable Portfolio Standard (RPS) policy took effect (intended to last through June 2012), mandating that electricity retailers use renewable energies for a certain percentage of their power source. In addition, an excess electricity purchasing scheme, the Feed-in Tariff (FIT), began in November 2009, superseding the RPS. Under the FIT, electric power companies purchase surplus energy unused by photovoltaic (PV) power generators themselves at a fixed price. Since July 2012, electric power companies have had to purchase all power generated by facilities using renewable energy sources such as PV, small- and medium-scale hydroelectric, wind, geothermal, and biomass (except for residential PV power generation systems) at fixed prices during a period determined by the government. At the moment, the tariff for excess electricity from residential PV power generation systems is JPY 26 per kWh in Tokyo and the duration is ten (12.10) years.

In addition to various regulatory measures, electric power companies and other entities have voluntarily launched incentives such as the green electricity fund (GEF) and carbon-offsets in an attempt to encourage consumers to use more eco-friendly energy. In the GEF system, for example, an electricity consumer pays JPY 500 per month to an electric power generation company, which contributes the same amount to promote eco-friendly activities such as environmental education in public schools and constructing power plants sourced by renewable energies. By the end of fiscal year 2009, the fund had facilitated approximately 1% of the total PV power generation capacity (24 MW of 2,627 MW). However, electric power companies abolished the fund after the FIT was introduced.

Despite the aforementioned efforts, the share of electricity production from renewable sources, including hydroelectric power sources, was only approximately 15% in fiscal year 2016.

## 6.3 Literature Review

This study examines the structure of the Japanese electricity market, which is determined by competitive situations among firms to produce electricity and consumer selection among power sources. The horizontal and vertical differentiation models (Lancaster 1979) identify the market structure in which firms produce a different quality of goods or use a different technology. Consider, for example, a consumer purchasing a car; cars have several attributes, such as design, performance, and safety, unrelated to the differences in the products' relative merits. Similarly, among cars in the same price range, consumers with different design preferences may choose differently designed cars. Thus, different attributes attract different consumers, causing horizontal differentiation.[1]

In vertical differentiation, all consumers have identical preferences if products were identical. Without differences in the product information that consumers receive, vertical differentiation is an endpoint solution. Let us assume that cars differ on only one environmental attribute and they exhibit clear differences in advantages and disadvantages, such as a green product versus a brown product. Given an option between identically priced products, consumers will always choose a green product for environmental superiority. Thus, products are only vertically differentiated. However, if the price of a brown product is lower than that of the green product because of low production costs, some consumers may choose the brown product. In the vertical differentiation model, differences in product qualities such as eco-friendliness cause different consumer choice patterns. In this case, a green consumer chooses an eco-friendly car despite its high price, but a brown consumer purchases a non-eco-friendly car for its lower price. Shaked and Sutton (1982) and Moorthy (1988), for example, developed a game theoretic vertical differentiation model to examine firms' strategic product quality decisionmaking behavior. More recently, Cremer and Thisse (1999), Lombardini-Riipinen (2005), André et al. (2009), Toshimitsu (2010), and Lambertini and Tampieri (2011) analyzed vertical differentiation models to examine the equilibrium characteristics in Cournot or Bertrand competition, and investigated the effectiveness of taxes or subsidies to improve social welfare. Heterogeneity assumptions of consumers' choice between high (green) and low (brown) production technology or products resulted in various conclusions depending on both the market condition and the consumer choice behavior.

Shaked and Sutton (1982) and Moorthy (1988) investigated firms' strategies concerning products' quality decision using a two-stage game framework. Under full

[1] A pioneering study in horizontal differentiation is Hotelling (1929).

**Table 6.1** Recent studies on vertical differentiation

| Classification / Authors | Coverage: Full / Partial | Competition: Bertrand / Cournot | Policy: Regulation Tax Subsidy | Notes |
|---|---|---|---|---|
| Shaked and Sutton (1982) | Partial | Bertrand | - | Assuming two firms and the non-existent production cost, the authors showed that the firms will choose distinct products' qualities, and that both will enjoy a positive profit at equilibrium. The intuitive idea behind this result is that, as their qualities become more similar, the price competition between the two firms will reduce the profit of both firms. |
| Motta (1993) | Partial | Bertrand<br>Cournot | - | The author analyzed two types of models of vertical differentiation to study the influence of price and quantity competition in the Nash equilibrium solution. The author showed that an optimal product differentiation is higher in Bertrand competition rather than in Cournot, because competition will be fiercer in Bertrand than in Cournot without differentiation. |
| Cremer and Thisse (1994) | Partial | Bertrand | Tax | Following the specification introduced by Mussa and Rosen (1978), the authors showed that a uniform ad valorem tax, where the same rate applies to all variants of the product, lowers both equilibrium qualities, distorts the allocation of consumers between firms, and lowers the consumer prices of both variants. A small uniform tax is always welfare improving over the non-tax equilibrium. |
| Lombardini-Riipinen (2005) | Full | Bertrand | Tax, Subsidy | Using a similar theoretical model as Cremer and Thisse (1994), the auhor examined the effectiveness of the emission tax, ad valorem tax, and subsidies for eco-friendly consumers. Unlike Cremer and Thisse (1994), the author incorporated the environmental externalities in the analysis. The author concluded that the combination of a uniform ad valorem tax and emission tax can lead to the social optimum. In addition, the same result is obtained by coupling a uniform ad valorem tax and a subsidy to consumers who choose the green products. |
| Bansal (2008) | Partial | Bertrand | Tax, Subsidy | Using an approach similar to Lombardini-Riipinen (2005) and assuming a more general variable cost function, the author analyzed effects of ad valorem taxes/subsidies and emission taxes on firms. In addition, the optimal policy shifts from ad valorem taxes to ad valorem subsidies as the magnitude of the damage parameter associated with the environmental externality increases. |
| André *et al* .(2009) | Partial | Bertrand | Tax | In the similar theoretical framework as of Shaked and Sutton (1982), the authors extended the model to treat the environmental quality as a discrete variable rather than a continuous one. They supported the Porter Hypothesis in a vertically differentiated duopoly model with Bertrand competition, where firms choose to adopt the green standard under the regulation policy that a lump-sum tax is levied on brown technology. |
| Toshimitsu (2010) | Partial | Cournot | Subsidy | The author considered the effects of environmental subsidies on the outside market, i.e., a market with implicit alternatives for consumers (a bicycle is always a green good, outside the car market which comprises both eco-friendly cars and non eco-friendly cars). From this idea, he obtained the unique result that the subsidy for clean cars degrades the environment. |
| Lambertini and Tampieri (2011) | Partial | Cournot | - | The authors extended the analysis conducted by André et al.(2009), assuming Cournot competition between firms. The background of their idea is that several car manufacturers extensively invest in R&D, without the taxation on brown technology. They indicated that a sufficiently low asymmetry in costs drives firms to the green outcome without regulations. |

market coverage, wherein products are provided to every consumer, Cournot competition may lead to non-existence of equilibrium (Motta 1993). In the vertical differentiation model, many studies assumed Bertrand competition between firms and full market coverage. André et al. (2009) demonstrated that a Bertrand competition between duopolies when a lump-sum tax was imposed on the brown technology would make both firms use the green technology. Lambertini and Tampieri (2011) extended André's analysis to include a Cournot competition with a restriction on production scale. Accordingly, in the Bertrand competition market structure, policy measures that affect equilibrium are important in the vertical differentiation models. Cremer et al. (2003), Lombardini-Riipinen (2005), and Bansal (2008) investigated vertical differentiation models to examine environmental policies such as taxes and subsidies in the presence of green consumers.

Table 6.1 presents the recent arguments about the application of the vertical differentiation models to various market aspects, such as product coverage, competition among firms, and policy measures, to attain social welfare optimality. Applying previous studies' theoretical aspects of vertical differentiation, duopolistic competition, and consumers' green choice to the development of the Japanese electricity market, this study examines the institutional design of Japan's electricity market and analyzes the different outcomes concerning social welfare.

## 6.4 The Model

### 6.4.1 Model Features

Having reviewed the Japanese electricity market's historical background in Sect. 6.2, this section theoretically examines the method to enhance the effective expansion of renewable energies. The model utilized here reflects the varied consumers' WTP for power sources, considering both the production cost structure and the Bertrand competition market structure. Here, we construct the model framework with consumer selection behavior to demonstrate how the price and market share of power sources are determined at equilibrium, and to analyze the factors affecting social welfare. Although electricity cannot be physically differentiated, the model assumes that consumers have a varied WTP for each power source that generates electricity: renewable energy or fossil fuel energy. Therefore, this model features Bertrand competition between the firms generating power through thermal and solar energy sources.

### 6.4.2 Model Structure

The research reviewed in Sect. 6.3 reveals that the differences between production methods and their resultant environmental factors such as $CO_2$ emission have some kind of effect on consumer choices through a decision-making process (Bansal 2008; Eriksson 2004; Yabuta and Scott 2010). Eco-friendly product qualities affect consumer consumption patterns because environmental attributes influence consumer decisions in purchasing such goods. Altruism is an important factor affecting consumer behavior. Consumer contribution to improve the environment by the purchase and use of green products can enhance individual consumer utility. This is partly because consumers can then enjoy a better environment, and a higher reputation for contributing to the environment (Andreoni 1989; Cornes and Sandler 1994; and Kotchen 2005, 2007). Therefore, the model integrates an altruism factor that affects consumer selection.[2]

Assume that a solar power generating firm ($i = 1$) and a thermal power generating firm ($i = 2$) compete in the electricity market. There are considerable differences between the firms' cost functions. The typical thermal power generating firm represents economies of scale necessitating large facilities to supply sufficient services. The generating capacity that was built between 2009 and 2013 is 600–1,520 MW,[3]

[2]Several authors such as Bruvoll and Nyborg (2004) argue that people engage in eco-friendly behavior because of peer pressure.

[3]The generating capacity range indicates the capacities of LNG and coal power plants that began operating between 2009 and 2013 (Power Generation Cost Analysis Working Group HP).

and the average cost of production is 12.3–13.7 JPY/kWh.[4] In contrast, solar power facilities have relatively lesser generating capacity per site. The average operating capacity of mega solar power plants supported by the FIT, as of the end of September 2017, was approximately 2 MW.[5] The average generation cost is 24.2 JPY/kWh.[6] In this situation, the power generating company uses only thermal generation as its source. However, solar power generating companies generate electricity because of policy supports to solar power generating firms or consumer WTP for solar power's environmental benefits.

#### 6.4.2.1 Electricity Supply

With respect to each firm's environmental attribute, $e_i$ denotes eco-friendly efforts, and we assume $e_1 > e_2$. Here, we assume the opportunity cost, $c$, of the solar power generating firm to be larger than that of the thermal power generating firm, $g$.[7] The total amount of power generation is normalized to 1. Thus, the profit of each firm is given by

$$\pi_1 = x(p_1 - (1 - s)\,(c + e_1)), \tag{6.1}$$

$$\pi_2 = y(p_2 - (g + e_2)) \tag{6.2}$$

where $x$ is the generation share of the solar power generating firm, $y$ $(= 1 - x)$ is the generation share of the thermal power generating firm, $p_i$ is the price paid by consumers, and $s$ is the subsidy rate.

#### 6.4.2.2 Electricity Consumption

From the consumers perspective, there is no difference in the electrical power generated. The difference in consumer selection results primarily from the difference between firms' power sources. Consumers must consider it important whether the source of power is solar or thermal, the latter emitting more $CO_2$ than the former. However, the structure of the electricity market determines consumers' choice

---

[4]The cost is calculated from the model plant of coal and LNG as of 2014 (Power Generation Cost Analysis Working Group HP).

[5]The calculation relied upon data downloaded from the Agency for Natural Resources and Energy HP.

[6]The figures were calculated from the model plant of 2 MW as of 2014 (Power Generation Cost Analysis Working Group HP).

[7]We also assume that $(1 - s)\ \ c > g$, meaning that the average cost of the solar power generating firm is greater than that of the thermal generating power firm to generate 1 kW of electricity. The reality is that a solar power generating firm changes its capacity utilization to adjust production, whereas a thermal power generating firm adjusts production by changing its quantities of fuel inputs. Therefore, we assume the costs $(c, e_1)$ of the solar power firm to be larger than those of the thermal power firm.

between solar and thermal power. Until recently, the market structure deterred consumers from freely choosing power generation methods. Consumers in Tokyo, for example, could obtain only mixed electricity provided by TEPCO, with no information on the source of this power. As described below, liberalizing the retail electricity market enabled consumers to choose among power generation methods partially on the basis of their WTP. Thus, Japan's recent electricity market development changed the market structure enabling consumer selection. In such a market, it is critical that consumers with sufficiently high WTP for solar power are aware of the generation method of the electricity consumed. Without power source information, consumers cannot evaluate their WTP for environmental advantages. With information on solar power, consumers can choose a power source on the basis of their marginal WTP. Here, each consumer's marginal WTP is expressed by

$$W_i = \theta e_i,\ i = 1, 2 \tag{6.3}$$

where $\theta$ is a consumer's evaluation of $e_i$ and is assumed to be a uniform distribution bounded in $\left[\underline{\theta}, \overline{\theta}\right]$. Thus, the average is $\mu = (\underline{\theta} + \overline{\theta})/2$, and the variance is $\sigma = (\overline{\theta} - \underline{\theta})^2/12$. In general, although eco-friendly consumers choose the solar power generating firm to have a large $\theta$, the non-eco-friendly consumers choose the thermal power generating firm. In consumer's equilibrium, we assume that

$$\overline{u} - p_1 + \theta e_1 + \rho(e_1 - e_2) = \overline{u} - p_2 + \theta e_2 \tag{6.4}$$

where $\overline{u}$ is the intrinsic utility obtained from a single unit of electricity, irrespective of the variant's unit emission level, and $\rho$ is the marginal utility of social-related evaluation, which gives solar power consumers a sense of satisfaction from social recognition for their contribution toward environment preservation. If the market structure does not permit consumers to choose their preferred power source, no difference occurs in their evaluation of power sources, and consumers choose only thermal power for its low price. However, if solar power is subsidized, one consumer may select solar power and another select thermal power.

#### 6.4.2.3 Market Structures

Considering the aforementioned points, the relationship between the market structure and consumers' free choice among power sources, the following three types of markets merit analysis (Fig. 6.1).

1. Consumers are aware that there are two types of power sources but are unable to choose a power source because the power generation company having monopoly power provides only mixed-source electricity. In this market, the policymaker's

| Case | Choice of Consumers | Condition of Competition between Firms | Scheme | Reference Figures |
|---|---|---|---|---|
| (1) | actually impossible | Regulation of Price/ Quota | Subsidy for Solar Power<br>FIT or RPS | 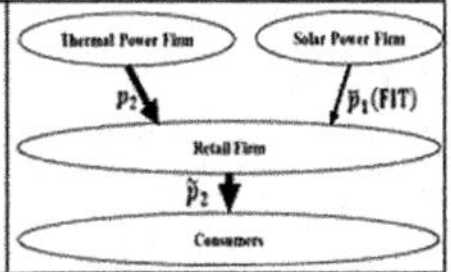 |
| | | Bertrand | | |
| (2) | partly possible | Regulation of Price/ Quota | Retail Electricity Market Liberalization<br>Subsidy for Solar Power<br>FIT or RPS | 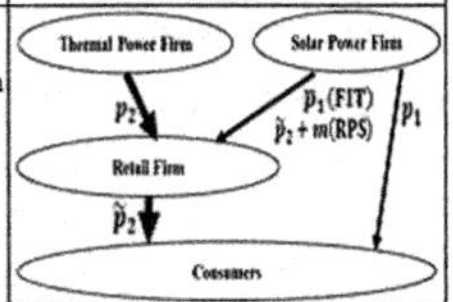 |
| | | Bertrand | | |
| (3) | possible | Bertrand | Retail Electricity Market<br>LiberalizationSubsidy for Solar Power | 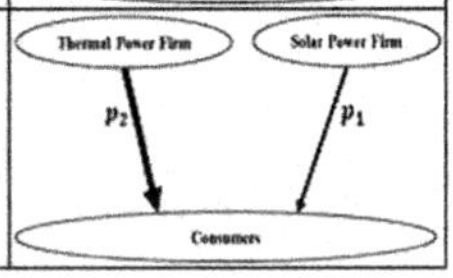 |

**Fig. 6.1** Framework of model markets

objective is the composition of power sources. To enhance the share of solar power in the total power sources, the policymaker introduces the FIT or RPS.
2. Consumers are aware that there are two types of power sources. As in (15.1), though the power generation company provides mixed-source electricity, consumers are able to select solar power under the retail electricity market liberalization.
3. Consumers are aware that there are two types of power sources and are able to freely and directly choose one power source depending upon their WTP for the environment.

From the consumers' free choice perspective, this electricity market classification is close to that of Eriksson (2004). Most proceeding studies, including Eriksson, analyze consumers' choice between green and brown technologies. Although technology substitutions are difficult in the electricity sector, consumer preferences can be reflected in the generation mix comprising sources such as thermal and solar power. Assume that firms' production technology for generating electricity cannot change flexibly, and that there are two types of firms: a thermal power generating firm and a solar power generating firm. They compete to determine the share of each power source for electricity generation.

## 6.5 Analysis

### 6.5.1 *Consumers Can Choose a Supplier (Competitive Model: Fig. 6.1, Case (3))*

In this case, consumers choose a supplier freely in the retail electricity market among the power generating firms competing in the market. Thus, we obtain

$$\theta^* = \frac{p_1 - p_2}{e_1 - e_2} - \rho \tag{6.5}$$

on the basis of consumer behavior such that the consumers are indifferent between electricity generated by solar and thermal power. Therefore, the demand for solar power can be given by (6.6).

$$x\left(p_1, p_2\right) = [\overline{\theta} - \theta^*]/[\overline{\theta} - \underline{\theta}] = \left[\left(\overline{\theta} + \rho\right)\left(e_1 - e_2\right) - \left(p_1 - p_2\right)\right] / \left(\overline{\theta} - \underline{\theta}\right)\left(e_1 - e_2\right). \tag{6.6}$$

In the model, each power generating firm has a strategic variable: the price of electricity it supplies. The analysis is suited to the situation where the demand and supply are determined based on the price as of each firm's strategic variable.[8] Consumers choose a power source on the basis of these prices. In the Bertrand–Nash competition, the reaction functions of each firm are given by

$$p_1 = \left[p_2 + \left(\overline{\theta} + \rho\right)\left(e_1 - e_2\right) + (1 - s)\left(c + e_1\right)\right]/2, \tag{6.7}$$

$$p_2 = \left[p_1 - \left(\underline{\theta} + \rho\right)\left(e_1 - e_2\right) + \left(g + e_2\right)\right]/2, \tag{6.8}$$

respectively. From (6.7) and (6.8), we obtain

$$p_1^* = \frac{\left(2\overline{\theta} - \underline{\theta} + \rho\right)\left(e_1 - e_2\right) + 2(1 - s)\left(c + e_1\right) + \left(g + e_2\right)}{3}, \tag{6.9}$$

and

$$p_2^* = \frac{\left(\overline{\theta} - 2\underline{\theta} - \rho\right)\left(e_1 - e_2\right) + (1 - s)\left(c + e_1\right) + 2\left(g + e_2\right)}{3} \tag{6.10}$$

Thus, the difference in prices between both power generating firms becomes

[8]The model assumes that each power generating firm adjusts the electricity price, not its generation level, so as to maximize its profit.

$$p_1^* - p_2^* = \frac{\left[\left\{\left(\overline{\theta}+\underline{\theta}+2\rho\right)\right\}(e_1-e_2)+(1-s)(c+e_1)-(g+e_2)\right]}{3}$$
$$= \frac{\left(\overline{\theta}+\underline{\theta}+2\rho+1-s\right)e_1-\left(\overline{\theta}+\underline{\theta}+2\rho+1\right)e_2+((1-s)c-g)}{3}. \tag{6.11}$$

Taking (6.5), (6.6), and (6.11) together causes

$$x^* = \frac{\left(2\overline{\theta}-\underline{\theta}+\rho\right)(e_1-e_2)-[(1-s)(c+e_1)-(g+e_2)]}{3\left(\overline{\theta}-\underline{\theta}\right)(e_1-e_2)}. \tag{6.12}$$

**Lemma 6.1** *From (6.12), under the assumption that* $e_1 > e_2$*, the condition that enables solar power consumption becomes*

$$\text{Numerator of } x^* = Ae_1 - Be_2 + C$$
$$A = B + s > B = 2\overline{\theta} - \underline{\theta} + \rho - 1, C = -((1-s)c - g) \tag{6.13}$$

*where* $C < 0$ *under the assumption of the cost function (i.e.,* $(1-s)c > g$*).*[9]

Figure 6.2 demonstrates that as a result of Bertrand competition, the solar power generating firm can generate electricity represented by the shaded portion bounded by the curbs of $x = 0$ and $x = 1$ under the condition that $e_1 > e_2$. Consider the conditions where each power source is utilized by using (6.6) and (6.12). When only thermal power is utilized, that is, when no consumer prefers solar power to thermal power, $\left(\overline{\theta}+\rho\right)(e_1-e_2) = p_1^* - p_2^*$ holds. However, when only solar power is utilized, that is, when every consumer chooses the solar power generating firm, $\left(\underline{\theta}+\rho\right)(e_1-e_2) = p_1^* - p_2^*$ holds. This result suggests the following proposition.

**Proposition 6.1** *The difference between the prices of solar and thermal power depends on consumer evaluation of* $e_i$ *(marginal WTP for* $e_i$*), and on the marginal utility of social-related evaluation.*

In Fig. 6.2, we take the example of Proposition 6.1. Because solar power is more expensive than thermal power, the share of solar power in the market decreases. In this relationship, the expansion of the subsidy rate, $s$, in (6.12) decreases the difference between prices and increases the share for solar power.

#### 6.5.1.1 Consumers Can Partially Choose a Supplier (Fig. 6.1, Case (2))

In this case, consumers are able to partly choose a power source under the liberalized retail electricity market. Assume the retail electricity liberalization that enables

[9] $c$ is much smaller than $g$. In addition, the subsidies for installing solar panels by the Japanese central government and some local governments were abolished. Therefore, the subsidy rate is getting smaller. Because of this, we assume $(1-s)c > g$.

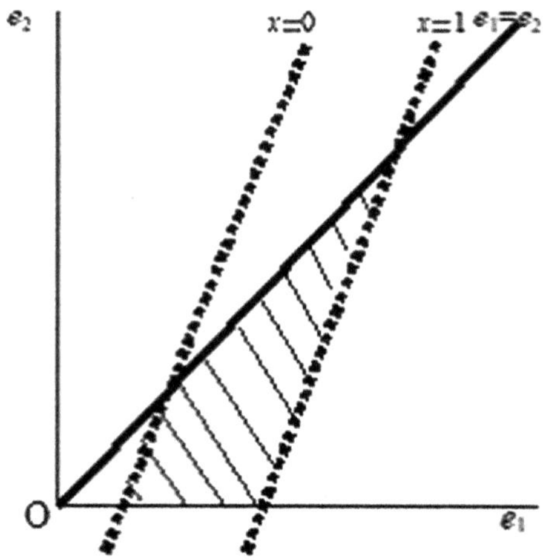


**Fig. 6.2** Bertrand competition and the solar power

consumers to purchase green power directly from the solar power generating firm. As Fig. 6.1 illustrates, customers largely purchase mixed power from the retail firm which needs to buy some amount of electricity from the solar power generating firm under the FIT. Thus, the consumer equilibrium is expressed as

$$\bar{u} - p_1 + \theta e_1 + \rho(e_1 - e_2) = \bar{u} - \tilde{p}_2 + \theta e_2, \tag{6.14}$$

where $\tilde{p}_2$ is the price of electricity from mixed power (solar and thermal)[10] $\rho'$. Equation (6.14) obtains $\theta^{**}$; here consumers are indifferent between purchases of solar and mixed power:

$$\theta^{**} = \frac{p_1 - \tilde{p}_2}{e_1 - e_2} - \rho. \tag{6.15}$$

The demand share for $x$ by the solar power generating firm and for $\tilde{y}$ by the retail firm is

$$x(p_1, \tilde{p}_2) = (\overline{\theta} - \theta^{**})/(\overline{\theta} - \underline{\theta}) = \left[\left(\overline{\theta} + \rho\right)(e_1 - e_2) - (p_1 - \tilde{p}_2)\right] / \left(\overline{\theta} - \underline{\theta}\right)(e_1 - e_2), \tag{6.16}$$

$$\tilde{y} = 1 - x(p_1, \tilde{p}_2) = (\theta^{**} - \underline{\theta})/(\overline{\theta} - \underline{\theta}) = [(p_1 - \tilde{p}_2) - (\underline{\theta} + \rho)(e_1 - e_2)] / \left(\overline{\theta} - \underline{\theta}\right)(e_1 - e_2). \tag{6.17}$$

Section 6.5.1.2 analyzes the equilibrium in which the retail firm is required to utilize a certain amount of solar power (i.e., $\bar{z}$ in (6.19) under the FIT or in (6.28) under the RPS).

[10] Here consumers fully recognize that the retail firm supplies mixed power, (6.14) is rewritten as $u - p_1 + \theta e_1 + \rho(e_1 - e_2) = u - \tilde{p}_2 + \theta e_2 + \rho'(e_1 - e_2)$ and (6.15) is rewritten as $\theta^{**} = [(p_1 - \tilde{p}_2)/(e_1 - e_2)] - (\rho - \rho')$. As a result, the electricity consumption share of $x$ is considered to decrease where $\rho'$ is the marginal utility of social-related evaluation.

#### 6.5.1.2 Liberalized Retail Electricity Market with FIT

Here, we assume that the retail firm purchases electricity from the thermal power generating firm belonging to the same parent company and must buy a certain amount of electricity, $\bar{z}$, at $\overline{p}_1$, which is higher than $\tilde{p}_2$ from the solar power generating firm through the FIT. In this case, the solar power generating firm has two options: supply electricity to the retail firm or supply electricity directly to consumers with high marginal WTP. Here, we assume that a solar power generating firm supplies $\bar{z}$ of the supply power to a retail company at a price of $\bar{p}_1$ to secure a guaranteed profit.[11] On that basis, we also assume that the solar power generating firm supplies the remaining power, $x$, at the price of $p_1$ to consumers who wish to purchase directly. In this case, the profit function of the solar power generating firm is given by

$$\pi_1 = x[p_1 - (1-s)(c+e_1)] + \bar{z}[\overline{p}_1 - (1-s)(c+e_1)]. \tag{6.18}$$

The profit function of the retail firm is given by

$$\pi_2 = \tilde{p}_2\tilde{y} - (\tilde{y}-\bar{z})(g+e_2) - \overline{p}_1\bar{z} = (\tilde{y}-\bar{z})p_2 + \bar{z}\overline{p}_1 - (\tilde{y}-\bar{z})(g+e_2) - \overline{p}_1\bar{z}, \tag{6.19}$$

where $(g+e_2)$ is the cost of the thermal power generating firm assumed in Sect. 6.5.1; $\overline{p}_1\bar{z}$ denotes the purchase cost from the solar power generating firm; $\tilde{y}(=1-x)$ expresses the retail firm supply share; the thermal power generating firm's share is expressed as $\tilde{y}-\bar{z}$. The price mixed power (solar and thermal power) supplied by the retail firm is set at $\tilde{p}_2 = \left[(\tilde{y}-\bar{z})\,p_2 + \bar{z}\overline{p}_1\right]/\tilde{y}$.

In the following equations, the solar power generating firm ($i=1$) and the retail firm ($i=2$) determine each price under given $\overline{p}_1$ and $\bar{z}$. As discussed in Sect. 6.4.1, the reaction functions of each firm are

$$p_1 = \left[\tilde{p}_2 + \left(\overline{\theta}+\rho\right)(e_1-e_2) + (1-s)(c+e_1)\right]/2, \tag{6.20}$$

$$\tilde{p}_2 = \left[p_1 - \left(\underline{\theta}+\rho\right)(e_1-e_2) + (g+e_2)\right]/2, \tag{6.21}$$

respectively. From (6.20) and (6.21), each price at equilibrium is given as

$$p_1^{**} = \frac{\left(2\overline{\theta}-\underline{\theta}+\rho\right)(e_1-e_2) + (g+e_2) + 2(1-s)(c+e_1)}{3} \tag{6.22}$$

$$\tilde{p}_2^{**} = \frac{\left(\overline{\theta}-2\underline{\theta}-\rho\right)(e_1-e_2) + 2(g+e_2) + (1-s)(c+e_1)}{3}, \tag{6.23}$$

[11] We assume here that both the purchase price ($\overline{p}_1$) and quantities ($\bar{z}$) are regulated under the FIT. For the FIT in a country introducing a large amount of renewable energy, both the price and quantity is regulated. In Japan, quantities should be regulated by technical factors, such as insufficient network capacity.

and their difference is given as

$$p_1^{**} - \tilde{p}_2^{**} = \frac{(\bar{\theta} + \underline{\theta} + 2\rho)(e_1 - e_2) - (g + e_2) + (1 - s)(c + e_1)}{3}$$
$$= \frac{(\bar{\theta} + \underline{\theta} + 2\rho + 1 - s)e_1 - (\bar{\theta} + \underline{\theta} + 2\rho + 1 - s)e_2 + ((1 - s)c - g)}{3} \tag{6.24}$$

Taking (6.16), (6.17), and (6.24), the demand share for $x$ and $\tilde{y}$ is

$$x^{**} = \left[\left(2\overline{\theta} - \underline{\theta} + \rho\right)(e_1 - e_2) - (1 - s)(c + e_1) - (g + e_2)\right]/3\left(\overline{\theta} - \underline{\theta}\right)(e_1 - e_2) \tag{6.25}$$

$$\tilde{y}^{**} = (1 - x)^{**}$$
$$= [\left(\overline{\theta} - 2\underline{\theta} - \rho\right)(e_1 - e_2) + (1 - s)(c + e_1) - (g + e_2)]/3\left(\overline{\theta} - \underline{\theta}\right)(e_1 - e_2). \tag{6.26}$$

Taking (6.23), (6.24), and $\tilde{p}_2 = \left[(\tilde{y} - \bar{z})\, p_2 + \bar{z}\overline{p}_1\right]/\tilde{y}$, we obtain

$$p_2^{**} = \frac{\tilde{y}^{**}\tilde{p}_2^{**} - \bar{z}\bar{p}_1}{\tilde{y}^{**} - \bar{z}} \tag{6.27}$$

**Proposition 6.2** *(a) Considering the analyses in Sects. 6.5.1 and 6.5.1.1, it is noteworthy that the price and the quantity at which the consumers purchase directly from the solar power generating firm are identical in both cases. (b) The price and quantity at which the thermal power firm in Sect. 6.5.1 and the retail firm in Sect. 6.5.1.1 supply electricity are also identical. (c) The difference is in the quantities that the solar power generating firm supplies because it can supply $\bar{z}$ in addition to $x$ in Sect. 6.5.1.2 with FIT support. In this case, although the solar power generating firm supplies a quantity of $(x^{**} + \bar{z})$, the thermal power firm supply quantity decreases by $\bar{z}$.*

#### 6.5.1.3 Liberalized Retail Electricity Market with RPS

Here, we assume that the retail firm ($i = 2$) purchases electricity from the thermal power generating firm that belongs to the same parent company and is required to purchase a certain amount of electricity, $\bar{z}$, at $(p_2 + m)$, from the solar power generating firm ($i = 1$) under the RPS policy.[12] As in the previous case, the power generating firm has two options: supply electricity to the retail firm or supply electricity directly

[12]Under Japan's RPS, a retail firm had to use a certain percentage of renewable energy as their power source. In general, the purchase price is a competitive price that reflects both the physical and the environmental value. Therefore, we assume that the retail firm purchases a certain amount of electricity from the solar power generating firm, and that the purchase price is $\tilde{p}_2$, a weighted average of $p_1$ and $p_2$, and of $m$as an environmental value.

to consumers who have a high marginal WTP. In this case, the profit functions of the solar power generating firm and the retail firm are given by

$$\pi_1 = x[p_1 - (1-s)(c+e_1)] + \bar{z}[\tilde{p}_2 + m - (1-s)(c+e_1)], \tag{6.28}$$

$$\pi_2 = \tilde{p}_2\tilde{y} - (\tilde{y} - \bar{z})(g+e_2) - (\tilde{p}_2 + m)\bar{z}, \tag{6.29}$$

respectively.

From (6.28) and (6.29), the reaction functions of each firm are

$$p_1 = \left[\tilde{p}_2 + \left(\overline{\theta} + \rho\right)(e_1 - e_2) + (1-s)(c+e_1)\right]/2, \tag{6.30}$$

$$\tilde{p}_2 = [p_1 - \left(\underline{\theta} + \rho\right)(e_1 - e_2) + (g+e_2) - \bar{z}(\bar{\theta} - \underline{\theta})(e_1 - e_2)]/2, \tag{6.31}$$

respectively. From (6.30) and (6.31), the prices at equilibrium and their differences are given as

$$p_1^{***} = \frac{\left(2\overline{\theta} - \underline{\theta} + \rho\right)(e_1 - e_2) + (g+e_2) + 2(1-s)(c+e_1) - \bar{z}(\overline{\theta} - \underline{\theta})(e_1 - e_2)}{3} \tag{6.32}$$

$$\tilde{p}_2^{***} = \frac{\left(\overline{\theta} - 2\underline{\theta} - \rho\right)(e_1 - e_2) + 2(g+e_2) + (1-s)(c+e_1) - 2\bar{z}\left(\overline{\theta} - \underline{\theta}\right)(e_1 - e_2)}{3}, \tag{6.33}$$

$$p_1^{***} - \tilde{p}_2^{***} = \frac{\left(\overline{\theta} + \underline{\theta} + 2\rho\right)(e_1 - e_2) - (g+e_2) + (1-s)(c+e_1) + \bar{z}\left(\overline{\theta} - \underline{\theta}\right)(e_1 - e_2)}{3}. \tag{6.34}$$

Considering (6.16), (6.17), and (6.34), the demand shares for $x$ and $\tilde{y}$ are

$$x^{***} = [\left(2\overline{\theta} - \underline{\theta} + \rho\right)(e_1 - e_2) + (g+e_2) - (1-s)(c+e_1)$$
$$-\bar{z}\left(\overline{\theta} - \underline{\theta}\right)(e_1 - e_2)]/3\left(\overline{\theta} - \underline{\theta}\right)(e_1 - e_2), \tag{6.35}$$

$$\tilde{y}^{***} = (1 - \mathrm{x})^* = [\left(\overline{\theta} - 2\underline{\theta} - \rho\right)(e_1 - e_2) - (g+e_2) + (1-s)(c+e_1) + \bar{z}(\overline{\theta} -$$
$$\underline{\theta})(e_1 - e_2)]/3\left(\overline{\theta} - \underline{\theta}\right)(e_1 - e_2) \tag{6.36}$$

Thus, equilibrium prices in Sects. 6.5.1.2 and 6.5.1.3 are those depicted in Fig. 6.3.

The solar power generating firm has the same reaction function in both cases. The retail firm reaction function shifts downward from (6.21) to (6.30). In this relationship, though the slope of the solar power generating firm in both cases is 2, the slope of the reaction function of the retail firm is 50%. Therefore, the solar power generating firm's decrease in electricity price is smaller than that of the retail firm, and the difference between their prices is larger in Sect. 6.5.1.2, as (6.24) and (6.33) demonstrate. This outcome suggests the following proposition.

**Proposition 6.3** *The retail firm market share becomes larger in Sect. 6.5.1.3 than in Sect. 6.5.1.2.*

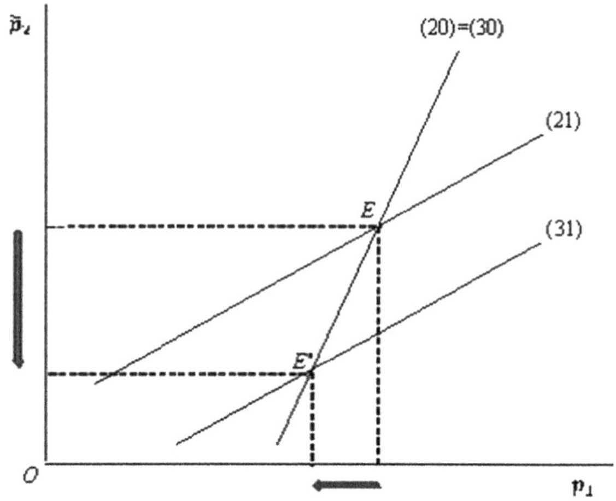


**Fig. 6.3** Reaction functions of solar power generating firm and retail firm

#### 6.5.1.4 Consumers Cannot Choose a Supplier (Fig. 6.1, Case (1))

In competitive markets, consumers are able to freely select goods and services to purchase. A consumer chooses a car among a range of cars produced by many different companies in a competitive market, granting them free choice among eco-friendly cars. However, as noted in Sect. 6.2, Japan's electricity market was far from being competitive for a number of reasons, including regional monopolies such as TEPCO and a market system that prevents consumer choice among power resources. Figure 6.1, case (3) describes the opposite "free choice" model.

Section 6.5.1, using (6.6), discussed the condition where consumers directly purchase solar power. The condition in Sect. 6.5.1 is the same as in Sect. 6.5.1.1 with the retail electricity market liberalization and the FIT. No consumer demand for direct purchase from the solar power generating firm occurs unless the numerator of (6.16), $\left(\bar{\theta}+\rho\right)(e_1-e_2)-(p_1-p_2)$, becomes positive. Therefore, the key variables are $\rho$, $p_1$, and $\tilde{p}_2$. When $\rho$ increases, and when the difference between $p_1$ and $\tilde{p}_2$ decreases, consumer demand for direct purchase from the solar power generating firm increases. As (6.25) shows, the subsidy to the solar power generating firm, $s$, reduces the difference. Because $c$ is the marginal cost to install an additional 1 MW solar panel, increasing $s$ reduces $c$. In this relationship, it is noteworthy that because of the combination of the subsidy paid for residents who install solar panels and of the power generating companies' voluntary purchase of surplus energy unused by residential customers who install solar panels, Japan had ranked No.1 in the world for PV power generating capacity from 1994 to 2004. The self-consumption system using subsidized solar panels represents one form of the combination of a green electricity program and subsidy. However, after suspending the subsidy, Japan has lost its ranking for installation capacity since 2005. Given this background, Japan re-instituted the subsidy in fiscal year 2009.

### 6.5.2 Welfare Analysis

#### 6.5.2.1 Framework

This section examines the welfare factors of the electricity market focusing on the market structures depicted in Fig. 6.1, especially the economic and social surplus in the frameworks shown in Sects. 6.5.1 and 6.5.1.1. The consumer surplus (*CS*) in Sect. 6.5.1.1 is defined as

$$CS_1 = \int_{\theta^*}^{\bar{\theta}} [\,\bar{u} - p_1 + \theta e_1 + \rho\,(e_1 - e_2)]\,d\theta + \int_{\underline{\theta}}^{\theta^*} [\bar{u} - p_2 + \theta e_2]d\theta. \quad (6.35)$$

In contrast, the consumer surplus in Sect. 6.5.1.1 is defined as

$$CS_2 = \int_{\theta^{**}}^{\bar{\theta}} [\bar{u} - p_1 + \theta e_1 + \rho(e_1 - e_2)]d\theta + \int_{\theta}^{\theta^{**}} [\bar{u} - \tilde{p}_2 + \theta e_2]d\theta. \quad (6.36)$$

#### 6.5.2.2 A Comparison of the Surplus

The consumer surpluses in Sects. 6.5.1 and in 6.5.1.1 are identical, because we confirmed in Sect. 6.5.1 that the value of $p_1$ in Sects. 6.5.1 and 6.5.1.1 is identical, $p_2 = \tilde{p}_2$, and $\theta^* = \theta^{**}$. Thus, the surplus of consumers obtaining electricity directly from the solar power generating firm is computed as

$$CS_{11} = CS_{21} = A[6\bar{u}\,(e_1 - e_2) - A\,(e_1 - 2e_2) + 6\,(1 - s)\,(c + e_1)\,(e_1 - e_2)$$
$$+ 6\rho(e_1 - e_2)^2]/18(e_1 - e_2)^2,$$

where $A = \left(2\bar{\theta} - \underline{\theta} + \rho\right)(e_1 - e_2) - [(1 - s)\,(c + e_1) - (\text{g}{+}e_2)]$.

The surplus of consumers obtaining electricity from the thermal power generating firm in Sect. 6.5.1 and the retail firm in Sect. 6.5.1.1 are computed as

$$CS_{12} = CS_{22} = B\,[6\bar{u}\,(e_1 - e_2) - B\,(2e_1 - 3e_2) + 6\,(g + e_2)\,(e_1 - e_2)]\,/18(e_1 - e_2)^2, \quad (6.37)$$

where $B = \left(\bar{\theta} - 2\underline{\theta} - \rho\right)(e_1 - e_2) + (1 - s)\,(c + e_1) - (\text{g}{+}e_2)$.

The producer surpluses of the solar power generating firm in Sects. 6.5.1 ($PS_{11}$) and 6.5.1.2 ($PS_{21}$) are calculated, respectively, as

$$PS_{11} = A^2/9(\bar{\theta} - \underline{\theta})\,(e_1 - e_2) \quad (6.38)$$

$$PS_{21} = [A^2/9(\bar{\theta} - \underline{\theta})\,(e_1 - e_2)] + \bar{z}[\bar{p}_1 - (1 - s)\,(c + e_1)]. \quad (6.39)$$

Comparing (6.38) and (6.39), we clearly find that the latter is larger by $\bar{z}[\bar{p}_1 - (1 - s)\,(c + e_1)]$. The thermal power firm producer surpluses in Sect. 6.5.1.1 ($PS_{12}$) and those of the retail firm in Sect. 6.5.1.2 ($PS_{22}$) are calculated, respectively, as

$$PS_{12} = B^2/9(\bar{\theta} - \underline{\theta})\,(e_1 - e_2)\,, \tag{6.40}$$

$$PS_{22} = B^2/9(\bar{\theta} - \underline{\theta})\,(e_1 - e_2) - \bar{z}[\overline{p}_1 - (g + e_2)]. \tag{6.41}$$

Comparing (6.40) and (6.41), we find that the latter is smaller by $\bar{z}[\overline{p}_1 - (g + e_2)]$. Moreover, the environmental burden in (6.38) is larger than in (6.42), the difference between them being equal to $[(\bar{e} - e_2) - (\bar{e} - e_1)]\,\bar{z}$. Governmental spending for the solar power generating firm in (6.41) is clearly larger than in (6.40), and the difference is $\bar{z}s\,(c + e_1)$.

Summarizing these outcomes, we calculate the difference between the social welfare in Sects. 6.5.1 and 6.5.1.1 as

$$\begin{aligned} W_2 - W_1 = {} & \bar{z}[\bar{p}_1 - (1 - s)(c + e_1)] - \bar{z}[\overline{p}_1 - (g + e_2)] + \bar{z}[(\bar{e} - e_2) - (\bar{e} - e_1)] \\ & - \bar{z}s(c + e_1) = \bar{z}(-c + g) < 0 \end{aligned} \tag{6.42}$$

Therefore, we can state the following proposition.

**Proposition 6.4** *The social welfare in the competitive market in Sect. 6.5.1 is larger than that in the market in Sect. 6.5.1.1 where mixed power is supplied under the FIT policy in the retail electricity market liberalization.*

## 6.6 Conclusion and Further Remarks

This study theoretically examined the restructuring and development pattern of the Japanese electricity market structure. One major issue is consumers' free choice between electricity suppliers who generate electricity via different power sources. The study makes the important finding that social welfare where the FIT is enforced (case (2), Fig. 6.1) is lower than that of the competitive market (case (3)), suggesting that social welfare is not enhanced with only mixed power. This study also finds that the demand for direct purchase of solar power depends on the marginal WTP for eco-friendliness, the marginal utility of social-related evaluation, and the price difference between the solar power generating firm and the thermal power generating firm (case (3), Fig. 6.1), or the price difference between the solar power generating firm and the retail firm (case (2)). If the numerator of Eqs. (6.6) and (6.16) is negative, demand for direct purchase from the solar power generating firm does not occur.

The aforementioned findings suggest important considerations for the current discussion about Japan's future energy policy. The most controversial issue is the share of power sources which Japan should target through 2030. However, if political viewpoints determine the share of power generation sources, each consumer's WTP is neither reflected nor estimated. Achieving the target may require certain policies, such as the FIT and the subsidy we investigated here. If the FIT, which forces some consumers to continue purchasing mixed power, is enforced, the optimal use of power sources will be unavailable.[13] Thus, any policy measures to increase the share of renewable power sources should be supported by environmentally oriented consumer behavior. To support these policies, green consumers require information disclosure on power sources because the optimal distribution of power sources can be attained only in a market system that accurately reflects consumer preference, that is, their marginal WTP for eco-friendly attributes.

Finally, let us consider future research. This study examined the electricity market using the vertical differentiation model under the assumption of full coverage because electricity is an essential good. However, if alternative energy services such as provided by gas utilities become available, electricity does not have to cover 100% of energy needs, and we can relax the assumption of full market coverage. We plan to extend our research in those directions.

## References

André, F.J., P. González, and N. Porteiro. 2009. Strategic Quality Competition and the Porter Hypothesis. *Journal of Environmental Economics and Management* 57: 182–194.
Andreoni, J. 1989. Impure Altruism and Donations to Public Goods: A Theory of Warm Glow Giving. *Journal of Political Economy* 97: 1447–1458.
Bansal, S. 2008. Choice and Design of Regulatory Instruments in the Presence of Green Consumers. *Resource and Energy Economics* 30: 345–368.
Bruvoll, A., and K. Nyborg. 2004. The Cold Shiver of Not Giving Enough: On the Social Cost of Recycling Campaigns. *Land Economics* 80 (4): 539–549.
Cornes, R., and T. Sandler. 1994. The Comparative Static Properties of the Impure Public Good Model. *Journal of Public Economics* 54 (3): 403–421.
Cremer, H., and J.F. Thisse. 1994. Commodity Taxation in a Differentiated Oligopoly. *International Economic Review* 35 (3): 613–633.
Cremer, H., and J.F. Thisse. 1999. On the Taxation of Polluting Products in a Differentiated Industry. *European Economic Review* 43: 575–594.
Cremer, H., F. Gahvari, and N. Ladoux. 2003. Environmental Taxes with Heterogeneous Consumers; An Application to Energy Consumption in France. *Journal of Public Economics* 87: 2791–2815.
Eriksson, C. 2004. Can Green Consumerism Replace Environmental Regulation? A Differentiated Products Example. *Resource and Energy Economics* 26: 281–293.
Hotelling, H. 1929. Stability in Competition. *Economic Journal* 39: 41–57.
Kotchen, J. 2005. Impure Public Goods and Comparative Statics of Environmentally Friendly Consumption. *Journal of Environmental Economics and Management* 49: 281–300.
Kotchen, J. 2007. Private Provision of Environmental Public Goods: Household Participation in Green-Electricity Programs. *Journal of Environmental Economics and Management* 53: 1–16.

[13]The policy paper announced by the Energy and Environment Council on September 14, 2012 indicates that the share of each power source should be determined as a result of competition among power generating firms and consumers' free choice. The paper also set the numerical goal of tripling the output of electricity generated from renewable energy sources from 110 billion kWh in 2010 to 300 billion kWh by 2030. To reach the target, the paper envisages FIT as an important policy measure. However, it seems impossible that outcomes of free competition will correspond with those envisioned by the regulatory policy. Thus, a considerable discrepancy may exist in the final report (see The Energy and Environment Council HP).

Lambertini, L., A. Tampieri. 2011. Vertical Differentiation in a Cournot Industry: The Porter Hypothesis and Beyond. http://www2.dse.unibo.it/wp/WP730.pdf. Accessed 30 April 2012.
Lancaster, K.J. 1979. *Variety, Equity, and Efficiency*. New York: Columbia University Press.
Lombardini-Riipinen, C. 2005. Optimal Tax Policy under Environmental Quality Competition. *Environmental & Resource Economics* 32: 317–336.
Moorthy, K.S. 1988. Product and Price Competition in a Duopoly. *Marketing Science* 7 (2): 141–168.
Motta, M. 1993. Endogenous Quality Choice: Price vs. Quantity Competition. *The Journal of Industrial Economics* XLI: 113–131.
Mussa, M., and S. Rosen. 1978. Monopoly and Product Quality. *Journal of Economic Theory* 18: 301–317.
Shaked, A., and J. Sutton. 1982. Relaxing Price Competition through Product Differentiation. *Review of Economic Studies* 49: 3–13.
Toshimitsu, T. 2010. On the Paradoxical Case of a Consumer-based Environmental Subsidy Policy. *Economic Modelling* 27: 159–164.
Yabuta, M., N. Scott. 2010. Ecotourist Behaviour as a Green Consumer. http://www2.tamacc.chuo-u.ac.jp/keizaiken/discussno146.pdf. Accessed 30 April 2012.

## Web References

Power Generation Cost Analysis Working Group HP. http://www.enecho.meti.go.jp/committee/council/basic_policy_subcommittee/mitoshi/cost_wg/pdf/cost_wg_03.pdf. Accessed 15 April 2018.
The Agency for Natural Resources and Energy HP. https://www.fit-portal.go.jp/PublicInfoSummary. Accessed 15 April 2018.
The Energy and Environment Council HP. http://www.npu.go.jp/policy/policy09/archive01_14.html#haifu. Accessed 15 Sept 2012.

# Part II
# International Trade and Investment

# Chapter 7
# Global Supply Chain and Japanese Electronics Firms' Location in East Asia: A Case of Final Goods Production Sites

**Suminori Tokunaga and Maria Ikegawa**

## 7.1 Introduction

Japanese companies in the global-type electrical/electronics industry continued to locate in ASEAN and other countries instead of China from the 1990s up until 2009, but the proportion located in ASEAN and other countries declined so that the number of locations in China and in ASEAN and other countries was about equal as of 2009. Although this sector's expansion proceeded at about the same rate in both China and ASEAN and other countries, the number of locations in China has grown rapidly since the mid-2000s. To this purpose, this paper surveys the trends in overseas locations in East Asia among the relevant Japanese multinational firms (MNFs), focusing on the global-type electrical/electronics industry. It also conducts an empirical analysis of the factors involved in choosing overseas locations for the relevant MNFs' production sites for final goods by looking at these companies' final production sites in East Asia.[1]

This chapter is structured as follows. Focusing on the global-type electrical/electronics industry in East Asia, Sect. 7.2 reviews the trend toward supply chain globalization at the relevant Japanese electronics firms in East Asia, particularly the trend of setting up production sites for final goods in overseas locations. Section 7.3 follows with an analysis of the factors that Japanese electronics firms consider when choosing overseas locations for final goods production sites and shows overseas

[1]In this paper, the global-type electrical/electronics industry refers to the manufacture of electronic parts, devices and electronic circuits per JSIC Code 28, the manufacture of electrical machinery, equipment and supplies per JSIC Code 29, and the manufacture of information and communication electronics equipment per JSIC Code 30.

S. Tokunaga (✉)
Reitaku University, Kashiwa, Japan
e-mail: tokunaga@reitaku-u.ac.jp

M. Ikegawa
Policy Research Institute of MAFF, Tokyo, Japan



M. Hosoe et al. (eds.), *Applied Analysis of Growth, Trade, and Public Policy*,
https://doi.org/10.1007/978-981-13-1876-4_7

location choice model. Section 7.4 shows the data source and model specification. Specifically, we conduct our analysis using an overseas location selection model based on the new economic geography (NEG) model and focusing on market potential, supply access, and vertical agglomeration of industry as factors involved in Japanese electronics firms' choice of overseas locations. In Sect. 7.5, we show the estimation results using the conditional logit model. The final section presents our conclusions and shows some policy implications.

## 7.2 Trend in Japanese Electronics Firms' Locations in East Asia

First, we will analyze the trends in overseas locations for Japanese electronics firms in East Asia, focusing on the final goods production sites of the global-type electrical/electronics industry. In view of the vertical coagglomeration between intermediate and final goods in Japanese domestic manufacturing agglomeration (Tokunaga et al. 2015), we focus on the analysis of firms' production sites for final and intermediate goods.[2] Figure 7.1a, b show total overseas production site locations of final and intermediate goods for Japanese-affiliated electrical/electronics companies' production sites as of 2009, respectively. Some spatial fragmentation is observed. From these figures, most global-type Japanese electrical/electronics companies have chosen China for locating both their final and intermediate goods production sites, followed by Thailand, Indonesia, and other ASEAN countries. However, production sites for intermediate goods far outnumber those for final goods.

Next, we review the country-by-country trend in the number of new locations for Japanese electrical/electrics industry between 1995 and 2009 in Fig. 7.2.[3] For this industry, the total number of Japanese domestic locations bottomed out around the time of the Asian currency crisis in the mid-1990s, while new overseas locations peaked around the mid-2000s. Japanese electrical/electronics companies gravitated toward China, with its inexpensive, high-quality labor and large market, followed by Thailand, Indonesia, Malaysia, South Korea, and others from the mid-1990s to the early 2000s, including during the Asian currency crisis in 1998–99. From the early to mid-2000s, however, these companies were entering China faster than they were entering Thailand, South Korea, and Indonesia. When Chinese wages later rose precipitously, the number of companies locating there declined, and more companies started locating in such countries as India, Indonesia, and Vietnam.

From the country-by-country trends over time, we found that Japanese electrical/electronics firms' production sites in East Asia shifted as these companies pursued the best locations with inexpensive, high-quality labor and large domestic markets.

---

[2]In addition to Venables (1996) employing the NEG model, Fujita and Hamaguchi (2001, 2014), Todo et al. (2015), and other papers have analyzed the supply chain and knowledge dissemination.

[3]See Tokunaga, Akune, Ikegawa, and Okiyama (2015, Fig. 6) for this point.

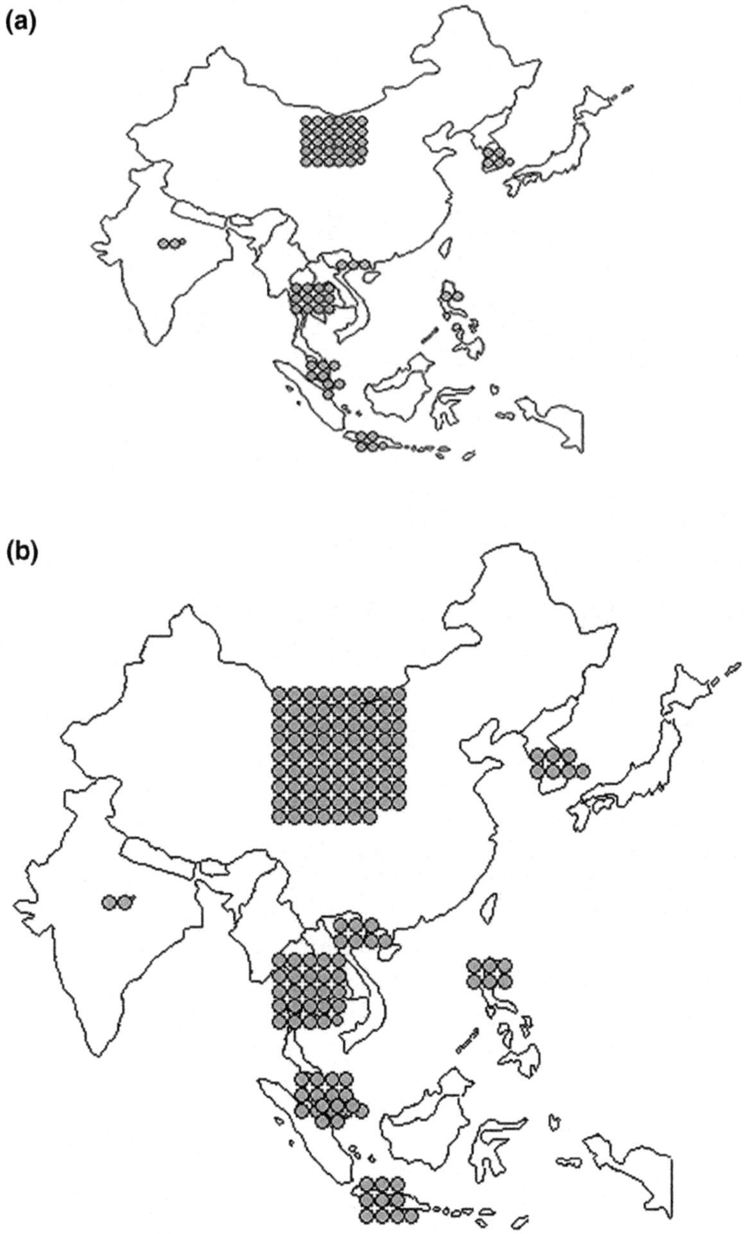


**Fig. 7.1** **a** Location of new production plants for Japanese electronics firms in East Asia (2009), Final goods (• is 5 locations, total is 337). (Source: *Toyo Keizai Directory of Japanese Overseas Affiliates 2011*, Toyo Keizai). **b** Location of new production plants for Japanese electronics firms in East Asia (2009), Intermediate goods (• is 20 locations, total is 3188). (Source: *Toyo Keizai Directory of Japanese Overseas Affiliates 2011*, Toyo Keizai)

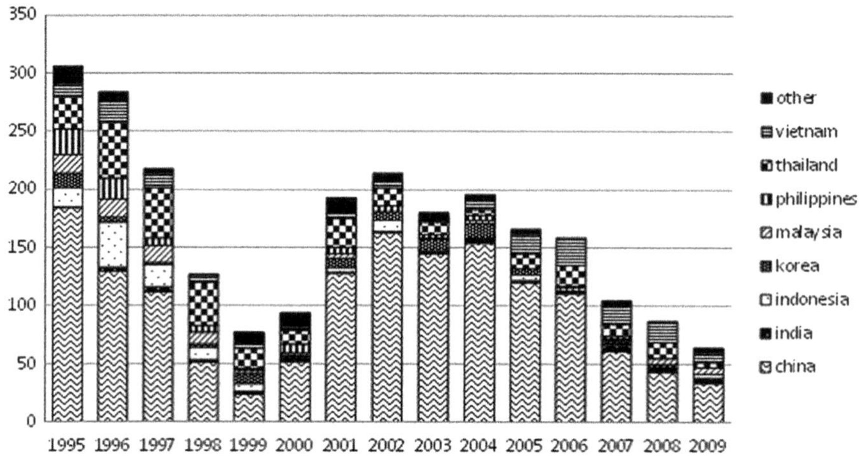


**Fig. 7.2** Number of new locations of Japanese electronics industries in East Asia (Source: *Toyo Keizai Directory of Japanese Overseas Affiliates 2011*, Toyo Keizai)

## 7.3 Overseas Location Choice Model for Japanese Electronics Firms' Production Sites

Next, in light of the foregoing and focusing on the important role played by the final goods and conduct an empirical analysis of the factors involved in choosing overseas locations for final goods production sites in East Asia by Japanese electrical/electronics companies. So, which variables are key factors in Japanese companies' location choices? This leads us to summarize the "deciding factors for investment" given in the Ministry of Economy, Tradeand Industry's annual "Basic Survey on Overseas Business Activities (Parent Company Version)." This shows that parent companies considered in deciding whether to make new or additional investments in local subsidiaries overseas. The following investment factors are especially notable. Reasons for global-type Japanese electrical/electronics industries to invest overseas were, for final goods production sites, "local product demand is strong or demand is anticipated in the future" in first place, "high-quality inexpensive labor can be secured" in second place, and "other Japanese companies are there, including delivery destinations" in third place. However, for "product demand in neighboring countries is strong or demand is anticipated in the future" and "easy to procure parts and other supplies locally," both in fourth place, it was significant that the trend was flat for intermediate goods production sites but increasing for final goods production sites. These were followed by "tax and financing incentives" and "social infrastructure improvements." We adopted these results as theoretical assumptions and then used them as explanatory variables in our model for overseas location choice for final goods production sites in this industry.

Many empirical analyses have been conducted in recent years using the market potential and supplier access variables introduced in the NEG model built by Krugman (1991a, b) and Fujita et al. (1999) (e.g., Head and Mayer 2004; Redding and Venables 2004; Redding 2011 and Tokunaga and Jin 2011). Therefore, in this section, we explicitly introduce market potential and supplier access, as proposed in the NEG model, as explanatory variables along with the previously mentioned variables to our analysis of the factors considered by Japanese electronics firms in choosing overseas locations.

In our overseas location selection model, we assume that firm $i$ locates in East Asian country $j$ in year $t$ in order to maximize Profit $\pi_{ijt}$.

$$\pi_{ijt} = \beta X_{ijt} + \varepsilon_{ij} \tag{7.1}$$

Here, $\beta$ is the vector for the unknown parameter, the variable $X_{ijt}$ is the economic characteristics of firm $i$'s location in country $j$ in year $t$, and $\varepsilon_{ij}$ is an error term. If the error term $\varepsilon_{ij}$ in Eq. (7.1) follows an independent and identical Gumbel distribution, the probability $\Pr(y^*_{ijt} = 1)$ that firm $i$ will choose an overseas location in country $j$ can be expressed by the following conditional logit model equation (McFadden 1974):

$$\Pr(y^*_{ijt} = 1) = \frac{\exp(\beta X_{ijt})}{\sum_{j=1}^{J} \exp(\beta X_{ijt})} \tag{7.2}$$

The value is 1 if the location is new and 0 if the location is not.

## 7.4 Data Sources and Model Specification

We used the following data sources. The source of the data for the explained variable of presence/absence of Japanese electronics firms overseas production site locations and the data for the explanatory variable of total number of Japanese electronics firms locations producing final goods is the 2011 edition of "Overseas Japanese Affiliates" published by Toyo Keizai Inc.[4] Data on wages came from the International Labor Organization's LABORSTA database, data on total distance of highways by country came from the World Bank's "World Development Indicator" and Taiwan's Statistical Bureau, and that on total distance of superhighways by country came from the respective countries' statistics bureaus. The estimation period was 1995 through 2009, and the analysis covered 11 countries: China, Hong Kong, South Korea, Thailand, Indonesia, Malaysia, Philippines, Singapore, Vietnam, India, and Japan. Therefore, the number of panel data totaled (number of Japanese companies for each industry) × (11 location countries) × (the 15-year survey period of 1995–2009).

[4]We eliminated those firms whose entry date was unknown.

The explained variable is the presence/absence of a final goods production site location in country $j$ for Japanese MNF $i$ (in the electrical/electronics industry) in year $t$, with 1 denoting presence and 0 indicating absence. The number of firms in this industry being studied, as shown below, was those making final goods, depending on the business description given in the 2011 edition of Toyo Keizai's "Overseas Japanese Companies." Final goods production site for the electrical/electronics industry numbered 143.

In light of the above-mentioned factors in overseas investment decisions, we use the following seven variables as explanatory variables in our overseas location selection model. [1] Real Wages (RWAGE), "high-quality inexpensive labor can be secured" was a major factor in determining overseas locations, as was shown in the reasons for investment in the "Basic Survey on Overseas Business Activities". We therefore take as real wages the logarithm of the US dollar-denominated real wages in the target industries in the location countries divided by US dollar-denominated real wages in Japanese manufacturing industries. Because one goal of production locations is to minimize costs, we can hypothesize that "Japanese electronics firms locate in those countries where the real wages of the industries concerned are lower than real wages in Japan." Therefore, the expected sign condition is negative. [2] Infrastructure (INFRA), "social infrastructure improvement" is a key factor for firms locating overseas, according to the reasons for investment in the "Basic Survey on Overseas Business Activities." Many manufacturing production sites desire social infrastructure more than anything else. From the standpoint of facilitating the distribution of goods, they especially want to locate in places that have well-developed transportation networks, including superhighways. We therefore took the relative value of superhighway distance divided by total highway network distance within a country as the infrastructure metric. In our opinion, "Japanese electronics firms like to locate in places with good infrastructure," so the expected sign condition is positive. [3] Industry agglomeration [vertical agglomeration (Agglomeration_intermediate), horizontal agglomeration (agglomeration_final)] of the reasons for investment cited in the "Basic Survey on Overseas Business Activities," a key factor in location choice is "other Japanese companies are there, including delivery destinations," so in light of the vertical and horizontal agglomeration that exists in Japanese domestic manufacturing locations, particularly for the electrical/electronics industry, we introduced industry agglomeration variables for Japanese firms as the third factor in overseas location choice (see Tokunaga et al. 2018). By vertical agglomeration in Japanese electronics firms' final goods production site locations, we mean that industry agglomeration of Japanese firms' intermediate goods production sites in a target country is present if the cumulative number of locations of Japanese firms' intermediate production sites in a target country for a target industry was large as of the previous year, and because benefits can be obtained from Japanese firms' vertical agglomeration, production sites for final goods will be located in that country. At the same time, horizontal agglomeration means the presence of industry agglomeration in a target country for Japanese firms' final production sites if the cumulative number of Japanese firms' final goods production sites in a target industry was large as of the previous year, and because benefits can be obtained from Japanese firms' horizontal agglomeration, production sites for final goods will be located in that country.[5] Previous research by Tokunaga et al. (2006, 2014, 2018), Nakamura (1985, 2008), Klein and Crafts (2012), and others, as well as the results of interviews, have demonstrated the existence of vertical and horizontal agglomeration in Japan's manufacturing industries and that agglomeration and coagglomeration exert positive external economies on production (Ellison and Glaeser 1997). Japanese MNFs thus place value on proximity in locating their final goods production sites in East Asia. Therefore, if agglomeration (that is, vertical agglomeration) of Japanese firms' intermediate goods production sites and agglomeration (that is, horizontal agglomeration) of final goods production sites exist in the country of location, Japanese firms will regard this as a benefit of agglomeration and therefore locate in that country. In our opinion, "the greater the degree of vertical or horizontal agglomeration of Japanese firms in the countries where they are located, the greater the economies of agglomeration, thus inducing Japanese MNFs to locate their production sites in those countries." Therefore, the expected sign condition is positive. [4] Market potential (MPK), domestic (for a target country) MPK (DMPK) and foreign (neighboring countries) MPK (FMPK). The "Basic Survey of Overseas Business Activities" showed that "local product demand is strong or demand is anticipated in the future" and "product demand in neighboring countries is strong or demand is anticipated in the future" are major reasons that Japanese firms decide to make overseas investments.[6] In NEG model, we took this to be market potential (market access) and determined a geographical distribution of firms according to the relative strengths of this market potential (market access) effect and the market crowding effect. We then introduced this market potential variable as the explanatory variable for location. For the estimation, we used the estimated values gained from a gravity model as the variable of market potential (see Tokunaga et al. 2015 in the appended estimation results from the gravity model for the electrical/electronics industry). Previous research by Redding and Venables (2004), Head and Mayer (2004), and Lu and Tokunaga (2008) used a dummy variable for two countries sharing a language and a dummy variable for landlocked borders, but our paper revises the empirical model of Lu and Tokunaga (2008) as a gravity model and uses relative export prices, market size of importing countries, time distance, and the year of completing a bilateral or multilateral FTA or EPA as dummy variables. The market potential for firms producing final goods is expressed as market potential for final goods (MPK_final),

[5]Tokunaga and Ishii (2000), Tokunaga and Jin (2011), and Tokunaga et al. (2018) demonstrated that the agglomeration variable is a key explanatory variable in overseas location choice because economies of agglomeration are at work, but this paper is the first to demonstrate the vertical and horizontal coagglomeration effect on location by separating production sites into those for final goods and those for intermediate goods for the electrical/electronics and automotive industries. Yamashita et al. (2014) demonstrated the importance of the agglomeration effect in Japanese MNFs' location choices in China.

[6]See Ikegawa, Tan, and Tokunaga, Chugoku Dairen ni okeru nikkei shokuhin, denki denshi, jidosha kanren kigyo oyobi JETRO Dairen jimusho no genchi chosa (2013, Nov.), [On-site survey of Japanese food, electrical/electronics, and automotive-related companies in Dalian, China, and JETRO's Dalian office (Nov. 2013)], (Ikegawa and Tokunaga 2018).

domestic market potential for final goods (DMPK_final), and surrounding country market potential for final goods (FMPK_final) (see Fig. 7.3). In our opinion, "Japanese MNFs producing final goods locate in those countries with the greatest market growth potential domestically," so the respective expected sign conditions are positive. Although, "Japanese electronics firms producing final goods locate in those countries with the greatest market growth potential in surrounding to countries," the respective expected sign conditions are ambiguous. [5] Supplier Access for intermediate goods (SA_intermediate), domestic supplier access for intermediate goods (DSA_intermediate) and supplier access to surrounding countries for intermediate goods (FSA_intermediate). In the "Basic Survey on Overseas Business Activities," electrical/electronics companies with final goods production sites placed relatively high importance on "easy to procure parts and other supplies locally" among the reasons for Japanese companies to invest overseas. Therefore, as determined in the previous section of our analysis, for a final goods production site of a Japanese electronics firm located, if supplier access of intermediate goods (upstream industries) in a target location country (SA_intermediate, DSA_intermediate) increases, then the degree of vertical coagglomeration will increase in that country, thereby strengthening the supply chain. Meanwhile, if supplier access of intermediate goods (upstream industries) in neighboring countries (FSA_intermediate) increases, the degree of global vertical coagglomeration between that country and its neighbors will increase, thereby strengthening that country's global supply chain with its neighbors. We thus introduced these supplier access variables as explanatory variables in choosing overseas locations.[7] For the estimation, we calculated these variables gained from a gravity model, as was also the case for the market potential variables. Supplier access for firms producing final goods is supplier access for intermediate goods both domestically and in neighboring countries (SA_intermediate), supplier access for intermediate goods domestically (DSA_intermediate), and supplier access for intermediate goods in neighboring countries (FSA_intermediate). Figure 7.3 illustrates the supplier access values over time for intermediate goods in China for the period from 1995 through 2009. In our opinion, "Japanese MNFs producing final goods locate in countries where the supply chain expands if supplier access of intermediate goods increases in those countries and their neighbors." It follows that even though we consider these various expected sign conditions to be positive, as put forth by spatial economic theory, if more firms locate in the same region, they will face fiercer price competition. This will generate the market crowding effect, and the expected sign condition could even turn negative.[8] Table 7.1 lists the variables we used as explanatory variables, classifying them according to final goods for the Japanese electronics industry in our study.

[7]This paper is the first to conduct an empirical analysis of the market potential (market access) and supplier access variables involved in choosing locations for the final goods production sites in the electrical/electronics by clearly differentiating between period 1995–2000 and period 2001–2009 and looking at domestic and neighboring countries' markets separately. Tokunaga et al. (2018) and Ikegawa and Tokunaga (2018) have studied for Japanese MNFs using the same methodology.

[8]Regarding this point, see Fujita and Thisse (2013), Chap. 9.

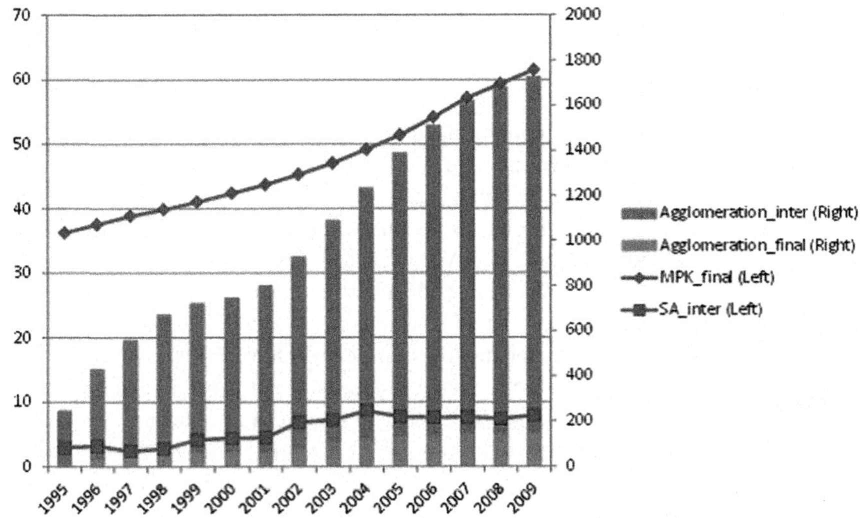


**Fig. 7.3** Cumulative number of location, MPK, and SA for the Japanese electronics industry in China (1995–2009) (Source: Tokunaga et al. (2015, p. 84))

**Table 7.1** Description of independent variables

| | Variables | Signs | Discriptions |
|---|---|---|---|
| RWAGE | Real Wage | − | Logarithm of Real wages of employee in manufacturing industry in US$. (Relative value of located country to Japan) |
| INFRA | Infrastructure | + | Relative value of highway distance to all road distance in located country |
| Agglomeration_ Intermediate | Vertical Agglomeration Index (Intermediate) | + | Total number of Japanese firms located in the host country. (Intermediate) (t − 1) |
| Agglomeration_final | Horizontal Agglomeration Index (Final) | + | Total number of Japanese firms located in the host country. (Final) (t − 1) |
| MPK_final | Market Potential (final goods) | + | Market potential in located country |
| DMPK_final | Domestic Market Potential (final goods) | ? | Domestic market potential in located country |
| FMPK_final | Foreign Market Potential (final goods) | ? | Foreign market potential in located country |
| SA_intermediate | Supplier Access (Intermediate goods) | + | Supplier access in located country |
| DSA_intermediate | Domestic Supplier Access (Intermediate goods) | ? | Domestic supplier access in located country |
| FSA_intermediate | Foreign Supplier Access (Intermediate goods) | ? | Foreign supplier access in located country |

## 7.5 Estimation Results of the Overseas Location Choice Model

The estimation results of the conditional logit model of the location choice of Japanese electrical/electronics firms' final goods production sites in East Asian countries (1995–2009) are presented in Table 7.2.

We first look at the results based on the fundamental explanatory variables in overseas location choice in Table 7.1. As the table shows, the sign conditions for the variables for real wages (RWAGE) and infrastructure metric (INFRA), which have traditionally been important factors in overseas location choice, have been satisfied, and these results were statistically significant at the 1% level. These results verify the hypotheses "Japanese electronics firms locate in those countries where real wages in the target industries are lower than real wages in Japan" and "Japanese electronics firms locate in places with good infrastructure." Therefore, the policy variables we used in location choice factors are limited to the variables of real wages and infrastructure, which are factors traditionally used in choosing locations.

Next, we look at the existence of vertical and horizontal agglomeration of Japanese manufacturing industries' domestic locations, which were analyzed in the previous section and this factor's middle ranking among the reasons for investment in the "Basic Survey of Overseas Business Activities." Here, the sign condition in regard to Japanese firms' industrial agglomeration, the third factor in location choice, was satisfied, and the results were statistically significant at the 5% level. For final goods production sites of electrical/electronics company, in the case of the cumulative number of locations as of the previous year of these companies' intermediate production sites, which exhibit vertical agglomeration, and the cumulative number of locations as of the previous year of these companies' final goods production sites, which exhibit horizontal agglomeration, the positive sign condition was satisfied, and the results were statistically significant at the 1% level. In other words, both variables are key factors because Japanese electrical/electronics company place value on proximity when locating final goods production sites in East Asia, and because the existence of scale economies is taken into consideration in Japanese firms' agglomeration of their intermediate goods production sites (vertical agglomeration) and agglomeration of their final goods production sites (horizontal agglomeration) in these countries (Tokunaga et al. 2018). Therefore, the hypothesis "the greater the degree of vertical or horizontal agglomeration of Japanese firms in the countries where they are located, the greater the economies of agglomeration, thus inducing Japanese electronics firms to locate their production sites in those countries" was verified. In particular, the use of agglomeration of intermediate goods production sites in a target country as a factor in overseas location choice for Japanese firms' final goods production sites in a location country verifies, albeit indirectly, that "agglomeration of the final goods sector in a particular region is the outcome of the concentration of intermediate goods industries in that region; the reverse is also the case," as asserted in Krugman

**Table 7.2** Results of Japanese Electrical/Electronics Companies (1995–2009) <final goods production site>

| | (1) | (2) | (3) | (4) | (5) | (6) | (7) |
|---|---|---|---|---|---|---|---|
| ln RWAGE | -0.6147 *** | -0.527 *** | -0.52004 *** | -0.92566 *** | -0.77481 *** | -0.27146 *** | -0.96777 *** |
| ln(rwage) | (-12.94) | (-10.54) | (-10.49) | (-18.51) | (-17.65) | (-6.18) | (-17.92) |
| INFRA | 0.092184 *** | 0.076505 *** | 0.056846 *** | 0.285854 *** | 0.345551 *** | 0.105461 *** | 0.276152 *** |
| (highway/road) | (2.69) | (2.4) | (2.62) | (10.26) | (9.72) | (4.55) | (10.04) |
| Agglomeration | | 0.001901 *** | | | | | |
| _intermediate | | (19.51) | | | | | |
| Agglomeration | | | 0.019156 *** | | | | |
| _final | | | (19.27) | | | | |
| ln MPK | | | | 3.40208 *** | | | 3.350046 *** |
| _final | | | | (15.8) | | | (15.99) |
| ln DMPK | | | | | 2.02115 *** | | |
| _final | | | | | (14.01) | | |
| ln FMPK | | | | | | -0.61552 *** | |
| _final | | | | | | (-7.11) | |
| ln SA | | | | | | | 0.227191 *** |
| _intermediate | | | | | | | (2.74) |
| ln DSA | | | | | | | |
| _intermediate | | | | | | | |
| ln FSA | | | | | | | |
| _intermediate | | | | | | | |
| Log likelihood | -1672.62 | -1556.34 | -1557.97 | -1586.22 | -1593.59 | -1665.27 | -1491.41 |
| No. of Sample | 22595 | 22595 | 22595 | 22595 | 22595 | 22595 | 21736 |
| No. of Firms | 142 | 142 | 142 | 142 | 142 | 142 | 142 |

| | (8) | (9) | (10) | (11) | (12) | (13) | (14) |
|---|---|---|---|---|---|---|---|
| ln RWAGE | -0.70412 *** | -0.96657 *** | -0.64766 *** | -0.64601 *** | -0.94658 *** | -0.64269 *** | -0.93206 *** |
| ln(rwage) | (-11.12) | (-18.07) | (-10.75) | (-10.8) | (-17.52) | (-10) | (-17.46) |
| INFRA | 0.30211 *** | 0.262651 *** | 0.146018 *** | 0.125665 *** | 0.258422 *** | 0.272582 *** | 0.246075 *** |
| (highway/road) | (11.12) | (9.51) | (4.72) | (4.24) | (10.14) | (10.44) | (9.71) |
| Agglomeration | | | 0.001415 *** | | | | |
| _intermediate | | | (6.29) | | | | |
| Agglomeration | | | | 0.014022 *** | | | |
| _final | | | | (6.16) | | | |
| ln MPK | 3.260329 *** | 3.267391 *** | 1.086071 *** | 1.157557 *** | | | |
| _final | (14.66) | (15.95) | (3.31) | (3.54) | | | |
| ln DMPK | | | | | 2.372197 *** | 2.206223 *** | 2.324659 *** |
| _final | | | | | (16.9) | (12.19) | (17.07) |
| ln FMPK | | | | | | | |
| _final | | | | | | | |
| ln SA | | | | | 0.729241 *** | | |
| _intermediate | | | | | (7.9) | | |
| ln DSA | -0.76925 *** | | | | | -0.40154 *** | |
| _intermediate | (-4.99) | | | | | (-2.25) | |
| ln FSA | | 0.296571 *** | | | | | 0.702102 *** |
| _intermediate | | (5.55) | | | | | (9.27) |
| Log likelihood | -1455.46 | -1482.29 | -1550.71 | -1551.57 | -1496.95 | -1496.15 | -1451.95 |
| No. of Sample | 21736 | 21736 | 22595 | 22595 | 21736 | 21736 | 21736 |
| No. of Firms | 142 | 142 | 142 | 142 | 142 | 142 | 142 |

| | (15) | (16) | (17) | (18) | (19) | (20) | (21) |
|---|---|---|---|---|---|---|---|
| ln RWAGE | -0.62904 *** | -0.62215 *** | -0.35266 *** | -0.26094 *** | -0.32952 *** | -0.46661 *** | -0.46921 *** |
| ln(rwage) | (-12.26) | (-12.2) | (-6.97) | (-4.72) | (-6.35) | (-8.44) | (-8.55) |
| INFRA | 0.152244 *** | 0.140246 *** | 0.161441 *** | 0.111315 *** | 0.162809 *** | 0.100977 *** | 0.061295 *** |
| (highway/road) | (5.77) | (5.22) | (6.86) | (4.82) | (6.94) | (4.25) | (2.5) |
| Agglomeration | 0.001265 *** | | | | | 0.001781 *** | |
| _intermediate | (9.9) | | | | | (17.36) | |
| Agglomeration | | 0.0127 *** | | | | | 0.018051 *** |
| _final | | (9.71) | | | | | (17.08) |
| ln MPK | | | | | | | |
| _final | | | | | | | |
| ln DMPK | 0.859655 *** | 0.86648 *** | | | | | |
| _final | (5.04) | (5.02) | | | | | |
| ln FMPK | | | -1.61192 *** | -0.4211 *** | -1.93225 *** | -0.31306 *** | -0.27195 *** |
| _final | | | (-12.77) | (-2.69) | (-14.12) | (-2.12) | (-2.71) |
| ln SA | | | 1.410207 *** | | | | |
| _intermediate | | | (11.75) | | | | |
| ln DSA | | | | -0.65742 *** | | | |
| _intermediate | | | | (-4.21) | | | |
| ln FSA | | | | | 1.210972 *** | | |
| _intermediate | | | | | (14.2) | | |
| Log likelihood | -1542 | -1544.8 | -1529.57 | -1591.64 | -1495.92 | -1551.31 | -1554.71 |
| No. of Sample | 22595 | 22595 | 21736 | 21736 | 21736 | 22595 | 22595 |
| No. of Firms | 142 | 142 | 142 | 142 | 142 | 142 | 142 |

and Venables (1995) and Venables (1996).[9] Also, the use of a horizontal industrial agglomeration variable as an overseas location choice factor indirectly verifies the traditional proposition of industrial agglomeration, which is that agglomeration of a target industry breeds agglomeration of that industry.

The lower transportation costs for final goods in a target country stimulate trade in final goods, thereby inducing companies to locate not only their final goods production sites but also their intermediate goods production sites in that country.[10] Thus, in the estimates below, we do not make direct use of this trade variable. Instead, we employ the estimated values of the gravity model to construct new data of the market potential and supplier access variables for location country and those for neighboring countries. Then we conduct the estimation using the market potential and supplier access variables. For locations of final goods production sites, all sign conditions were satisfied and the results were statistically significant at the 1% level for the final goods market potential in the locational country and neighboring countries combined and the final goods market potential in the locational country. However, all sign conditions were not satisfied for the final goods market potential in the neighboring countries. From these results of estimation, we found that the final goods domestic market potential in the locational country is very important determinants in the plant location level. These results are partly consistent with the hypothesis that, for global-type electrical/electronics companies, "locational product demand is strong" is an important factor in the location of final good production sites. This shows that the home market effect is a key factor in the location of a target company's final goods production sites.

For intermediate goods supplier access, the sign condition was satisfied in the case of supplier access for the home country and neighboring countries combined and for the neighboring countries, and results were statistically significant at the 1% level. However, the sign condition for domestic supplier access was not satisfied due to market crowding effect. For estimates using both the market potential variable and the Japanese industrial agglomeration variable, both variables satisfied the sign condition and were significant at the 1% level. This shows that strength of demand and strength of agglomeration exerted through horizontal and vertical agglomeration are key to the location of Japanese electrical/electronics companies' final goods production sites in a target country.

Next, we estimate this model for both period 1995–2000 and period 2001–2009. The estimation results are presented in Tables 7.3 and 7.4, respectively.

---

[9]Regarding this point, see Fujita and Thisse (2013, p. 335).

[10]Fujita and Thisse (2013, Chap. 8) used a simple NEG model to show that a region experiences coagglomeration of the intermediate goods sector and the final goods sector when the transportation costs for intermediate goods exceed the transportation costs for final goods in that region.

**Table 7.3** Results of Japanese Electrical/Electronics Companies (1995–2000) <final goods production site>

| | (1) | (2) | (3) | (4) | (5) | (6) | (7) |
|---|---|---|---|---|---|---|---|
| ln RWAGE | -0.5070*** | -0.5219*** | -0.5237*** | -0.6297*** | -0.7407*** | -0.4959*** | -0.9973*** |
| ln(rwage) | (-6) | (-5.27) | (-5.61) | (-7.74) | (-7.91) | (-5.54) | (-7.81) |
| INFRA | 0.0640 | 0.0485 | 0.0202 | 0.2186*** | 0.1902*** | 0.0972** | 0.2552*** |
| (highway/road) | (1.47) | (1.18) | (0.72) | (3.97) | (4.01) | (2.2) | (4.8) |
| Agglomeration | | 0.0029*** | | | | | |
| _intermediate | | (6.36) | | | | | |
| Agglomeration | | | 0.0245*** | | | | |
| _final | | | (5.32) | | | | |
| ln MPK | | | | 2.6040*** | | | 3.2736*** |
| _final | | | | (4.55) | | | (5.46) |
| ln DMPK | | | | | 1.2616*** | | |
| _final | | | | | (4.69) | | |
| ln FMPK | | | | | | -0.2526* | |
| _final | | | | | | (-1.76) | |
| ln SA | | | | | | | 0.4567** |
| _intermediate | | | | | | | (1.97) |
| ln DSA | | | | | | | |
| _intermediate | | | | | | | |
| ln FSA | | | | | | | |
| _intermediate | | | | | | | |
| Log likelihood | -342.56 | -325.71 | -321.24 | -322.99 | -321.32 | -342.35 | -273.93 |
| No. of Sample | 2970 | 2970 | 2970 | 2970 | 2970 | 2970 | 2268 |
| No. of Firms | 45 | 45 | 45 | 45 | 45 | 45 | 42 |

**Table 7.4** Results of Japanese Electrical/Electronics Companies (2001–2009) <final goods production site>

| | (8) | (9) | (10) | (11) | (12) | (13) | (14) |
|---|---|---|---|---|---|---|---|
| ln RWAGE | -0.4566*** | -1.0022*** | -0.6022*** | -0.6715*** | -0.9667*** | -0.3362** | -0.9606*** |
| ln(rwage) | (-2.97) | (-8.41) | (-5.1) | (-5.6) | (-7.72) | (-2.26) | (-8.25) |
| INFRA | 0.2513*** | 0.2491*** | 0.0966* | 0.1212* | 0.2588*** | 0.2257*** | 0.2518*** |
| (highway/road) | (4.75) | (4.64) | (1.67) | (1.95) | (4.99) | (4.45) | (4.92) |
| Agglomeration | | | 0.0024*** | | | | |
| _intermediate | | | (4.02) | | | | |
| Agglomeration | | | | 0.0167*** | | | |
| _final | | | | (2.77) | | | |
| ln MPK | 2.2245*** | 2.3491*** | 0.5036 | 1.2542** | | | |
| _final | (2.66) | (5.76) | (1.21) | (2.01) | | | |
| ln DMPK | | | | | 2.5694*** | 1.2191*** | 2.6255*** |
| _final | | | | | (5.81) | (3.1) | (6.32) |
| ln FMPK | | | | | | | |
| _final | | | | | | | |
| ln SA | | | | | 0.9261*** | | |
| _intermediate | | | | | (2.39) | | |
| ln DSA | -1.2605*** | | | | | -1.2645*** | |
| _intermediate | (-3.57) | | | | | (-3.42) | |
| ln FSA | | 0.5554*** | | | | | 0.9416*** |
| _intermediate | | (3.16) | | | | | (4.42) |
| Log likelihood | -269.04 | -270.61 | -224.96 | -229.14 | -270.81 | -270.90 | -263.77 |
| No. of Sample | 2268 | 2268 | 2970 | 2970 | 2268 | 2268 | 2268 |
| No. of Firms | 42 | 42 | 45 | 45 | 42 | 42 | 42 |

(continued)

From two tables, we found that for two periods, many variables were almost the same estimation results, but the sign conditions for domestic supplier access were different for two periods. The sign condition for domestic supplier access for period 1995–2000 was negative, but the sign condition for domestic supplier access for period 2001–2009 was positive as predicted, because the supplier access of intermediate goods increases over time in China for the period from 2001 through 2009 in Fig. 7.2.These results were statistically significant at the 1% level. In addition, the sign condition for neighboring countries supplier access for period 2001–2009 was positive as mentioned and these results were statistically significant at the 1% level.

**Table 7.4** (continued)

| | (15) | (16) | (17) | (18) | (19) | (20) | (21) |
|---|---|---|---|---|---|---|---|
| ln *RWAGE* | -0.6100 *** | -0.6492 *** | -0.5572 *** | -0.4236 *** | -0.4686 *** | -0.5117 *** | -0.5090 *** |
| ln(rwage) | (-5.79) | (-6.22) | (-4.6) | (-2.69) | (-2.85) | (-5.02) | (-5.21) |
| *INFRA* | 0.1071 ** | 0.1207 ** | 0.1022 ** | 0.1193 *** | 0.1152 *** | 0.0533 | 0.0354 |
| (highway/road) | (2.1) | (2.26) | (2.27) | (2.68) | (2.64) | (1.23) | (0.87) |
| *Agglomeration* | 0.0022 *** | | | | | 0.0029 *** | |
| _intermediate | (2.84) | | | | | (3.97) | |
| *Agglomeration* | | 0.0154 *** | | | | | 0.0241 *** |
| _final | | (2.7) | | | | | (4.94) |
| ln *MPK* | | | | | | | |
| _final | | | | | | | |
| ln *DMPK* | 0.6400 * | 0.5786 *** | | | | | |
| _final | (1.9) | (2.61) | | | | | |
| ln *FMPK* | | | -0.3199 | 0.7159 ** | -1.1170 *** | -0.0646 | -0.0960 |
| _final | | | (-0.8) | (2.44) | (-2.66) | (-0.34) | (-0.51) |
| ln *SA* | | | 0.3146 | | | | |
| _intermediate | | | (0.88) | | | | |
| ln *DSA* | | | | -2.0477 *** | | | |
| _intermediate | | | | (-5.72) | | | |
| ln *FSA* | | | | | 0.9179 *** | | |
| _intermediate | | | | | (2.22) | | |
| Log likelihood | -222.85 | -227.69 | -289.47 | -272.24 | -284.43 | -225.63 | -221.11 |
| No. of Sample | 2970 | 2970 | 2268 | 2268 | 2268 | 2970 | 2970 |
| No. of Firms | 45 | 45 | 42 | 42 | 42 | 45 | 45 |

| | (1) | (2) | (3) | (4) | (5) | (6) | (7) |
|---|---|---|---|---|---|---|---|
| ln *RWAGE* | -0.6557 *** | -0.4719 *** | -0.4555 *** | -0.9994 *** | -0.6002 *** | -0.2270 *** | -1.1026 *** |
| ln(rwage) | (-6.02) | (-5.26) | (-5.07) | (-12.56) | (-11.67) | (-2.06) | (-12.58) |
| *INFRA* | 0.0299 | 0.0216 | 0.0056 | 0.3117 *** | 0.2741 *** | 0.0655 | 0.2556 *** |
| (highway/road) | (0.72) | (0.48) | (0.12) | (6.22) | (5.75) | (1.44) | (4.85) |
| *Agglomeration* | | 0.0021 *** | | | | | |
| _intermediate | | (15.26) | | | | | |
| *Agglomeration* | | | 0.0224 *** | | | | |
| _final | | | (15.54) | | | | |
| ln *MPK* | | | | 4.2956 *** | | | 4.1255 *** |
| _final | | | | (13.21) | | | (13.62) |
| ln *DMPK* | | | | | 2.5589 *** | | |
| _final | | | | | (11.28) | | |
| ln *FMPK* | | | | | | -0.9272 *** | |
| _final | | | | | | (-6.09) | |
| ln *SA* | | | | | | | 0.8019 *** |
| _intermediate | | | | | | | (5.26) |
| ln *DSA* | | | | | | | |
| _intermediate | | | | | | | |
| ln *FSA* | | | | | | | |
| _intermediate | | | | | | | |
| Log likelihood | -622.81 | -570.42 | -561.02 | -583.72 | -594.47 | -660.01 | -567.69 |
| No. of Sample | 6415 | 6415 | 6415 | 6415 | 6415 | 6415 | 6230 |
| No. of Firms | 85 | 85 | 85 | 85 | 85 | 85 | 85 |

| | (8) | (9) | (10) | (11) | (12) | (13) | (14) |
|---|---|---|---|---|---|---|---|
| ln *RWAGE* | -1.1512 *** | -1.0596 *** | -0.6312 *** | -0.5626 *** | -1.0621 *** | -1.2579 *** | -1.0157 *** |
| ln(rwage) | (-10.25) | (-12.27) | (-6.16) | (-5.46) | (-12.27) | (-9.82) | (-11.7) |
| *INFRA* | 0.2164 *** | 0.2281 *** | 0.1346 ** | 0.0816 | 0.2311 *** | 0.3045 *** | 0.2128 *** |
| (highway/road) | (6.26) | (4.46) | (2.16) | (1.41) | (4.85) | (6.4) | (4.42) |
| *Agglomeration* | | | 0.0015 *** | | | | |
| _intermediate | | | (5.66) | | | | |
| *Agglomeration* | | | | 0.0176 *** | | | |
| _final | | | | (6.67) | | | |
| ln *MPK* | 4.6264 *** | 2.9752 *** | 1.5104 *** | 1.0602 * | | | |
| _final | (13.05) | (13.26) | (2.74) | (1.96) | | | |
| ln *DMPK* | | | | | 2.7971 *** | 2.4256 *** | 2.0655 *** |
| _final | | | | | (12.89) | (12.11) | (12.47) |
| ln *FMPK* | | | | | | | |
| _final | | | | | | | |
| ln *SA* | | | | | 1.3162 *** | | |
| _intermediate | | | | | (7.67) | | |
| ln *DSA* | 0.5522 ** | | | | | 1.5544 *** | |
| _intermediate | (2.12) | | | | | (4.62) | |
| ln *FSA* | | 0.7150 *** | | | | | 1.0715 *** |
| _intermediate | | (5.69) | | | | | (5.06) |
| Log likelihood | -550.72 | -564.16 | -596.52 | -539.07 | -555.24 | -561.67 | -551.80 |
| No. of Sample | 6230 | 6230 | 6415 | 6415 | 6230 | 6230 | 6230 |
| No. of Firms | 85 | 85 | 85 | 85 | 85 | 85 | 85 |

(continued)

**Table 7.4** (continued)

| | (15) | (16) | (17) | (18) | (19) | (20) | (21) |
|---|---|---|---|---|---|---|---|
| ln *RWAGE* | -0.5529 *** | -0.5407 *** | -0.2135 *** | -0.2167 *** | -0.2768 *** | -0.2246 *** | -0.2529 *** |
| ln(rwage) | (-6.7) | (-5.99) | (-3.62) | (-4.16) | (-2.24) | (-2.26) | (-2.69) |
| *INFRA* | 0.1160 ** | 0.0828 | 0.1676 *** | 0.0969 ** | 0.1664 *** | 0.0718 | 0.0444 |
| (highway road) | (2.22) | (1.61) | (4.07) | (2.19) | (3.6) | (1.56) | (0.96) |
| *Agglomeration* | 0.0015 *** | | | | | 0.0019 *** | |
| _intermediate | (7.27) | | | | | (12.42) | |
| *Agglomeration* | | 0.0177 *** | | | | | 0.0210 *** |
| _final | | (7.88) | | | | | (12.6) |
| ln *MPK* | | | | | | | |
| _final | | | | | | | |
| ln *DMPK* | 1.0116 *** | 0.7640 ** | | | | | |
| _final | (2.22) | (2.51) | | | | | |
| ln *FMPK* | | | -2.6760 *** | -1.4276 *** | -2.6614 *** | -0.5228 *** | -0.4021 ** |
| _final | | | (-12.12) | (-6.71) | (-11.98) | (-2.74) | (-2.05) |
| ln *SA* | | | 2.5510 *** | | | | |
| _intermediate | | | (11.95) | | | | |
| ln *DSA* | | | | 1.0779 *** | | | |
| _intermediate | | | | (3.45) | | | |
| ln *FSA* | | | | | 1.9627 *** | | |
| _intermediate | | | | | (12.36) | | |
| Log likelihood | -564.62 | -557.76 | -564.20 | -652.08 | -557.58 | -566.41 | -558.82 |
| No. of Sample | 6415 | 6415 | 6330 | 6330 | 6330 | 6415 | 6415 |
| No. of Firms | 65 | 65 | 65 | 65 | 65 | 65 | 65 |

(continued)

These mean that Japanese MNFs producing final goods locate in countries where the supply chain expands if supplier access of intermediate goods increases in those countries and their neighbors.

The foregoing results for the this industry show that along with the wage and infrastructure variables, which are traditional factors in location choice, the NEG model variables of market potential, domestic supplier access, and Japanese industrial agglomeration (not only Japanese horizontal agglomeration but Japanese vertical agglomeration as well) are key as well. The results confirm the following. Even in overseas locations of Japanese MNFs' final goods production sites in East Asia, the traditional variables of wages and infrastructure are important, as are also the demand factor of market potential and the supply factor of supplier access, especially vertical supplier access.

## 7.6 Conclusion

In this paper we conducted an empirical analysis using an NEG model to investigate the relationship between global supply chain and overseas location choice for target Japanese MNFs' final goods production sites from 1995 through 2009 in East Asia. In doing so, we focused on the major Japanese industry: the global-type Japanese electrical/electronics industry. The results of this analysis revealed the following three points.

First, the results showed the importance not only of the traditional location factors of the wage and infrastructure variables, but also of such variables based on the NEG model as market potential and domestic supplier access variables and Japanese industrial agglomeration variables, especially the Japanese horizontal and vertical industrial agglomeration variables.

Second, for final goods production site locations, the final goods market potential variable for the home country and neighboring countries combined satisfied the sign conditions and was statistically significant, verifying that the home market effect is a key factor. In the case of intermediate goods supplier access, only supplier access for domestic and neighboring countries combined was a key factor. Therefore, both the market potential variable and the Japanese industrial agglomeration variable met the sign condition and were statistically significant, showing that strength of demand and strength of agglomeration exerted through horizontal and vertical agglomeration are key to the location of Japanese electrical/electronics companies' final goods production sites in a target country.

Third, comparing the period 1995–2000 with the period 2001–2009, we found that the sign conditions for domestic supplier access were different for two periods. The sign condition for domestic supplier access for period 1995–2000 was negative, but the sign condition for domestic supplier access for period 2001–2009 was positive as predicted, because the supplier access of intermediate goods increases over time in East Asia for this period. These results were statistically significant at the 1% level. In addition, the sign condition for neighboring countries supplier access for period 2001–2009 was positive and these results were statistically significant at the 1% level. These mean that Japanese electronics firms producing final goods locate in countries where the supply chain expands if supplier access of intermediate goods increases in those countries and their neighbors.

## References

Ellison, G., and E. Glaeser. 1997. Geographic Concentration in U.S. Manufacturing Industries: A Dartboard Approach. *Journal of Political Economy* 105 (5): 898–927.

Fujita, Masahisa, and N. Hamaguchi. 2001. Intermediate goods and the spatial structure of an economy. *Regional Science and Urban Economics* 31: 79–109.

Fujita, Masahisa, and N. Hamaguchi. 2014. Supply Chain Internationalization in East Asia: Inclusiveness and risk, *RIETI Discussion Paper Series*, 14-E-066, pp. 1–23.

Fujita, Masahisa, and Thisse. 2013. *Economics of Agglomeration* (second edition), Cambridge University · D

Fujita, Masahisa, P. Krugman, and A.J. Venables. 1999. *The Spatial Economy : Cities, Regions, and International Trade*. Cambridge, MA: MIT Press.

Head, K., and T. Mayer. 2004. Market Potential and the Location of Japanese investment in the Europe union. *Review of Economics and Statistics* 86 (4): 959–972.

Ikegawa, M., and S. Tokunaga. 2018. Location Choice for Japanese Frozen Food Industry in East Asia using Domestic Market Access with the Penetration Rate of Refrigerators. *Annals of Regional Science* 60. https://doi.org/10.1007/s00168-018-0865-6.

Klein, A., and N. Crafts. 2012. Making sense of the manufacturing belt: determinants of U.S. industrial location, 1880–1920. *Journal of Economic Geography* 12: 775–807.

Krugman, P. 1991a. Increasing Returns and Economic Geography. *Journal of Political Economy* 99: 483–499.

Krugman, P. 1991b. *Geography and Trade*. Cambridge, USA: MIT Press.

Krugman, P., and A.J. Venables. 1995. Globalization and the Inequality of Nations. *Quarterly Journal of Economics* 110: 857–880.
Lu, J., and Suminori Tokunaga. 2008. Supplier access and the location choice of Japanese food industry FDI in East Asia. *Letter in Spatial and Resource Science* 2 (1): 1–10.
McFadden, D. 1974. Conditional logit analysis of qualitative choice behaviour. In *Frontiers in Econometrics*, ed. P. Zarembka, 105–142. New York: Academic Press.
Nakamura, R. 1985. Agglomeration economies in urban manufacturing industries, a case of Japanese cities. *Journal of Urban Economics* 17: 108–124.
Nakamura, R. 2008. Changes in Agglomeration economies and Linkage Externalities for Japanese Urban Manufacturing industries: 1990 and 2000, *RIETI Discussion Paper Series* 08-E-040, pp. 1-27.
Redding, Stephan. 2011. *Economic Geography: A Review of the Theoretical and Empirical Literature, edited Bernhofen, Falvey, Greenaway, and Kreickemeier*, 497–531. UK, PALGRAVE MACMILLAN: Palgrave Handbook of International Trade.
Redding, Stephan, and Anthony J. Venables. 2004. Economic geography and international inequality. *Journal of International Economics* 62: 53–82.
Todo, Y., P. Matous, and H. Inoue. 2015. The Strength of Long Ties and the Weakness of Strong Ties: Knowledge diffusion through supply chain networks, *RIETI Discussion Paper Series* 15-E-034, pp. 1–39.
Tokunaga, S., and R. Ishii. 2000. An Empirical Analysis of Agglomeration Effects and Locational Choice of Japanese Electronics Firms in East Asia, *Regional Cohesion and Competition in the Age of Globalization*, pp. 127–143.
Tokunaga, S., and S. Jin. 2011. Market potential, agglomeration and location of Japanese manufacturers in China. *Letter in Spatial and Resource Science* 4 (1): 9–19.
Tokunaga, S., M. Kageyama, and Y. Akune. 2006. An Empirical Analysis of Scale Economies and Agglomeration Effects in Japanese Manufacturing Industries. *Journal of Applied Regional Science* 11: 55–69.
Tokunaga, S., M. Kageyama, Y. Akune, and R. Nakamura. 2014. Empirical Analyses of Agglomeration Economies in Japanese Assembly-type Manufacturing Industry for 1985–2000: Using Agglomeration and Coagglomeration Indices. *Review of Urban & Regional Development Studies* 26 (1): 57–79.
Tokunaga, S., Y. Akune, M. Ikegawa, and M. Okiyama. 2015. Measures of the Agglomeration in Japanese Manufacturing Industries and location of Japanese manufacturers in East Asia, *RIETI Policy Discussion Paper Series*, 15-P-021, pp. 1–116 (in Japanese).
Tokunaga, S., Y. Akune, and M. Ikegawa. 2018. Complex Industrial Agglomeration. *Supplier Accesses and Location of Japanese FDI: Case of Japanese Electronics Firms in East Asia, Studies in Regional Science* 47 (2): 95–103.
Venables, A.J. 1996. Equilibrium locations of vertically linked industries. *International Economic Review* 37: 341–359.
Yamashita, N., T. Matsuura, and K. Nakajima. 2014. Agglomeration effects of inter-firm backward and forward linkages: Evidence from Japanese manufacturing investment in China. *Journal of the Japanese and International Economies* 34: 24–41.

# Chapter 8
# A Measure of the Spillover Effects Among Companies of Same Nationality in the Location Choice of FDIs

**S.-J. Hwang and X. Li**

## 8.1 Introduction

Foreign direct investments (FDIs) have grown rapidly with globalization. Despite the recent emergence of protectionism, this increase in FDIs will not reverse. Nonetheless, a recent article in *The Economist* predicts the decrease of FDIs.[1] Both the convergence of technologies according to globalization and the decrease of transportation costs due to technological advances are mentioned as the main causes. However, if there are strong incentives to attract FDIs, then this prediction will not be realized. It is important to find out strong attractions in investment destinations and measure their intensities. If these intensities are large enough, the increasing trend of FDIs can be retained but how can these intensities be identified and measured?

Ellison and Glaeser (1997) suggested, what they called the "dartboard approach" to explain the geographical concentration of US manufacturers. (From now on, the index based on this approach is called the EG index.) They proposed a methodology for scientifically measuring agglomerations among companies that are spatially concentrated through probabilistic processes, based on a choice theory. This approach suggests that these spatial agglomerations can be a powerful incentive for a company to decide its location. However, the suggested index cannot identify whether a new firm has chosen a location in light of its "natural advantage," or in a pursuit of "spillover effects" such as knowledge spillovers with preexisting firms. Ellison and Glaeser (1997) admit this identification problem and call it an "observational equivalence."

However, if the focus is on location choices of new FDIs, there is a way to identify the "spillover effect" and the "natural advantage effect" respectively. When a firm chooses its location, it will consider the profits it will make in the chosen location.

[1]The retreat of the global company, *The Economist*, Jan. 28th, 2017.

S.-J. Hwang (✉) · X. Li
Kyungpook National University, Daegu, South Korea
e-mail: sxh219@knu.ac.kr



M. Hosoe et al. (eds.), *Applied Analysis of Growth, Trade, and Public Policy*,
https://doi.org/10.1007/978-981-13-1876-4_8

These profits are called potential profits in alternative locations. The geographical distribution of preexisting firms can represent the geographical distribution of potential profits. A new FDI choosing its location in the host country will have two different geographic distributions of potential profits. One is the distribution of domestic firms, that is, the firms of the host country, while the other is that of preexisting FDIs with the same nationality in the host country. If these two reference groups are separable, there is a way to identify the types of agglomeration effects on location choice under certain assumptions.

In this research, a method to identify the type of agglomeration effect is suggested. The index obtained according to the proposed method is applied to measure the agglomeration effects on location choices of new Japanese FDIs in Korea. The proposed measure in this research could be used to assess the quality of FDI for local development, as well as to devise policies to attract foreign companies in a given region.

Section 8.2 provides a short literature review. Section 8.3 explains how to identify the agglomeration effects and Sect. 8.4 shows the empirical application of the proposed method. Section 8.5 provides the conclusion.

## 8.2 A Short Literature Review

Efforts have been made to measure the agglomeration effect and explain the relationship between agglomeration and firm location choices. Kominers (2008) well explains the literature on coherent methods of measuring agglomeration. He introduces two ways to measure agglomeration, one based on a discrete spatial distance model and the other based on a continuous spatial distance model. The big difference between them is as follows: in a discrete spatial distance model, equidistance among companies that are included in the same administrative district is assumed. However, in a continuous spatial distance model, physical distance information becomes important and cannot be ignored simply by assuming equidistance among companies. Therefore, because continuous spatial distance models require more micro-data than discrete ones, it is difficult to measure the agglomeration effect based on continuous models in situations where the data are not practically sufficient. If the data are not sufficient, the EG index is an excellent index in theoretical and empirical practice, since it does not require as great a data burden as those indices based not only on discrete spatial distance models, but also derived from a location choice theory in economics.

Even though the EG index is excellent one, it has been proved by its originators that it cannot identify the type of agglomeration effect, given their dataset. In their subsequent studies, Ellison and Glaeser (1999) well explain the importance of natural advantage effects on the location choice of a company. However, they still cannot show how to identify the effects of spillovers on companies' location decisions. Ellison et al. (2010) measure spillover effects with another index suggested by Duranton and Overman (2005), and further indices have been proposed to identify spillover effects. One of these is a coagglomeration index suggested by Howard et al. (2016). Kopczewska (2016) suggests an improved index based on that of Howard et al. (2016). However, these indices are not entirely based on location choice theory in economics. In this respect, of the available methods to identify spillover effects, the EG index has theoretical underpinning that allow it to capture explicitly agglomeration effects.

Many studies have focused on domestic companies' location choices for domestic regions using the indices described above. In some respects, it would be somewhat easier to measure and identify the agglomeration effect through the process of FDI location choice for the region of its destination. Alfaro and Chen (2016) use the index suggested by Duranton and Overman (2005) to estimate spillover effects in their study of multinational companies' destination country choice. Duranton and Overman (2005) suggest a kernel estimation to estimate a spillover index, of which a key point is the grouping of data based on the physical distances between companies. Since Alfaro and Chen (2016) investigated the destination country choice, their distance measurement is based on the distances between countries. However, although it can capture spillover effects in macro terms, it is not adequate to investigate micro-based spillovers.

In this research, a way to identify the spillover effect is suggested, that differs from those proposed in the existing literature. The key to this approach is the fact that when a new FDI chooses a location, multiple reference groups can be used to infer profitability in alternative regions. If the location choice process of domestic companies for domestic regions is used as control information, then the spillover effects among companies with the same nationality can be identified relative to those among domestic companies. The same method is also used to identify the natural advantages of the alternative. This approach is explained in the next section.

## 8.3 A Relative Identification of Agglomeration Effects

The basic model setup of Ellison and Glaeser (1997) is as follows: first, an industry is composed of N individual companies and the individual company chooses a location among M regions in a nation. When these individual companies choose their locations, they choose the respective location that can provide the highest profits. When the $k$th company chooses its location, the chosen location is indexed as $r_k$ and if it is in region $i$, then $r_k = i$. The profit function is then defined as (8.1)

$$\log \pi_{ki} = \log \bar{\pi}_i + g_i\left(r_1, \ldots, r_{k-1}\right) + \xi_{ki}, \tag{8.1}$$

Here, $\bar{\pi}_i$ represents average potential profits when a typical firm $k$ chooses its location in $i$, while $g_i$ is a function of the externality caused by companies 1 to $k-1$ that have already decided their location in $i$. $\xi_{ki}$ represents the error term of $k$ at $i$. Natural advantage is reflected on $\bar{\pi}_i$. If $\xi_{ki}$ is assumed to have a Weibull distribution and there is no externality, then the probability of company $k$ locating in $i$ has a standard logit form and can be expressed as (8.2):

$$prob\{r_k = i|\bar{\pi}_1\ ,\ \ldots, \bar{\pi}_M\} = \frac{\bar{\pi}_i}{\sum_j \bar{\pi}_j} \tag{8.2}$$

According to Ellison and Glaeser (1997), the distribution of $\bar{\pi}_i$ } can be chosen such that it satisfies two parametric restrictions of conditional mean and variance, given as (8.3) and (8.4):

$$E_{\bar{\pi}_1.,.\bar{\pi}_M} \frac{\bar{\pi}_i}{\sum_j \bar{\pi}_j} = x_i \tag{8.3}$$

$$var\left(\frac{\bar{\pi}_i}{\sum_j \bar{\pi}_j}\right) = \gamma^{na} x_i(1 - x_i) \tag{8.4}$$

Here, $x_i$ is the share of employment in region $i$ out of total employment. $\gamma^{na} \in [0, 1]$ is the correlation between the natural advantage and the profitability of a typical firm locating there. Then the standardized distribution of $\bar{\pi}_i$ } is as follows:

$$2\left(\frac{1-\gamma^{na}}{\gamma^{na}}\right)\bar{\pi}_i \sim \chi^2\left(2\left(\frac{1-\gamma^{na}}{\gamma^{na}}\right)\bar{\pi}_i\, df.\right),\quad E\left(\bar{\pi}_i\right) = x_i \quad,\quad var\left(\bar{\pi}_i\right) = \left(\frac{1-\gamma^{na}}{\gamma^{na}}\right)x_i$$

Ellison and Glaeser (1997) assume an "all or nothing" pattern of spillover effects. That is, as long as companies are located in a common region, the degree of spillover effects is infinite. This means that if the locations are different, there are no spillover effects at all. They assume further that the spillover effect can be measured as $\gamma^s \in [0, 1]$ and is defined as follows:

$$\log \pi_{ki} = \log \bar{\pi}_i + \sum\nolimits_{l \neq k} e_{kl}(1 - u_{li})(- \bowtie) + \xi_{ki} \tag{8.5}$$

Here, $\{e_{kl}\}$ is the random variable of a Bernoulli distribution with probability $\gamma^s$, while $u_{il}$ is the index function when a company $l$ chooses its location in $i$; then $u_{il} = 1$. Otherwise, $u_{il} = 0$. This random variable satisfies symmetricity and transitivity.

With the above setup, Ellison and Glaeser (1997) show that when a measure of geographical concentration of industry is defined as follows:

$$G \equiv \sum\nolimits_i (s_i - x_i)^2 \tag{8.6}$$

Here, $\mathrm{s_i} = \sum_k z_k u_{ki}$: $z_k$ means the share of $k$th company workers among total workers of the industry that includes the $k$th company.

they can derive properties such as (14.7):

$$E\,(G) = \left(1 - \sum_i x_i^2\right)[\gamma + (1-\gamma)\,H] \tag{8.7}$$

Here, $=E\,(^{\mathrm{na}} + \gamma^s - \gamma^{na}\gamma^s)$, and $H = \sum_k z_k^2$ is the Herfindahl index.

Ellison and Glaeser (1997) derive equation (8.6) from the profit-maximizing behavior of a company in choosing the region that gives the most profit out of the alternatives. They further prove that the calculated  is the unbiased estimator of $^{\mathrm{na}} + \gamma^s - \gamma^{na}\gamma^s$.[2] Property (8.7) shows that the agglomeration can be decomposed into two correlations: one is a correlation between potential profits and the natural advantage of a region, while the other is between potential profits and the spillover effects among firms that locate in the same place. However, they argue that while  can be estimated from the data, neither $\gamma^{na}$ nor $\gamma^s$ can be discerned with their dataset. They call this "observational equivalence."

This equivalence is true of their dataset. However, if the focus is on the FDI's location choice, then their observational equivalence can be avoided. When a company chooses its location, it refers the geographical distribution of companies as a probability distribution of potential profits in alternative regions. When the company is a new FDI, because it is foreign investment, its information on the potential profitability of alternatives can depend on the nationality of pre-existing companies. That is, a new FDI in a particular country can have two sources for the information on the potential profitability of alternatives when choosing a location: one is a spatial distribution of domestic (or host country) companies and the other is the spatial distribution of companies of the same nationality that already exist in the host country. In this context, two different values of the EG index can be estimated, based on the two different probability distributions of the potential profitability for alternatives derived from the two different reference groups. Then, with certain assumptions, both correlations of natural advantage and spillover effects can be identified respectively from the location choices of FDIs.

One of the important assumptions required to identify the types of agglomeration effects is that the natural advantage effects and the spillover effects are independent of each other. While natural advantage is caused by the given environment conditions, spillover effects arise from interactions among people. The independence of the two effects can therefore be assumed. Further, if we assume that $E\,(\gamma^{na}) = \gamma^{na}$ and $E\,(\gamma^s) = \gamma^s$, then these assumptions can help to discern between the two effects respectively.[3] Therefore, as long as the companies are in the same industry and the two agglomeration effects are independent, Eq. (8.8) can be derived as follows:

$$E\left(\gamma^{na} + \gamma^s - \gamma^{na}\gamma^s\right) = E\left(\gamma^{na}\right) + E\left(\gamma^s\right) - E\left(\gamma^{na}\right)E\left(\gamma^s\right) = \gamma^{na} + \gamma^s - \gamma^{na}\gamma^s \tag{8.8}$$

[2]Ellison and Glaeser (1997) show this in the Proposition 1E of their paper, pp. 895–896.

[3]Actually, the effect of natural advantage can be common to individual companies that are in the same industry. Moreover, because we set up "all or nothing" spillover effects, spillover effects also have the same shared properties as the common effect of natural advantages among individual companies in the same industry.

We then need two more technical assumptions about the behavior of companies with different nationalities. These assumptions are explained below.

**Assumption 8.1** $\gamma_d^{na} = \gamma_{jd}^{na}$: When referring to the geographical distribution of domestic firms in terms of potential profitability, there is no difference in assessing the degree of correlation of natural advantage between when a new FDI chooses its location and when a new domestic company does in the host country.

This Assumption 8.1 is based on a situation as follows: domestic companies in the host country are familiar with the natural environment in the country, such that production technology and operational skills are developed in accordance with its environmental conditions in the host country. From the standpoint of new FDIs, it will be cost-saving for them to follow the location choice of domestic companies, because they do not have detailed information on these environmental conditions of the host country. On the other hand, preexisting FDIs can maintain those technologies that suit the environmental conditions of their home country. New FDIs may need to share information with preexisting FDIs. Then $\gamma_j^{na}$ can be different from $\gamma_{jd}^{na}$ and $\gamma_d^{na}$, furthermore, the Assumption 8.1 becomes plausible.

**Assumption 8.2** $\gamma_{jd}^{s} = \gamma_j^{s}$: Regardless of whether a new FDI in determining its location refers to the geographical distribution of FDIs or domestic firms, there is no difference in assessing the correlation of spillover effects with FDIs or domestic firms.

The spillover effect on the location choice is in contrast with the effect of natural advantage. The correlation of spillover effect is relatively more influenced by the interactions between people. Barriers due to differences in culture and language can exist between countries. As a result, the correlation of spillover effects with FDI agglomeration when a new FDI choose its location may differ from the correlation with domestic agglomeration when a new domestic company chooses its location. However, if the interaction between FDI and host country companies is active, then the barrier of culture and language can be overcome. If the FDI has more efficient technology, the correlation of spillover effect with domestic agglomeration could be same as that with FDI agglomeration when a new FDI chooses its location.[4] In line with that, Assumption 8.2 could be feasible.

Let us now consider the location choice of new country $j$ FDIs. Let us suppose that a new FDI from country $j$ can regard the geographical distribution of preexisting country $j$ companies in the host country as a probability distribution of potential profits in alternative regions. From the distribution of country $j$ FDIs in the host country, the following measurement (8.9) is re-written in the same way as the derivation of (8.6) and (8.7).

$$E\left(G^j\right) = \left(1 - \sum_i x_i^{j2}\right)\left[\gamma^j + \left(1 - \gamma^j\right) H^j\right] \tag{8.9}$$

[4]We assume that relatively more efficient companies can invest in a foreign country because their efficiency allows for them to overcome barriers from the different language and culture. Refer to Helpman et al. (2004).

As in (8.8), $\gamma^j = \gamma_j^{na} + \gamma_j^s - \gamma_j^{na}\gamma_j^s$, where $_j$ is the correlation of total agglomeration effects caused by country $j$ firms with the potential profitability of a specific location where FDIs of the same origin gather together. This correlation can be decomposed into $\gamma_j^{na}$, $^s_j$, and the cross effect of these two correlations. $\gamma_j^{na}$ is the correlation of natural advantages with the potential profitability of a specific location where FDIs of the same origin gather together. This implies that when FDIs of the same origin locate there, the potential profit in the location is the greatest available to them in view of natural environments or amenities. From now on, we call this "the correlation of natural advantage with FDI agglomeration."[5] $\gamma_j^s$ is the correlation of spillover effects among FDIs of the same nationality with the potential profitability of the location where they gather together. From now on, in a similar fashion, that is called "the correlation of spillover effects with FDI agglomeration." Then $^j$ is derived as follows and let us define this as $k_1$.

$$\gamma^j = \frac{1}{(1-H^j)}\left[\frac{E(G^j)}{1-\sum_i x_i^{j2}} - H^j\right] = \gamma^{na} + \gamma^s - \gamma^{na}\gamma^s = k_1 \tag{8.10}$$

Next, let us suppose that a new FDI from country $j$ can regard the geographical distribution of domestic companies in the host country as a probability distribution of potential profits in alternative regions. While the derivation of the correlation of total agglomeration effects is same as that of (8.9), the degree and interpretations of the index are different. The following Eq. (8.11) is the result of derivation, defined as $k_2$, and the index is rewritten with sub- and superscripts $jd$, where $d$ means that the reference group is domestic country firms.

$$\gamma^{jd} = \frac{1}{(1-H^d)}\left[\frac{E(G^{jd})}{1-\sum_i x_i^{d2}} - H^d\right] = \gamma_{jd}^{na} + \gamma_{jd}^s - \gamma_{jd}^{na}\gamma_{jd}^s = k_2 \tag{8.11}$$

where, $E\left(G^{jd}\right) = \left(1-\sum_i x_i^{d2}\right)\left[\gamma^{jd} + \left(1-\gamma^{jd}\right)H^d\right]$.

As before, $\gamma_{jd}^{na}$ is the correlation of natural advantages with the potential profitability of a specific location where domestic firms gather together, when new FDI from country $j$ chooses its location. From now on, this is called "the correlation of natural advantage with domestic agglomeration." $\gamma_{jd}^s$ is the correlation of spillover effects among domestic firms with the potential profitability of the location where they gather together under the same condition. In similar fashion, this is called "the correlation of spillover effects with domestic agglomeration."

Lastly, the location choice of new domestic firms is considered in order to identify the types of agglomeration effects. The same approach can be applied, but the decision makers are not new FDIs, but new domestic companies in the host country. Then Eq. (8.12) is derived as follows:

[5]From now on, FDI means FDI with the same nationality. If it has a different meaning, then it will be mentioned.

$$\gamma^d = \frac{1}{(1-H^d)}\left[\frac{E(G^d)}{1-\sum_i x_i^{d2}} - H^d\right] = \gamma_d^{na} + \gamma_d^s - \gamma_d^{na}\gamma_d^s = k_3 \tag{8.12}$$

where, $E\left(G^d\right) = \left(1-\sum_i x_i^{d2}\right)\left[\gamma^d + \left(1-\gamma^d\right)H^d\right]$

The interpretations of the agglomeration effects are then the same, but the situation is different when a new domestic company chooses its location. The indices are summarized as follows;

(1) $\gamma^j$: the correlation of agglomeration effect with FDI agglomeration when a new FDI chooses its location.

(2) $\gamma^{jd}$: the correlation of agglomeration effect with domestic agglomeration when a new FDI chooses its location.

(3) $\gamma^d$: the correlation of agglomeration effect with domestic agglomeration when a new domestic company chooses its location.

Even though the above two assumptions are somewhat strong, they are very helpful in identifying the types of agglomeration effects. With these two assumptions and Eqs. (8.10)–(8.12), the simultaneous equation system can be setup and solved. Then, two solutions (8.13) and (8.14) are obtained as follows:

$$\frac{\left(1-\gamma_j^s\right)}{\left(1-\gamma_d^s\right)} = \frac{k_2-1}{k_3-1} \tag{8.13}$$

$$\frac{\left(1-\gamma_j^{na}\right)}{\left(1-\gamma_d^{na}\right)} = \frac{k_1-1}{k_2-1} \tag{8.14}$$

Equation (8.13) shows the relative degree of the correlation of spillover effects with FDI agglomeration when a new FDI chooses its location relative to that of domestic agglomeration, when a new domestic company chooses its location. To be precise, it measures relatively how far the correlation of spillover effects with FDI agglomeration is from perfect correlation. When the value of (8.13) is larger than 1, that is $\left(1-\gamma_j^s\right) > \left(1-\gamma_d^s\right)$, the spillover effect of FDI agglomeration when a new FDI chooses its location is less than that of domestic agglomeration when a new domestic company chooses its location. When we remember the inference of Assumption 8.2, that is $\gamma_{jd}^s = \gamma_j^s$, it can be inferred that the interaction between new FDI and domestic agglomeration can be less powerful in the process of a new FDI location choice, compared with the interactions of domestic companies when a new domestic firm chooses its location. The lager this value, the weaker is the correlation of spillover effects with FDI agglomeration. However, if it is less than 1, the correlation is reversed; that is, in this case, the correlation of spillover effects with FDI or domestic agglomeration when a new FDI chooses its location is relatively stronger than that when a new domestic firm chooses its location. The smaller the value is, the stronger is the correlation of spillover effects with FDI or domestic agglomeration. Then, the industry can be classified depending on the degree of (8.13). If the value of (8.13) for a specific industry is relatively small, then the location choice pattern of the industry can be classified as "strong spillover chaser." However, it is not, then their location choice patterns can be classified as "weak spillover chaser."

Similarly, Eq. (8.14) shows the relative degree of the correlation of natural advantages with FDI agglomeration when a new FDI chooses its location relative to that with domestic agglomeration when a new domestic company chooses its location. However, here, <assumption 1> affects the value in the numerator, that is, $\gamma_d^{na} = \gamma_{jd}^{na}$. Therefore, if the value of (8.14) is greater than 1, it can be inferred that, when a new FDI chooses its location, the correlation of natural advantage with FDI agglomeration is relatively weaker than the correlation with domestic agglomeration. It thus explains that the location choices of new FDIs tend more to follow the location choices of domestic firms. Let us call this the "keeping up with the Joneses" style of location choice. The larger the value, the stronger is the tendency of "keeping up with the Joneses." If the value of (8.14) is less than 1, the direction of choice behavior is opposite. There is one point to note: the interpretation of the natural advantage is not limited to the state of the natural environment; rather, it captures the region's overall amenities in wide terms. This is well discussed in Ellison and Glaeser (1999). It is therefore preferable that the index be interpreted as representing regional amenities including business environments.

## 8.4 Empirical Analysis

The proposed logic is applied to identify the correlation of natural advantage and spillover effects of location choices of new Japanese FDIs in the manufacturing sector of South Korea. Information on FDI is collected from the homepage of the Ministry of Trade, Industry and Energy in Korea. Data were collected in August 2015. These data include starting of business, industrial classification based on the Korean Standard Industry Classification system (KSIC), address of the location, and source country of investment. However, it does not provide information such as employment, financial status, and other important company information, and these details are difficult to collect. Information on Korean companies is collected by the Microdata Integrated Service (MDIS) of Statistics Korea. Those two databases are based on the 9th amendment of the KSIC in 2007. The basic classification unit is four digits. In the case of regional classification, 15 regional local governments are used; they are Seoul, Busan, Daegu, Incheon, Gwangju, Daejeon, Ulsan, Gyeonggido, Gangwondo, Chungchungbukdo, Chungchungnamdo, Jeonlabukdo, Jeonlanamdo, Gyeongsangbukdo, and Gyeongsangnamdo. However, Jeju island is excluded.

First, Japanese FDIs are focused on, because of data limitations. Unfortunately, it is impossible to build continuous data for Korean companies, due to the lack of manufacturing data in 2010. In addition, the 9th KSIC amendment was applied from the 2007 data onward. Therefore, the scope of the data is restricted to 2008, 2009, 2012, 2013 and 2014 only. Since lag data are required in the estimation processes, the indices for 2007 and 2011 are not estimated.

The problem of indices should be discussed before the calculation because of the lack of data. First, it is difficult to know the size of employment of an FDI when it starts its business in Korea. Each individual company is therefore assumed to have the same weight. However, as Ellison and Glaeser (1997) point out, this will bias the calculated indices.[6] If sufficient data can be collected, this index should be calculated taking into account the employment scale information of FDI. The FDI stock in Korea cannot be measured without that information. However, knowing when FDIs have entered Korea since 1967, the FDI stock can be estimated according to the following suggestion. Buckley et al. (2013) estimate the lifespan of Japan's FDIs in the United Kingdom at 13.9 years in their study. Considering this, it is reasonable to construct FDI stock by accumulating new FDIs since 2000, when the currency crisis of Korea from 1997 was officially overcome. Lastly bias can come from the broad definition of geographical unit and the break in time series data generated in 2010. However, these are inevitable problems due to the lack of data. Next, the estimated results are provided.

### 8.4.1 EG Index in the Overall Industry

(1) Japanese companies versus Japanese companies: the calculation of $k_1$
In this section, the calculation value of the EG index is introduced when new Japanese FDI in the manufacturing sector considers the geographical distribution of preexisting Japanese FDIs in Korea as a probability distribution of potential profitability to alternative regions. EG indices can be calculated for each industry and for each year, but a weighted average for the EG index for all industries is provided in this section. The weight of each industry is the ratio of all new Japanese FDIs in a specific industry to the total number of new Japanese FDIs that occurred in the same year. The scope of industry examined here includes only those industries where new Japanese FDIs occurred in a specific year. Industries without preexisting Japanese FDIs before a new Japanese FDI takes place in a certain year are excluded from the weighted average calculation of the year, because they have no agglomeration effects among companies of the same origin. The following Table 8.1 shows the weighted average calculation results of the EG index. The component of this EG index, that is $k_1$, is shown in (12.10).

For example, in Table 8.1, there are 19 industries (4 digit KSIC) and 27 new Japanese FDIs in 2008. The weighted average of EG index by each industry is −0.057. Since the value is based on (8.10), the sign of the estimated weighted average means

[6]However, it is not expected that the bias will be large. First, the indices of this study are relative, not absolute measures. The same bias applies to the calculation of indices for FDI and domestic companies simultaneously. We hope that such biases will be offset by each other. Second, Howard et al. (2016) argue that the knowledge spillover is not always relevant to the size of the company, especially in developing countries. As an exception, small companies can have more impact on the knowledge spillover in those countries. Although the same weight assumption cannot be justified sufficiently by this assertion, we can expect that the bias may not be so strong.

**Table 8.1** The weighted average of EG index ($k_1$): new Japanese FDI versus Japanese FDI stock

| Year | 2008 | 2009 | 2010 | 2011 | 2012 | 2013 | 2014 | 2015 |
|---|---|---|---|---|---|---|---|---|
| The number of industry | 19 | 25 | 19 | 33 | 42 | 37 | 29 | 25 |
| The number of new FDI | 27 | 29 | 31 | 52 | 72 | 55 | 36 | 31 |
| Weighted average | −0.057 | −0.050 | −0.044 | −0.033 | −0.021 | 0.012 | −0.033 | −0.039 |

Note: (1) Only industries with pre-existing Japanese FDI before a new FDI occurs are included. The number of new FDIs is the number of new companies in those industries

**Table 8.2** The weighted average of EG index ($k_2$): new Japanese FDI versus host country firms

| Year | 2008 | 2009 | 2012 | 2013 | 2014 |
|---|---|---|---|---|---|
| The number of industries | 23 | 31 | 49 | 41 | 30 |
| The number of new FDIs | 31 | 35 | 79 | 59 | 37 |
| Weighted average | 0.203 | 0.202 | 0.201 | 0.210 | 0.199 |

that $E(\gamma_j^{na}) + E(\gamma_j^s) < E(\gamma_j^{na})E(\gamma_j^s)$. In other words, in 2008, the expected value of the cross effect of the spillover effect and the natural advantage is larger than the expected value of the effect of each individual one to a new Japanese FDI, when it chooses its location through considering the spatial distribution of pre-existing Japanese FDI stock in Korea. This tendency decreases over time, except for 2014 and 2015. In particular, the tendency is significantly weakened in 2012 and 2013. This phenomenon is presumably due to the 2011 Great East Japan Earthquake.[7] Therefore, the overall correlation of FDI agglomeration with potential profits when new Japanese FDIs choose their location is negative. These results are similar to the previous research on the location choice of Japanese FDIs. Hwang (2014) and Lee and Hwang (2016) cannot find statistically significant effects of Japanese FDI agglomeration on the location choices of new Japanese FDIs in Korea. These small negative correlations support their results in overall.

(2) Japanese companies versus host country companies: $k_2$

In this section, the EG index is calculated when the new Japanese FDI takes into account the geographical distribution of the host companies as a probability distribution of the potential profitability of alternative regions. Since the data for Korean companies are limited, the EG indices for 2008, 2009, 2012, 2013, and 2014 can be calculated. As before, only those industries where new Japanese FDI has occurred are considered. However, as long as a domestic company exists in an industry, the industry can be included in the calculation, even if there is only one company in the industry. Therefore, the number of industries in Table 8.2 is somewhat different from that in Table 8.1. However, the same weights used before are applied.

The distinct difference between Tables 8.1 and 8.2 is the sign of the weighted average EG index. In Table 8.2, the respective effects of the natural advantage and the spillover effect are dominant over cross effects. Thus it can be inferred that there exist

[7]The effects of the Great East Japan Earthquake on the location choice of new Japanese FDI in Korea are discussed in detail in Hwang and Li (*forthcoming*).

**Table 8.3** The weighted average of EG index ($k_3$): new domestic firm versus domestic firms

| Year | 2008 | 2009 | 2012 | 2013 | 2014 |
|---|---|---|---|---|---|
| The number of industries | 21 | 30 | 48 | 41 | 29 |
| The number of new FDIs | 496 | 522 | 1257 | 1402 | 897 |
| Weighted average | 0.195 | 0.195 | 0.181 | 0.189 | 0.185 |

a positive correlation of domestic agglomeration with the potential profits in a region when a new Japanese FDI chooses its location. However, the degree of correlation is stable over the periods studied, except 2013. This relatively large correlation with domestic agglomeration also supports the empirical findings of Hwang (2014) and Lee and Hwang (2016); they estimate the statistically significant positive effect of domestic firm agglomeration on the location choice of new Japanese FDIs.

(3) domestic companies versus domestic companies: $k_3$

Lastly, the EG index for the domestic case is calculated, when the new domestic company takes into account the spatial distribution of domestic companies as a probability distribution of the potential profitability of alternative regions. In this case, industries that do not have a new company in a certain year are excluded even if a new Japanese FDI occurs. The weight of each industry is the ratio of all new domestic companies in a specific industry to the total number of new companies that occurred in the same year. Thus, only those industries in which both a new domestic company and new Japanese FDI occurred are included in the calculation. The sign of the EG index is positive. The degree of the index is less than that in Table 8.2, while the degree of correlation in Table 8.3 is also stable. The aggregate calculation shows that the overall correlation of agglomeration with domestic agglomeration is positive for both new Japanese FDI and domestic firms' location choices. However, when the type of agglomeration is identified at each industry level, interesting results can be found.

### *8.4.2 The Correlation of Spillover and Natural Advantage at Individual Industry Level*

In the previous section, $k_1$, $k_2$, and $k_3$ are calculated. By using these values, both the relative correlation of spillover effects and the relative correlation of natural advantage can be identified by (12.13) and (12.14), assuming the independency of two agglomeration effects, Assumptions 8.1 and 8.2. The results are reported in Table 8.4. In this table, the measure of each effect is the arithmetic mean, and its value and variance are given together annually and for two time periods such as 2008–2009 and 2012–2014. 2008–2009 represents the time before the Great East Japan Earthquake and 2012–2014 is after the earthquake. The year of occurrence of the earthquake is 2011, but the Korean data for that year cannot be used because of

**Table 8.4** The relative correlations of both the spillover and the natural advantage with new Japanese FDI location choice; arithmetic mean

| | 2008 | 2009 | 2012 | 2013 | 2014 |
|---|---|---|---|---|---|
| Spillover | 0.988 (0.008) | 0.990 (0.009) | 0.977 (0.012) | 0.979 (0.015) | 0.981 (0.009) |
| Period mean | 0.990 (0.008) | | 0.980 (0.013) | | |
| Natural advan. | 1.398 (0.201) | 1.317 (0.207) | 1.341 (0.211) | 1.280 (0.141) | 1.296 (0.1836) |
| Period mean. | 1.379 (0.211) | | 1.348 (0.191) | | |
| Total number of industries | 17 | 24 | 41 | 37 | 28 |

Note: The standard deviation is in parentheses

the data problem explained before. The industries of interest are those in which there is new Japanese FDI, a new domestic company, and preexisting Japanese FDI stock before the choice of a new Japanese FDI.

Generally, the correlation of spillover effects with FDI agglomeration is close to 1 and that of natural advantage effects is more than 1. This means that the effects of FDI agglomeration on the location choice of new Japanese FDI are relatively weaker than those of domestic agglomeration. Thus, when new Japanese FDIs choose their location, the location pattern of the "keeping up with the Joneses" is dominant. However, it is found that the interactions with domestic firms can also work in the location choice process. After the Great East Japanese Earthquake, the location choice pattern pursuing to the spillover effects is relatively stronger and is shown in more industries. However, the pattern of the "keeping up with the Joneses" dynamic is weaker and occurred in fewer industry areas. This shows that an unexpected shock in the home country may change the motivation and strategies of FDI.[8]

Let us look at this in more detail within industries, for example KSIC-four-digit level. In each year, industries are ranked by the degree of their correlation with each type of agglomeration effect. The highest ranked (for example, ranked 1–4) and the lowest ranked industries are checked. Furthermore, the frequency that is, how many times an industry appears among the highest ranking or the lowest ranking of the correlations by each type of agglomeration effect during the sample periods is checked. Based on this, the following industries are sorted as follows in Table 8.5.

The industries in group (I) Table 8.5 are those that show relatively weak correlation of spillover effects with domestic agglomeration. In the case of group (II), the new Japanese FDIs in those industries show a relatively strong pattern of "keeping up with the Joneses." Thus, the new Japanese FDIs in the "manufacture of basic inorganic chemistry" industry chase the spillover effects less, but consume more regional natural advantages through following the location pattern of domestic companies. However, the new Japanese FDIs in the "manufacture of electronic integrated circuits" industry are looking more for spillover effects and natural advantage effects

[8]Refer to Hwang and Li (*forthcoming*).

**Table 8.5** The industries sorted by types of agglomeration effect[1]

| | Spillover effects | Natural advantage effects |
|---|---|---|
| High Correlation<br>(>0.985: s.e.)[2]<br>(>1.363: n.a.)[3] | Medicinal chem. **(I)**<br>Inorganic chem.<br>Nonmetal n.e.c.<br>Rolling steel.<br>(less spillover chaser group) | Irradiation appara. **(II)**<br>Elec. integ. circuits.<br>Sports goods<br>Inorganic chem.<br>(strong keeping up with the Joneses) |
| Low Correlation<br>(<0.985: s.e.)<br>(<1.363: n.a.) | Other elec. comp. **(III)**<br>Other elec. equip.<br>Diodes et al.<br>Elec. integ. circuits.<br>(more spillover chaser group) | Other elec. comp. **(IV)**<br>Other elec. equip.<br>Diodes et al.<br>Semiconductor mach.<br>(weak keeping up with the Joneses) |

Note: (1) The full name of industries are provided in the <Appendix>
(2) The average correlation of spillover effects. "s.e." means spillover effects
(3) The average correlation of natural advantage effects. "n.a." means natural advantage

with domestic agglomeration, because it is classified in the group (III) for spillover effects and group (II) for natural advantage effects. Two industries, that is, "basic inorganic chemistry" and "electronic integrated circuits," have a common pattern in that they want to share the regional production resources with domestic companies. However, they are different in that while the one is looking relatively more for cooperation with the companies located in the same region regardless of nationality, the other is looking relatively less for cooperation with companies located in the same region. The new Japanese FDIs in three industries such as "other electronic components except semiconductor and electronic integrated circuits," "other electrical equipment" and "diodes, transistors, and similar semiconductor devices" are looking for the spillover effects, but want to avoid competition with domestic companies in acquiring regional production resources relative to other industries. They are therefore shown in group (III) and (IV) at the same time. Lastly, new Japanese FDIs in such industries as "medicinal chemicals, antibiotics and biological products," "other non-metallic mineral products n.e.c." and "steel products by rolling, extrusion and drawing" are relatively less interested in cooperating with companies located in the region compared with the new domestic firms' location choice patterns.

As this estimate shows, there are heterogeneous types in location decisions. However, in general, one common thing can be found. Recalling that one of Korea's major exports is semiconductors, it can be inferred that it is reasonable for FDIs to pursue spillover effects in domestic or preexisting semiconductor and electronic component industries. However, what is of interest is that the resources in the host country in which new FDIs are looking to locate can be different depending on the industrial technology level. However, new Japanese FDIs in some Korean industries that are exceptional, but not outstanding from a global perspective, pursue the spillover with firms located in the same region relatively weakly. In some cases, maybe in extreme conditions, they can pursue only the regional production resources. Thus, the identification of which type of agglomeration is being pursuing by FDIs is helpful for regional policy makers to design and customize their regional development program.

## 8.5 Conclusion

The index suggested by Ellison and Glaeser (1997) is a measurement of the agglomeration effect based on the economic theory of location choice. However, it is not easy to distinguish between the effects of spillover and natural advantage from the agglomeration effects on the location choice of new companies. In order to identify these effects, we focus on the location choice process of new FDIs. Three assumptions are introduced to implement our approach. Even though the assumptions are somewhat strict, they are helpful in identifying the type of agglomeration that is attractive to new FDIs.

The first assumption is the independence of occurrence between spillover effects and natural advantage effects. In addition to that, the degree of these effects is common to the companies as long as they are classified in the same industry and are located in the same regional area. The second assumption is that $\gamma_d^{na} = \gamma_{jd}^{na}$. The last one is that $\gamma_{jd}^{s} = \gamma_j^{s}$. If such assumptions are satisfied, the new FDI has two reference groups for its location choice in the host country. One is the spatial distribution of preexisting FDIs of the same nationality, while the other is that of domestic companies. In this study, we show that the effects of spillover and natural advantage can be relatively identified within this context.

The effects of the location choice of new Japanese FDI in Korea are empirically measured by the proposed method. Even though the dataset is restrictive, interesting findings are revealed. First, it is estimated that, when new Japanese FDI chooses its location in Korea, they pursue the spillover effects more, relative to new domestic firms' location choice pattern. However a relatively strong estimation indicates that the natural advantage effect is influenced more by the agglomeration of Korean companies. We can infer that the new Japanese FDIs at looking local natural environment conditions and business amenities prefer to follow Korean companies, rather than pursuing knowledge spillover or corporate information-sharing with domestic companies. Second, at the KSIC-four-digit level, new Japanese FDIs show a relatively high correlation of spillover effect with companies located in the same region in major Korean industries, such as those related to semiconductors. However, the correlation of the spillover effect in the location choice is relatively low in some Korean industries that are exceptional, but not outstanding from a global perspective, such as the chemistry, steel, and medicine sectors. This implies that if the number of companies of the same origin in the same region and same industry is used to proxy for agglomeration effects, the quality of the agglomeration may not be appraised. This therefore shows the importance of the identification of these two effects. Last, the degree of the agglomeration effect with domestic companies changes with an unexpected shock in the home country, such as the Great East Japan Earthquake in

2011. The unexpected shock in the home country can therefore affect the trend and motivation of FDIs moving into neighboring countries.

A degree of bias cannot be avoided because of the lack of data that was mentioned earlier. Even though there is a bias, we argue that it is possible to discern the agglomeration effects qualitatively. Regional governments need to design policies to the attract FDIs into their region, if they want to have sophisticated regional development and growth strategies. Thus it will be necessary to estimate, identify, and analyze these effects with a more complete dataset for domestic companies and FDIs of various origins.

**Acknowledgements** This work was supported by the Ministry of Education of the Republic of Korea and the National Research Foundation of Korea (NRF-2017S1A5A2A01026341).

## References

Alfaro, Laura and Maggie Xiaoyang Chen. 2016. Location fundamentals, agglomeration economies, and the geography of multinational companies. In *Harvard Business School Working Paper, No. 17-014*.

Buckley, Peter, Sierk Horn, Adam Cross, and John Stillwell. 2013. The spatial redistribution of Japanese direct investment in the United Kingdom between 1991 and 2010. *Business History* 55 (3): 405–430.

Duranton, Gilles, and Henry Overman. 2005. Testing for localization using micro-geographic data. *The Review of Economic Studies* 72 (4): 1077–1106.

Ellison, Glenn, and Edward Glaeser. 1997. Geographic concentration in U.S. manufacturing industries: A dartboard approach. *Journal of Political Economy* 105 (5): 889–927.

Ellison, Glenn, and Edward Glaeser. 1999. The geographic concentration of industry: Does natural advantage explain agglomeration? *The American Economic Review* 89 (2): 311–316.

Ellison, Glenn, Edward Glaeser, and William Kerr. 2010. What causes industry agglomeration? Evidence from coagglomeration patterns. *The American Economic Review* 100 (3): 1195–1213.

Helpman, Elhana, Marc Melitz, and Stephen Yeaple. 2004. Export versus FDI with heterogeneous firms. *The American Economic Review* 94 (1): 300–316.

Howard, Emma, Carol Newman, and Finn Tarp. 2016. Measuring industry coagglomeration and identifying the driving forces. *Journal of Economic Geography* 16 (5): 1055–1078.

Hwang, Seok-Joon. 2014. Inward FDIs' location choices: Difference in source countries. *Korea and the World Economy* 15 (1): 129–154.

Hwang, Seok-Joon and Xiaomin Li.forthcoming. Location choice of inward FDIs in Korea: The case of Japanese FDIs with unexpected shock in home country, *Trade and Global Market (edited by Vito Bobek)*. IntechOpen Ltd: London.

Kominers, Scott. 2008, Measuring agglomeration. http://www.scottkom.com/articles/measuring_agglomeration.pdf.

Kopczewska, Katarzyna. 2016. Comment to XCL co-agglomeration index: Distance-weighted improved DCL index. *Papers in Reginal Science* 95 (4): 903–911.

Lee, Ki-Dong, and Seok-Joon Hwang. 2016. Regional characteristics, industry agglomeration and location choice: Evidence from Japanese manufacturing investments in Korea. *Asian Economic Journal* 30 (2): 123–145.

*The Economist*, Jan. 28th, 2017, The retreat of the global company.

# Appendix 8.1

Medicinal chemistry: Manufacture of medicinal chemicals, antibiotics and biological products.
Inorganic chemistry: Manufacture of basic inorganic chemicals.
Nonmetallic n.e.c.: Manufacture of other non-metallic mineral products n.e.c.
Rolling steel: Manufacture of steel products by rolling, extrusion and drawing.
Electronic integrated circuits: Manufacture of electronic integrated circuits.
Sports goods: Manufacture of sports and athletic goods.
Other electronic components: Manufacture of other electronic components except semiconductor and electronic integrated circuits.
Other electrical equipment: Manufacture of other electrical equipment.
Diodes et al.: Manufacture of diodes, transistors, and similar semi-conductor devices.
Semiconductor Machinery: Manufacture of semiconductor and flat display board manufacturing machinery.

# Chapter 9
# Econometric Analysis on Product Differentiation and Trade Liberalization of Beef in Japan

**Kohya Takahashi and Koshi Maeda**

## 9.1 Objective

Trade liberalization of agricultural products is progressing in Japan; the tariff on beef, which is one of the most important products, is reducing. Specifically, in the Trans-Pacific Partnership (TPP) Agreement, which was reached in principle in October 2015, after setting quantity safeguards for Japan's beef imports, beef tariff in Japan would be reduced over 16 years from 38.5% to 9%. Following that, in the Comprehensive and Progressive Agreement for Trans-Pacific Partnership (CPTPP), which was reached in principle in November 2017 in response to the United States withdrawing from the TPP Agreement, the tariff on Japan's beef imports would be reduced to the same level as in the TPP Agreement. Therefore, there are concerns in Japan about the impact this reduction in beef tariff will have on domestic production of beef, particularly production of dairy beef, which is close to imported beef in quality.

To analyze the impact, it is primarily necessary to econometrically analyze Japan's current demand structure for beef and clarify the degree of product differentiation between imported beef and domestically produced beef. Previous studies that have conducted an econometric analysis from this viewpoint are Mori and Lin (1990), Hayes et al. (1990), Wahl et al. (1991), Kawashima and Sari (2010), and Matsuda (2014).

However, a problem with the studies done by Hayes et al. (1990), Wahl et al. (1991), Kawashima and Sari (2010), and Matsuda (2014) is that they aggregated dairy beef with imported beef or Japanese beef (Wagyu beef) as one good and did not analyze the relationship between imported beef and dairy beef, which is currently particularly noteworthy.

K. Takahashi · K. Maeda (✉)
Kyushu University, Fukuoka, Japan
e-mail: kmaeda@agr.kyushu-u.ac.jp

K. Takahashi
e-mail: ktakahashi@agr.kyushu-u.ac.jp

 
M. Hosoe et al. (eds.), *Applied Analysis of Growth, Trade, and Public Policy*,
https://doi.org/10.1007/978-981-13-1876-4_9

Conversely, in Mori and Lin (1990), although the period of the analysis was set prior to the tariffication of beef imports, after disaggregating beef into three classes—Japanese beef, dairy beef, and imported beef—they conducted an analysis using a demand system model and clarified that Japanese beef and dairy beef did not compete with imported beef. However, after the tariffication in 1991, on one hand, the quantity demanded for imported beef increased, but on the other hand, the quantity demanded for dairy beef decreased, so it appeared that imported beef and dairy beef were in a competitive relationship.

Furthermore, a problem with the study of Mori and Lin (1990) is that they did not consider the non-stationarity of time series data. When using time series data, to prevent "spurious regression," it is necessary to use an analysis model and estimation method that takes into consideration the non-stationarity of the data; however, Mori and Lin (1990) did not consider this and conducted a regression analysis.

A study that considered the non-stationarity of time series data and that carried out the analysis using a demand system model is Matsuda (2014). After conducting a unit root test and co-integration test, Matsuda (2014) used first difference series data and analyzed the demand structure for meat in Japan. However, as previously touched upon, a problem with Matsuda (2014) is that it aggregated domestically produced beef as one good and did not analyze the relationship between imported beef and dairy beef, which is currently particularly noteworthy.

Therefore, to consider the impact of trade liberalization on domestic production of beef, it is important to carry out an analysis that overcomes the problems in both Mori and Lin (1990) and Matsuda (2014); namely, disaggregating the beef into classes and considering the non-stationarity of time series data. In addition, a problem in all the above studies is that they did not explicitly analyze the demand for hybridize type beef (first filial generation beef of Japanese beef and dairy beef), which currently occupies an important position in the domestic production of beef.

Therefore, after disaggregating beef into four classes—Japanese beef, hybridized type beef, dairy beef, and imported beef—and considering the non-stationarity of time series data, the objective of this study is to econometrically analyze the current demand structure for beef in Japan and clarify the respective degrees of product differentiation between imported beef and domestically produced beefs; subsequently the impact of trade liberalization on domestic production of beef is also considered by studying the case of the TPP Agreement.

The remainder of this chapter is structured as follows. First, in Sect. 9.2, the methods of selecting the analysis model and the estimation method will be explained, and in Sect. 9.3, the data will be described. Then, in Sect. 9.4, the unit root test and co-integration test will be carried out, and the method that is suitable for this study to estimate the time series data will be selected. In Sect. 9.5, the demand structures for meat and beef in Japan will be estimated, and the estimation results will be considered in Sect. 9.6. Furthermore, in Sect. 9.7, the impact of trade liberalization will be analyzed by considering the case of TPP Agreement and using the results obtained; subsequently, the impact of trade liberalization on domestic production of beef will be considered. Finally, in Sect. 9.8, this study will be summarized, and the remaining issues for future research will be described.

## 9.2 The Methods of Selecting the Analysis Model and Estimation Method

In this study, the demand structure for beef in Japan is estimated using the linear approximate almost ideal demand system (LA/AIDS) model, which is a linear approximation of the almost ideal demand system model (Deaton and Muellbauer 1980). The LA/AIDS model is expressed as follows.

$$w_{it}=\alpha_i+\sum_{j=1}^{n}\gamma_{ij}\ln p_{jt}+\beta_i\left[\ln X_t-\ln P_t\right]+u_{it} \tag{9.1}$$

Here, $w_{it}$ is the expenditure share of item $i$ in period $t$, $p_{jt}$ is the price of item $j$ in period $t$, $X_t$ is the total expenditure on the target items in period $t$, $P_t$ is the price index in period $t$, $u_{it}$ is the error term of item $i$ in period $t$, and $\alpha_i$, $\gamma_{ij}$, and $\beta_i$ are the parameters.

For the price index in the above-described model, the following log-linear analogue of the Laspeyres price index is used.

$$\ln P_t=\sum_{i=1}^{n}\bar{w}_i\ln p_{it} \tag{9.2}$$

Here, $\bar{w}_i$ is the sample mean value of the expenditure share of item $i$.

Also, in the above-described model, the adding-up restriction ($\sum_{i=1}^{n}\alpha_i=1$, $\sum_{i=1}^{n}\gamma_{ij}=\sum_{i=1}^{n}\beta_i=0$), the homogeneity restriction ($\sum_{j=1}^{n}\gamma_{ij}=0$), and the symmetry restriction ($\gamma_{ij}=\gamma_{ji}$) are imposed.

If the original series of the time series data is a stationary process, there will be no problems, even if a regression analysis is performed using Eq. 9.1. However, if the original series of the time series data is a non-stationary process, performing a regression analysis using Eq. 9.1 will result in "spurious regression," so it is necessary to take measures against this concern, such as differencing the data until they become stationary processes.

The time series data that becomes a stationary process after differencing d times is expressed as I (d) (integrated of order d). Matsuda (2014) stated that nearly all non-stationary economic time series are I (1); therefore, the following three methods will be primarily considered for estimating the analysis model. First, if all the variables in an analysis model are I (0), the regression estimation is performed using the original series. Second, if all the variables in an analysis model are I (1) and there is a cointegration relationship among the variables, the regression estimation is performed using the error correction model. Third, if all the variables in an analysis model are I (1) and there is no co-integration relationship among the variables, the regression estimation is performed using the first difference series.

In this study, a unit root test and co-integration test are carried out and the estimation method that is suitable for this study is selected from the three methods described above.

## 9.3 The Data

In this study, the subjects of the analysis are eight types of meat; specifically, four classes of beef—Japanese beef, hybridize type beef, dairy beef, and imported beef—as well as domestically produced pork, imported pork, domestically produced chicken, and imported chicken. The period of the analysis is set as January 2006 to February 2011.[1] The quantity demanded and the price of each type of meat are calculated as shown below, with reference to the supply and demand table published by the Agriculture & Livestock Industries Corporation (2015) for each of the meats.

First, the estimated marketing quantity for all the meats is used for the quantity demanded. The estimated marketing quantity of domestically produced meats is calculated by subtracting the export quantity and the quantity of stock increase from the production quantity.[2] However, only the quantity of stock increase is subtracted for domestically produced chicken. Also, the estimated marketing quantity of imported meats is calculated by subtracting the quantity of stock increase from the import quantity.

For the production quantities of Japanese beef, hybridize type beef, dairy beef, and domestically produced pork, the production quantity of dressed carcass is used, and for domestically produced chicken, the production quantity published by the Agriculture & Livestock Industries Corporation (2015) is used. Also, data on the stock quantity and export quantity for domestically produced beef by class—Japanese beef, hybridize type beef, and dairy beef—cannot be obtained. Therefore, the estimated marketing quantity of each class of beef is calculated by multiplying the respective ratios of the production quantity of each class to the total production quantity of domestically produced beef (= the dressed carcass production quantity of each class / the total dressed carcass production quantity of domestically produced beef) by the total estimated marketing quantity of domestically produced beef. Further, the estimated marketing quantities of beef and pork are converted to a cut meat basis;

[1]The period of analysis is set in consideration of the fact that monthly data on the dressed carcass production quantity for hybridize type beef can be obtained from January 2006, that the Great East Japan Earthquake occurred in March 2011, and moreover, that the price of imported chicken has not been published since April 2011.

[2]The export quantities of beef and pork do not include edible offal and boiled meat.

that of domestically produced chicken is converted to a boneless dressed carcass basis, and that of imported chicken is an actual quantity basis.

Next, concerning price, for Japanese beef, hybridize type beef, and dairy beef, the wholesale dressed carcass prices on the meat central wholesale markets converted to a cut meat basis are used, and for imported beef, the average market (trader's) price of beef produced in Australia and the United States is used. For domestically produced pork, the wholesale dressed carcass price on the meat central wholesale markets converted to a cut meat basis is used, and for imported pork, the average market (trader's) price of pork produced in the United States, Canada, Denmark, and Mexico is used. For domestically produced chicken, the wholesale boneless dressed carcass price in Tokyo is used, and for imported chicken, the average market price in the Kanto district of chicken produced in Brazil and the United States is used. All prices are converted to real prices using "All items" in the "Consumer Price Index (2010 standards)" of the Ministry of Internal Affairs and Communications, and converted to prices including consumption tax.

The prices of imported beef, imported pork, and imported chicken are all calculated as weighted averages of the prices of each respective country's produce, which is calculated as the simple average of the prices by cut of each country, with the import quantity of the produce of each country in the relevant month as the weights.[3] In addition, the price of domestically produced chicken is calculated by weighting the prices of "leg meat" and "breast meat," with the weight ratios of each respective cut obtained from one chicken as the weights.

Further, for the production quantities and prices of Japanese beef, hybridize type beef, and dairy beef, the data on "cow," "castrated," and "bull" are used. However, some data on Japanese beef, such as the wholesale dressed carcass value of "bull," is not published. Therefore, for the price of Japanese beef, only the data on "cow" and "castrated" are used.

---

[3]The specific procedure for processing the prices of imported meats is as follows.

First, with regards to imported beef, for the produce of Australia, the simple average price of a total of 31 cuts is calculated, including 11 frozen cuts, 8 chilled grain short-fed cuts, and 12 chilled grass-fed cuts. Next, for the produce of the United States, the simple average price of 6 chilled cuts is calculated. However, the prices of U.S. produced beef by cut were not published from January 2006 to March 2007 because of the decrease in the domestic distribution quantity of U.S. produced beef due to the impact of an outbreak of bovine spongiform encephalopathy (BSE) in the United States. Therefore, from January 2006 to March 2007, the simple average price of 31 Australian produced cuts is used, and from April 2007 to February 2011, the weighted average price of Australian and U.S. produced cuts calculated with the import quantities of these two countries in the relevant month as the weights is used.

Second, with regards to imported pork, first the simple average prices are calculated of 7 U.S. produced cuts, 9 Canadian produced cuts, 4 Danish produced cuts, and 2 Mexican produced cuts. With the import quantities of U.S., Canadian, Danish, and Mexican produce in the relevant month as the weights, the weighted average price of the produce from the four above-mentioned countries is calculated.

Third, for imported chicken, the weighted average price of Brazil-produced leg meat and U.S. produced leg meat with bones is calculated, with the import quantities from these two countries in the relevant month as the weights.

**Table 9.1** The sample means and sample standard deviations of the quantity demanded, price, and expenditure share (from January 2006 to February 2011) (Unit: thousand tons, yen/kg)

| | Japanese beef ($i = 1$) | Hybridize type beef ($i = 2$) | Dairy beef ($i = 3$) | Imported beef ($i = 4$) | Dom. pork ($i = 5$) | Imported pork ($i = 6$) | Dom. chicken ($i = 7$) | Imported chicken ($i = 8$) |
|---|---|---|---|---|---|---|---|---|
| Quantity demanded | 11.909<br>(2.065) | 7.467<br>(0.793) | 9.681<br>(0.814) | 39.159<br>(5.006) | 73.966<br>(5.323) | 63.128<br>(6.197) | 81.464<br>(5.693) | 32.030<br>(4.153) |
| Price | 2,623.0<br>(253.6) | 1,648.7<br>(170.5) | 804.9<br>(98.5) | 972.4<br>(86.9) | 611.1<br>(75.9) | 634.2<br>(24.4) | 469.7<br>(54.6) | 452.3<br>(45.6) |
| Expenditure share | 0.137<br>(0.017) | 0.054<br>(0.005) | 0.035<br>(0.006) | 0.167<br>(0.016) | 0.198<br>(0.013) | 0.177<br>(0.015) | 0.169<br>(0.018) | 0.064<br>(0.008) |

Notes: (1) Dom. stands for domestically produced. (2) The upper row shows the sample mean and the lower row in parentheses shows the sample standard deviation.

The following respective data sets are used for the above-described quantities and prices. First, data from the Agriculture & Livestock Industries Corporation (2015) is used for the market (trader's) or wholesale prices of imported beef, imported pork, domestically produced chicken, and imported chicken, and the stock quantities of each of the meats. Second, "Livestock Distribution Statistics" from the Ministry of Agriculture, Forestry and Fisheries is used for the dressed carcass production quantities and the wholesale dressed carcass prices in the meat central wholesale markets of beef and pork. Third, the "Trade Statistics of Japan" from the Ministry of Finance is used for the import and export quantities of each of the meats. Fourth, the Agriculture & Livestock Industries Corporation (2010) is used for the methods of aggregating each of the import quantities and export quantities, and the yields from a dressed carcass to cut meat of beef and pork; the Agriculture & Livestock Industries Corporation (2001) is used for the method of aggregating the import quantity of chicken; and the "Food Balance Sheet" from the Ministry of Agriculture, Forestry and Fisheries is used for the yield of domestically produced chicken from meat with bone to boneless dressed carcass; and the Policy Research Institute, Ministry of Agriculture, Forestry and Fisheries (2013) is used for the weight ratios of "leg meat" and "breast meat" obtained from one chicken.

Table 9.1 shows the sample means and the sample standard deviations of quantity demanded, price, and expenditure share from the above calculations.

## 9.4 The Results of the Unit Root Test and Co-integration Test

To select a method of estimating the time series data that is suitable for this study, first, a unit root test is carried out. In this study, for the total of 45 variables, the variables used in the LA/AIDS model, and the natural logarithms of the relative price variables, an augmented Dickey-Fuller test (Dickey and Fuller 1979; ADF test), a weighted symmetric test (Park and Fuller 1995, Pantula et al. 1994; WS test) and a Phillips-

Perron test (Phillips and Perron 1988; PP test) are carried out on each of (1) the original series, (2) the difference series (first difference from one period before), and (3) the seasonal difference series (first difference from 12 periods before).[4]

Based on the result of the tests, for the original series, the null hypothesis of "there is a unit root" cannot be rejected in all the tests for most of the variables.[5] For the seasonal difference series, the same null hypothesis cannot be rejected in all the tests for most of the variables.

Conversely, for the difference series, based on the ADF test, the null hypothesis of "there is a unit root" cannot be rejected even at the 10% level for 17 variables, but based on the WS test and PP test, the same null hypothesis can be rejected for all the variables at the 5% level. In other words, for the data used in this study, the tests indicate that most of the original series are unit root processes, and it is understood that all become stationary processes by taking the first difference from one period before.

Next, to perform the co-integration test, the test methodology of Engle and Granger (1987) is used. In this study, after including the monthly dummy variables in Eq. 9.1, a total of 4 co-integration tests are carried out: "single-equation estimations without the restrictions (homogeneity restriction and symmetry restriction) imposed" or "simultaneous estimation with the restrictions imposed," and "including trend variable" or "not including trend variable".[6] Table 9.2 shows the results of the co-integration test.

As shown in Table 9.2, in all the cases, the null hypothesis of "no co-integration" is not rejected even at the 10% level in the expenditure share equations of all the meats. Thus, it is not considered to be a problem even if analysis is performed under the assumption that there is no co-integration relationship for the expenditure share equations for all the meats. Therefore, in this study, regression estimation is carried out using a first difference series.

---

[4]Matsuda (2010, 2014) are referred to when performing the analysis in this study. We also followed Matsuda (2014) when deciding the lag length in the unit root test and the co-integration test, as follows. In the ADF test, WS test and co-integration test, if j means the lag length that minimizes AIC (Akaike's information criterion), the lag length is set as Min $(j + 2, 12)$. In addition, in the PP test, if T means a sample size, the lag length is set as 4; that is, the integer value closest to $T^{(1/3)}$. Also, asymptotic critical value is used for the unit root test and the co-integration test.

[5]DeJong et al. (1992) conducted a Monte Carlo experiment for the unit root test, and Haug (1996) conducted the same experiment for the co-integration test. They clarified that when the sample size is 100 or less, the results of both tests will not be sufficiently reliable. However, in this study, the sample size cannot be increased from 62 due to the data constraints. Therefore, it should be kept in mind that the results in this section are the results with a reservation on this point.

[6]When conducting simultaneous estimation with the restrictions imposed, except for the imported chicken expenditure share equation, the simultaneous estimation is carried out using the iterative seemingly unrelated regression method (Kmenta and Gilbert 1968) for the expenditure share equations of the other meats. In this case, the adding-up restriction is automatically established. Also, the time series of the error term in the imported chicken expenditure share equation is estimated ex post facto using the restrictions and data, etc.

Table 9.2 Results of the co-integration test

| Expenditure share equation | Co-integration test statistics | | | |
|---|---|---|---|---|
| | Single-equation estimations without the restrictions imposed | | Simultaneous estimation with the restrictions imposed | |
| | Including the trend variable | Not including the trend variable | Including the trend variable | Not including the trend variable |
| Japanese beef | −4.539 | −4.478 | −2.192 | −1.937 |
| Hybridize type beef | −2.028 | −2.064 | −1.673 | −1.198 |
| Dairy beef | −3.311 | −2.835 | −2.954 | −2.554 |
| Imported beef | −2.831 | −2.269 | −2.242 | −2.335 |
| Dom. pork | −4.074 | −4.154 | −3.848 | −3.574 |
| Imported pork | −3.701 | −4.603 | −4.709 | −2.951 |
| Dom. chicken | −3.698 | −3.619 | −3.255 | −3.305 |
| Imported chicken | −5.381 | −3.695 | −2.968 | −3.258 |
| Critical value | | | | |
| 1% level | −6.436 | −6.221 | −6.223 | −5.997 |
| 5% level | −5.909 | −5.692 | −5.694 | −5.467 |
| 10% level | −5.633 | −5.415 | −5.417 | −5.189 |

Notes: (1) Dom. stands for domestically produced. (2) The number of explanatory variables (not including the constant term, the monthly dummy variables and the trend variable) is 8 when the restrictions are imposed and 9 when the restrictions are not imposed. The asymptotic critical values are referred to MacKinnon (2010).

## 9.5 Estimation Results of the Demand Structure

Based on the results of the unit root test and the co-integration test, the following analysis model is used in this study to estimate the demand structures for meat and beef in Japan.

$$\Delta w_{it} = \sum_{j=1}^{n} \gamma_{ij} \Delta \ln p_{jt} + \beta_i \left[\Delta \ln X_t - \Delta \ln P_t\right] + \sum_{s=2}^{12} d_{is} \Delta DM_s + \Delta u_{it} \tag{9.3}$$

Here, $\Delta$ expresses the first difference from one period before, $DM_s$ is the monthly dummy variable that takes 1 for month $s$ and zero for all months other than month $s$, and $d_{is}$ is the parameter.

In addition, as serial correlation in the error term was implied by the previous estimation, the estimation is carried out assuming that there is a first-order serial correlation in the error term. Also, in the expenditure share equations of all the meats, the constant terms were not significant even at the 10% level, so the constant terms are not included when carrying out the estimation. Based on the above points,

**Table 9.3** Estimation results of the expenditure share equations for each meat

| | Japanese beef | Hybridize type beef | Dairy beef | Imported beef | Dom. pork | Imported pork | Dom. chicken | Imported chicken |
|---|---|---|---|---|---|---|---|---|
| $\rho$ | −0.456‡ | | | | | | | |
| $\beta_i$ | −0.081‡ | −0.039‡ | −0.021‡ | 0.194‡ | −0.056† | 0.076* | −0.144‡ | 0.071† |
| $\gamma_{i1}$ | 0.044 | | | | | | | |
| $\gamma_{i2}$ | −0.011 | 0.040‡ | | | | | | |
| $\gamma_{i3}$ | −0.013† | 0.000 | 0.032‡ | | | | | |
| $\gamma_{i4}$ | 0.022 | −0.004 | 0.013† | 0.059 | | | | |
| $\gamma_{i5}$ | −0.015 | −0.012† | −0.008‡ | 0.019 | 0.142‡ | | | |
| $\gamma_{i6}$ | 0.037 | −0.001 | −0.009 | −0.038 | −0.066‡ | 0.049 | | |
| $\gamma_{i7}$ | −0.036† | −0.000 | −0.009* | −0.059‡ | −0.047‡ | −0.000 | 0.134‡ | |
| $\gamma_{i8}$ | −0.029* | −0.012† | −0.006* | −0.012 | −0.013 | 0.027 | 0.017* | 0.028 |
| $d_{i2}$ | 0.010‡ | 0.003* | 0.000 | −0.011 | −0.013‡ | 0.012† | −0.004* | 0.004 |
| $d_{i3}$ | 0.012‡ | 0.004‡ | 0.002* | −0.012 | −0.012‡ | 0.006 | 0.003 | −0.003 |
| $d_{i4}$ | 0.030‡ | 0.010‡ | 0.001 | −0.017 | −0.028‡ | 0.004 | 0.001 | −0.002 |
| $d_{i5}$ | 0.009† | 0.004† | −0.000 | −0.024† | −0.018‡ | 0.019‡ | 0.006* | 0.004 |
| $d_{i6}$ | 0.004 | 0.001 | −0.001 | −0.012 | −0.025‡ | 0.027‡ | 0.002 | 0.002 |
| $d_{i7}$ | 0.026‡ | 0.006† | −0.001 | −0.026† | −0.028‡ | 0.026‡ | −0.003 | −0.000 |
| $d_{i8}$ | 0.007 | 0.003 | −0.001 | −0.015 | −0.029‡ | 0.037‡ | −0.007* | 0.005 |
| $d_{i9}$ | 0.013‡ | 0.005† | 0.001 | −0.017 | −0.017‡ | 0.016† | −0.003 | 0.003 |
| $d_{i10}$ | 0.019‡ | 0.006‡ | 0.002 | −0.028† | −0.013‡ | 0.010 | 0.011‡ | −0.006 |
| $d_{i11}$ | 0.049‡ | 0.009‡ | 0.002 | −0.045‡ | −0.012† | −0.001 | 0.009† | −0.010 |
| $d_{i12}$ | 0.066‡ | 0.010‡ | 0.000 | −0.051‡ | −0.018‡ | −0.022† | 0.028‡ | −0.014* |
| $R^2$ | 0.921 | 0.730 | 0.822 | 0.602 | 0.864 | 0.633 | 0.920 | |
| DW | 2.774 | 2.568 | 2.432 | 2.717 | 2.371 | 2.515 | 1.706 | |

Notes: (1) Dom. stands for domestically produced, $\rho$ stands for the first-order autocorrelation coefficient in error term, $R^2$ stands for the coefficient of determination, and DW stands for Durbin Watson statistic. (2) The critical value of the t distribution in the degrees of freedom for demand system of 307 is 1.650 at the 10% level, 1.968 at the 5% level, and 2.592 at the 1% level. Also, *, †, and ‡indicate that the estimated value is statistically significant at the 10% level, 5% level, and 1% level, respectively.

each of the meats' expenditure share equations are simultaneously estimated using the nonlinear iterative seemingly unrelated regression method (Gallant 1987).[7]

[7]In the estimation of Eq. 9.3, with $\rho$, $e_{it}$ as the parameter and the stochastic variable, assuming that there is the relationship of $\Delta u_{it} = \rho \Delta u_{it-1} + e_{it}$ in the error term, Yen and Chern (1992) method is used. With regard to the imported chicken parameters, after carrying out the simultaneous estimation of the expenditure share equations for all the meats except for imported chicken, it is estimated ex post facto using the restrictions, etc. Also, the delta method is used to calculate its standard error. Greene (2012) and others were referred to for the delta method.

**Table 9.4** The estimated values of the price elasticity and meat expenditure elasticity of demand

| | Quantity demanded | | | | | | | |
|---|---|---|---|---|---|---|---|---|
| Price | Japanese beef | Hybridize type beef | Dairy beef | Imported beef | Dom. pork | Imported pork | Dom. chicken | Imported chicken |
| Japanese beef | −0.599‡<br>(−3.028) | −0.101<br>(−0.482) | −0.292*<br>(−1.700) | −0.025<br>(−0.157) | −0.037<br>(−0.570) | 0.151<br>(0.705) | −0.095<br>(−1.113) | −0.602†<br>(−2.480) |
| Hybridize type beef | −0.047<br>(−0.564) | −0.224<br>(−1.613) | 0.035<br>(0.320) | −0.085<br>(−1.253) | −0.046*<br>(−1.708) | −0.029<br>(−0.301) | 0.046<br>(1.120) | −0.253†<br>(−2.555) |
| Dairy beef | −0.074*<br>(−1.707) | 0.026<br>(0.387) | −0.068<br>(−0.569) | 0.036<br>(0.946) | −0.028*<br>(−1.864) | −0.063<br>(−1.206) | −0.024<br>(−0.837) | −0.138†<br>(−2.546) |
| Imported beef | 0.262<br>(1.384) | 0.053<br>(0.265) | 0.469‡<br>(2.651) | −0.842†<br>(−2.110) | 0.141<br>(1.284) | −0.285<br>(−1.260) | −0.208*<br>(−1.902) | −0.376<br>(−0.853) |
| Dom. pork | 0.008<br>(0.080) | −0.082<br>(−0.796) | −0.101<br>(−1.114) | −0.119<br>(−0.806) | −0.230‡<br>(−3.416) | −0.456‡<br>(−3.780) | −0.108†<br>(−2.035) | −0.424†<br>(−2.098) |
| Imported pork | 0.376<br>(1.385) | 0.108<br>(0.349) | −0.143<br>(−0.539) | −0.431*<br>(−1.780) | −0.281‡<br>(−2.776) | −0.800†<br>(−2.021) | 0.151<br>(1.052) | 0.231<br>(0.621) |
| Dom. chicken | −0.162<br>(−1.494) | 0.121<br>(0.919) | −0.161<br>(−1.125) | −0.550‡<br>(−4.362) | −0.189‡<br>(−4.020) | −0.072<br>(−0.502) | −0.061<br>(−0.627) | 0.076<br>(0.442) |
| Imported chicken | −0.172<br>(−1.625) | −0.182*<br>(−1.656) | −0.145<br>(−1.561) | −0.146<br>(−0.914) | −0.047<br>(−0.836) | 0.128<br>(0.994) | 0.155‡<br>(2.768) | −0.631*<br>(−1.962) |
| Meat expenditure | 0.408†<br>(2.163) | 0.280<br>(1.429) | 0.406†<br>(2.463) | 2.162‡<br>(5.486) | 0.717‡<br>(5.887) | 1.427‡<br>(6.358) | 0.144<br>(1.487) | 2.117‡<br>(4.274) |

Notes: (1) Dom. stands for domestically produced. (2) The values are evaluated by mean of the expenditure share during the period of the analysis. The upper row shows the estimated value and the lower row in parentheses shows the t value. (3) The critical value of the t distribution in the degrees of freedom for demand system of 307 is 1.650 at the 10% level, 1.968 at the 5% level, and 2.592 at the 1% level. Also, *, †, and ‡indicate that the estimated value is statistically significant at the 10% level, 5% level, and 1% level, respectively.

Table 9.3 shows the estimation results of the expenditure share equations of each of the meats. The coefficients of determination are from 0.602 to 0.921, and it is considered that generally good estimation results can be obtained.

Furthermore, Table 9.4 shows the estimated values of the price elasticities of demand and the meat expenditure elasticities of demand for each meat. The delta method is used to obtain the standard error of each elasticity.

## 9.6 Demand Structures for Meat and Beef in Japan

Based on the elasticities shown in Table 9.4, demand structures for meat and beef in Japan are considered in this section. Empirically, it is expected that the uncompensated cross-price elasticity of demand shows a positive value, but as seen in Table 9.4, the cross-price elasticities among many of the meats, including domestically produced pork and imported pork, are estimated to be significantly negative values, and it is considered that there is a problem in accepting these significant gross complementary relationships.[8] Therefore, interpreting these estimation results is set as a future issue, and in this section, we shall consider those parts other than the significant gross complementary relationships.

First, focusing on the own price elasticity of each meat, although the absolute values of all the estimated values are less than 1, it is estimated that all the values of the imported meats are more elastic than the values of the domestically produced meats. In addition, domestically produced meats are estimated to be significant or not significant, but all imported meats are estimated to be significant. Therefore, it can be said that reducing the price of each of the imported meats will significantly increase the quantity demanded for each respective imported meat.

Second, focusing on the meat expenditure elasticity of each meat, on the one hand, all domestically produced meats are estimated to be significant or not significant with a value of less than 1, but on the other hand, all imported meats are estimated to be significant with a value of 1 or more. Considering these estimation results together with the estimation results of the own price elasticity, we understand that the responses to own price and meat expenditure are larger for the demand for imported meats than for domestically produced meats. The above results imply that imported meats and domestically produced meats have different consumption tendencies, and compared to domestically produced meats, there is more room for increasing demand for imported meats that are more elastic with respect to own price and meat expenditure.

Third, focusing on the cross-price elasticities between domestically produced chicken and imported chicken, the elasticity of demand for domestically produced chicken to the price of imported chicken is estimated to be 0.155 and significant, so it can be said that reducing the price of imported chicken will significantly decrease the demand for domestically produced chicken.

Fourth, focusing on the cross-price elasticities among the beef classes, neither of the elasticities of demand for Japanese beef or hybridize type beef to the price of imported beef are estimated to be significant, so it cannot be said that reducing the price of imported beef will significantly decrease the demand for Japanese beef and hybridize type beef. Conversely, the elasticity of demand for dairy beef to the price of imported beef is estimated to be 0.469 and significant, so it can be said that reducing the price of imported beef will significantly decrease the demand for dairy beef.

The estimation results of the demand structure for beef described above support the considerations of the Ministry of Agriculture, Forestry and Fisheries (2015) that Japanese beef and hybridize type beef are differentiated from imported beef, but dairy beef competes with imported beef. Furthermore, with regard to hybridize type beef, which has not been explicitly analyzed in previous research, the results support the conclusion that the development and expanded production of this beef has been greatly effective as a countermeasure to the past liberalization of beef imports.

[8]In Mori and Lin (1990) and Matsuda (2014), the significant gross complementary relationships were estimated among many of the meats.

On comparing the above estimation results of the demand structure for beef with the results of Mori and Lin (1990), they are the same on the point that there is no competitive relationship between Japanese beef and imported beef, but they differ on the point that there is a competitive relationship between dairy beef and imported beef, and it is understood that this study more accurately captures the actual situation after the tariffication in 1991. The difference between these results implies that there is a possibility that bias is created in the estimation result of the demand structure for beef when the non-stationarity of the time series data is not taken into consideration.

On the other hand, comparing the results to those of Matsuda (2014), 0.093, which is the value of the elasticity of demand for domestically produced beef to the price of imported beef estimated in Matsuda (2014), is a value in between 0.053 and 0.469, which are the elasticities of demand for the three classes of domestically produced beef to the price of imported beef estimated in this study. In other words, even though the degree of the substitution relationship with imported beef is different for each of the three classes of domestically produced beef, if all domestically produced beef are aggregated as one item, the estimation results in its average value; so it can be confirmed once again that it is necessary to disaggregate domestically produced beef into classes when estimating the demand structure for beef in Japan from the viewpoint of analyzing the impact of trade liberalization.

## 9.7 Analyzing the Impact of Trade Liberalization

### 9.7.1 *The Analysis Method*

In this section, the impact of trade liberalization will be analyzed by considering the case of TPP Agreement using price elasticities of demand as shown in Table 9.4.

The following method is used for the analysis. First, when the demand function of item $i$ $D_i = D_i\,(p_1, \ldots, p_8, y, DM_2, \ldots, DM_{12})$ is totally differentiated, the following equation can be obtained.

$$dD_i = \sum_{k=1}^{8} \frac{\partial D_i}{\partial p_k} dp_k + \frac{\partial D_i}{\partial y} dy + \sum_{s=2}^{12} \frac{\partial D_i}{\partial DM_s} dDM_s \tag{9.4}$$

Here, $D_i$ is the quantity demanded for item $i$, and $y$ is income.

Next, assuming that only the prices of imported meats change, using the price elasticities of demand, Eq. 9.4 can be approximated as the following.

$$\Delta D_i = \eta_{i4} \frac{\bar{D}_i}{\bar{p}_4} \Delta p_4 + \eta_{i6} \frac{\bar{D}_i}{\bar{p}_6} \Delta p_6 + \eta_{i8} \frac{\bar{D}_i}{\bar{p}_8} \Delta p_8 \tag{9.5}$$

Here, $\Delta D_i$ ($= D_{it} - D_{it-1}$) is the amount of change in the quantity demanded for item $i$, $\Delta p_k$ ($= p_{kt} - p_{kt-1}$) is the amount of change in the price of item $k$, $\eta_{ik}$ is the elasticity of demand for item $i$ to the price of item $k$, period $t-1$ is the period before trade liberalization, and period $t$ is the period after trade liberalization.

When approximating a differential by difference, it is necessary to use the mean value of before and after the change as levels values, so $\bar{D}_i$ and $\bar{p}_k$ are respectively expressed as follows.

$$\bar{D}_i = \frac{D_{it}+D_{it-1}}{2} \tag{9.6}$$

$$\bar{p}_k = \frac{p_{kt}+p_{kt-1}}{2} \tag{9.7}$$

Therefore, arranging Eq. 9.5 using Eqs. 9.6–9.7, the amount of change in quantity demanded $\Delta D_i$ due to trade liberalization can be expressed as follows.

$$\Delta D_i = \frac{\frac{\eta_{i4}}{\bar{p}_4}\Delta p_4 + \frac{\eta_{i6}}{\bar{p}_6}\Delta p_6 + \frac{\eta_{i8}}{\bar{p}_8}\Delta p_8}{1 - \frac{\eta_{i4}}{2\bar{p}_4}\Delta p_4 - \frac{\eta_{i6}}{2\bar{p}_6}\Delta p_6 - \frac{\eta_{i8}}{2\bar{p}_8}\Delta p_8} D_{it-1} \tag{9.8}$$

Also, $\Delta p_k$, which is the amount of change in the price of item $k$, is calculated as follows.

$$\Delta p_k = p_{kt-1}\frac{1+r_{1k}}{1+r_{2k}} - p_{kt-1} \tag{9.9}$$

Here, $r_{1k}$ is the tariff rate of item $k$ after trade liberalization, and $r_{2k}$ is the tariff rate of item $k$ before trade liberalization.

In this study, the impact of trade liberalization is analyzed using the analysis method described above. For the amount of changes in the quantity demanded for each item, the delta method is used to calculate its standard error, and whether these amounts are statistically significant is tested.

As the analysis scenario, based on the contents of the TPP Agreement, it is assumed that the respective tariff rates will be reduced or eliminated, with the beef tariff rate being reduced from 38.5% (temporary rate) to 9.0%, the pork tariff rate from 4.3% (temporary rate) to 0.0%, and the chicken tariff rate from 11.9% (World Trade Organization bound rate) to 0.0%.[9] From these reductions, the imported beef price will be reduced by 21.3%, the imported pork price by 4.1%, and the imported chicken price by 10.6%.[10] In other words, the quantity demanded of (from) the 16$^{th}$ year after

[9]Please refer to the Cabinet Secretariat (2016) for details on the contents of the TPP Agreement.

[10]For the pork tariff, in the TPP Agreement, after maintaining the gate-price system and its gate-price of 524 yen/kg, the specific tariff in the low-price band will be reduced from a maximum of 482 yen/kg to a maximum of 50 yen/kg, and the ad valorem tariff in the high-price band of 4.3% will be eliminated. On this point, the Ministry of Agriculture, Forestry and Fisheries (2015) assumed that for pork imports in the future, combination imports will be likely to continue, but the possibility that some low-price cuts would be imported irrespective of the combination cannot be denied. Therefore, although it is difficult to accurately forecast the movement in the imported pork

the TPP Agreement came into effect, when the tariff reduction and elimination period for all the imported meats ends, is analyzed.

A total of estimated marketing quantities from January to December in 2014 is used as the benchmark for the quantity demanded for each of the meats.[11]

## 9.7.2 Results of the Analysis

The analysis results of the impacts of the TPP Agreement are shown in Table 9.5.

First, focusing on the changes in the quantity demanded for each of the imported meats, the changes in the quantities demanded for imported pork and imported chicken are not estimated to be significant, so it cannot be said that the TPP Agreement will have a significant impact on the demand for these imported meats. Conversely, the quantity demanded for imported beef will be increased significantly by 26.7% (95% confidence interval is 4.7%–48.6%). Therefore, it is considered that beef is the meat whose imports will be increased the most by the TPP Agreement.

Second, focusing on the changes in the quantities demanded for each of the domestically produced meats, the changes in the quantities demanded for Japanese beef, hybridize type beef, domestically produced pork, and domestically produced chicken are not estimated to be significant, so it cannot be said that the TPP Agreement will have a significant impact on the demand for these domestically produced meats. Conversely, the quantity demanded for dairy beef will be decreased significantly by 8.6% (95% confidence interval is 1.1%–16.0%). Therefore, it is considered that

price after the TPP Agreement came into effect, in this study, it is assumed that the combination imports at gate-price will be continued, or in other words, the ad valorem tariff of 4.3% will be eliminated and the imported pork price will be reduced by 4.1%.

Also, for the chicken tariff, in the TPP Agreement, all the tariff, the whole chicken (not cut in pieces) tariff of 11.9%, the meat with bone (legs with bone in) tariff of 8.5%, and the other (boneless meat, etc.) tariffs of 11.9%, will be eliminated. The chicken import in 2014, the percentage of import quantity from countries joining the TPP Agreement out of the total import quantity was 5.4% (mainly meat with bone from the United States), and most of the imports are boneless meat from Brazil. Based on this point, the Ministry of Agriculture, Forestry and Fisheries (2015) expected that the impact of the TPP Agreement would be limited for chicken, but on the other hand, in the long-term, they are concerned that the price of domestically produced chicken will be reduced due to the changes of the import partner countries resulting from the tariff reduction or elimination, etc. Therefore, although it is difficult to accurately forecast the movement in the price of imported chicken after the TPP Agreement came into effect, in this study, the possibility that the import partner countries will be changed by the TPP Agreement is taken into consideration, and it is assumed that the tariff for boneless meat, which is currently the main imported item, of 11.9% will be eliminated and the imported chicken price will be reduced by 10.6%.

In addition, for beef imports, the percentage of import quantity from countries joining the TPP Agreement out of the total import quantity was 99.9% (2014), and for pork imports, the percentage of import quantity from countries joining the TPP Agreement out of the total import quantity was 62.0% (2014).

[11]In the analysis method used in this study, because $\frac{\Delta p_k}{p_k}$ in Eq. 9.8 is equal to $\frac{2(r_{1k}-r_{2k})}{2+r_{1k}+r_{2k}}$ and is a constant regardless of the price level, there is no need to set a benchmark for price.

**Table 9.5** Analysis results of the impacts of the TPP Agreement

| Meat | Benchmark of quantity demanded | Change in the quantity demanded due to the TPP Agreement | Percentage change | Quantity demanded after the TPP Agreement came into effect |
|---|---|---|---|---|
| Japanese beef | 160.990 | −9.224<br>[−22.222, 3.773] | −5.7<br>[−13.8, 2.3] | 151.766<br>[138.769, 164.763] |
| Hybridize type beef | 80.789 | 0.255<br>[−7.240, 7.749] | 0.3<br>[−9.0, 9.6] | 81.043<br>[73.549, 88.538] |
| Dairy beef | 106.461 | $-9.108^{\dagger}$<br>[−17.042, −1.173] | −8.6<br>[−16.0, −1.1] | 97.354<br>[89.419, 105.289] |
| Imported beef | 506.337 | $135.006^{\dagger}$<br>[24.009, 246.004] | 26.7<br>[4.7, 48.6] | 641.343<br>[530.346, 752.340] |
| Dom. pork | 886.177 | −14.557<br>[−56.747, 27.634] | −1.6<br>[−6.4, 3.1] | 871.620<br>[829.429, 913.811] |
| Imported pork | 787.931 | 71.899<br>[−14.615, 158.414] | 9.1<br>[−1.9, 20.1] | 859.830<br>[773.315, 946.344] |
| Dom. chicken | 1,066.696 | 27.924<br>[−27.728, 83.576] | 2.6<br>[−2.6, 7.8] | 1,094.620<br>[1,038.969 , 1,150.272] |
| Imported chicken | 451.229 | 73.555<br>[−22.057, 169.167] | 16.3<br>[−4.9, 37.5] | 524.784<br>[429.172, 620.397] |
| All Dom. beef | 348.240 | −18.077 – −9.108 | −5.2 – −2.6 | 330.163 – 339.133 |
| All beef | 854.577 | 116.929 – 125.899 | 13.7 – 14.7 | 971.506 – 980.476 |

Notes: (1) Dom. stands for domestically produced. (2) With regard to each meat, the upper row shows the estimated value and the lower row in brackets shows 95% confidence interval. Also, "Percentage change" and "Quantity demanded after the TPP Agreement came into effect" are calculated ex post facto based on the estimation result. (3) The critical value of the t distribution in the degrees of freedom for demand system of 307 is 1.650 at the 10% level, 1.968 at the 5% level, and 2.592 at the 1% level. Also, †indicate that the estimated value is statistically significant at the 5% level.

dairy beef is the domestically produced meat that will be most affected by the TPP Agreement.

Third, focusing on the changes in the quantity demanded for all domestically produced beef (Japanese beef, hybridize type beef, and dairy beef), on the one hand, the changes in the quantities demanded for Japanese beef and hybridize type beef are not estimated to be significant, but on the other hand, the change in the quantity demanded for dairy beef is estimated to be significant. Considering both cases, totaling only the significant changes in the quantities demanded and totaling all the changes, including the changes in the quantities demanded that are not significant, we find that the quantity demanded for all domestically produced beef will be decreased by 2.6%–5.2%.

Fourth, focusing on the changes in the quantity demanded for all beef (Japanese beef, hybridize type beef, dairy beef, and imported beef), although the quantity demanded for all domestically produced beef will be decreased by 2.6%–5.2%, the quantity demanded for imported beef will be increased by 26.7%, so we find that the quantity demanded for all beef will be increased by 13.7%–14.7%.

### 9.7.3 Impact on the Domestic Production of Beef

Based on the analysis results described above, the impact of trade liberalization on the domestic production of beef will be considered.

First, in the results of the analysis shown in Table 9.5, looking at all domestically produced beef, imported beef, and all beef, although there are differences in degree, it is considered that changes after trade liberalization will show the same tendency as after the tariffication of beef imports in April 1991. From fiscal 1990 to fiscal 2000—the year prior to the domestic outbreak of bovine spongiform encephalopathy (BSE)—the production quantity of all domestically produced beef had decreased by 4.5% (from 378.0 thousand tons to 360.9 thousand tons); however, the other hand, the import quantity of beef had increased by 91.5% (from 385.5 thousand tons to 738.4 thousand tons) and, as a result, the total production quantity of domestically produced beef and import quantity of beef had increased by 44.0% (from 763.5 thousand tons to 1,099.3 thousand tons).

On the other hand, in the results of the analysis shown in Table 9.5, looking at domestically produced beef by class, it is considered that changes after trade liberalization will show a different tendency than after the tariffication of beef imports. From fiscal 1990 to fiscal 2000, the production quantity of all domestically produced beef had decreased by 4.5%, which was because the production quantity of dairy-type beef (hybridize type beef and dairy beef) had decreased by 18.8% (from 242.6 thousand tons to 196.9 thousand tons), but the production quantity of Japanese beef had increased by 21.0% (from 135.4 thousand tons to 163.9 thousand tons). In the case of aiming to increase the production of Japanese beef, also after trade liberalization, it is considered that an important point on the demand side is whether demand for Japanese beef has the characteristics of a luxury good. But after comparing the estimation results in this study to the previous research, it seems that the characteristics of an essential good have been strengthened in the demand for Japanese beef since the tariffication of beef imports.[12] In other words, it can be said that the current situation is that it is more difficult to increase the production of Japanese beef compared to the situation after the tariffication of beef imports. Therefore, even though the production quantity of Japanese beef had recovered from fiscal 2004 (132.7 thousand tons) to fiscal 2012 (166.8 thousand tons) to the level before the outbreak of BSE, a further increase in production cannot be expected as of now.

[12]In Mori and Lin (1990) (analysis period: Q2 1978 to Q1 1988), the meat and fish expenditure elasticity of demand for Japanese beef was estimated to be 2.55, which indicated that Japanese beef was estimated as a luxury good. Also, in Matsuda (2014) (analysis period: January 1994 to March 2011), the meat expenditure elasticity of demand for domestically produced beef was estimated to be 0.812. Conversely in this study (analysis period: January 2006 to February 2011), the meat expenditure elasticities of demand are estimated to be 0.408 for Japanese beef, 0.280 for hybridize type beef, and 0.406 for dairy beef. These differences imply that from the tariffication of beef imports to the present time, the meat expenditure elasticity of demand for Japanese beef has become smaller.

## 9.8 Conclusion

In this study, based on the present concerns in Japan about the impact of trade liberalization on domestic production of beef, after econometrically analyzing the current demand structure for beef in Japan and clarifying the respective degrees of product differentiation between imported beef and domestically produced beefs, the impact of trade liberalization on domestic production of beef was considered by considering the case of the TPP Agreement. When analyzing the demand structure for beef, to overcome the problems in previous research, the estimation was carried out using a demand system model after disaggregating the beef into four classes—Japanese beef, hybridize type beef, dairy beef, and imported beef—and in addition, taking into consideration the non-stationarity of time series data. The results of the analysis revealed the following points.

First, regarding the time series data of Japan's meat, it is considered that most of the original series are unit root processes, and all the data become stationary processes by taking the first difference from one period before. Also, looking at the demand system as a whole, there is no co-integration relationship among the time series data for Japan's meats.

Second, in Japan, the responses of demand for imported meats are larger than those for domestically produced meats with respect to own price and meat expenditure.

Third, it cannot be said that the TPP Agreement will have significant impacts on the quantities demanded for domestically produced pork, imported pork, domestically produced chicken, and imported chicken.

Fourth, it cannot be said that the TPP Agreement will have significant impacts on quantities demanded for Japanese beef and hybridize type beef; on the other hand, the quantity demanded for dairy beef will be decreased by 8.6%. In addition, the quantity demanded for all domestically produced beef will be decreased by 2.6%–5.2%, but the quantity demanded for imported beef will be increased by 26.7%, and as a result, the quantity demanded for all beef will be increased by 13.7%–14.7%.

Fifth, after the tariffication of beef imports in 1991, the impact of trade liberalization had been mitigated because of compensating for the decrease in production of dairy beef etc. by the increase in production of Japanese beef. However, the same mitigation effect cannot be expected as of now.

Finally, future issues in this study are as follows. Due to data constraints, we could not consider the demand structure for beef after March 2011. In addition, to analyzing CPTPP or the free trade agreement between Japan and the United States, we need to aggregate imported beef for each import partner's country or group. Furthermore, for a more accurate analysis of the impact of trade liberalization, it will be necessary to consider the supply side.

### Postscript

This chapter is a revised and modified version of our article, Takahashi, K., and K. Maeda (2018) Impacts of the TPP Agreement on beef demand in Japan: An analysis by class. *Japanese Journal of Agricultural Economics* 20:1–17.

## References


Agriculture & Livestock Industries Corporation. 2001. Toriniku to keiran no Yunyūryou ni tsuite (About the import quantities of chicken meat and eggs). Chikusan no jouhou: Kokunai hen (Livestock industries information: Domestic edition) 137, 36–37.

Agriculture & Livestock Industries Corporation. 2010. Jukyū doukou wo haaku suru tameno toukei kaisetsu: Gyūniku butaniku hen (Commentary on the statistics for understanding supply and demand trends: Beef and pork edition). Livestock industries information 244, 46–54.

Agriculture & Livestock Industries Corporation. 2015. Chikusan, kokunai toukei shiryou (Livestock, domestic statistical data). http://www.alic.go.jp/joho-c/joho05_000073.html. Accessed 12 Sept 2015.

Cabinet Secretariat. 2016. TPP no naiyou (Contents of the Trans-Pacific Partnership Agreement). http://www.cas.go.jp/jp/tpp/naiyou/index.html. Accessed 3 Feb 2016.

Deaton, A., and J. Muellbauer. 1980. An almost ideal demand system. *American Economic Review* 70 (3): 312–326.

DeJong, D.N., J.C. Nankervis, N.E. Savin, and C.H. Whiteman. 1992. The power problems of unit root tests in time series with autoregressive errors. *Journal of Econometrics* 53(1-3):323–343. https://doi.org/10.1016/0304-4076(92)90090-E.

Dickey, D.A., and W.A. Fuller. 1979. Distribution of the estimators for autoregressive time series with a unit root. *Journal of the American Statistical Association* 74:427–431. https://doi.org/10.1080/01621459.1979.10482531.

Engle, R.F., and C.W.J. Granger. 1987. Co-integration and error correction: Representation, estimation, and testing. *Econometrica* 55(2):251–276. https://doi.org/10.2307/1913236.

Gallant, A.R. 1987. *Nonlinear statistical models*. New York: Wiley.

Greene, W.H. 2012. *Econometric analysis*, 7th ed., International edition. Essex: Pearson Education.

Haug, A.A. 1996. Tests for cointegration: A Monte Carlo comparison.*Journal of Econometrics* 71(1-2):89–115. https://doi.org/10.1016/0304-4076(94)01696-8.

Hayes, D.J., T.I. Wahl, G.W. Williams. 1990. Testing restrictions on a model of Japanese meat demand. *American Journal of Agricultural Economics* 72(3):556–566. https://doi.org/10.2307/1243024.

Kawashima, S., and D.A.P. Sari. 2010. Time-varying armington elasticity and country-of-origin bias: From the dynamic perspective of the Japanese demand for beef imports. *Australian Journal of Agricultural and Resource Economics* 54(1):27–41. https://doi.org/10.1111/j.1467-8489.2009.00477.x.

Kmenta, J., and R.F. Gilbert. 1968. Small sample properties of alternative estimators of seemingly unrelated regressions. *Journal of the American Statistical Association* 63:1180–1200. https://doi.org/10.1080/01621459.1968.10480919.

MacKinnon, J.G. 2010. Critical values for cointegration tests. *Queen's Economics Department Working Paper* 1227.

Matsuda, T. 2010. Shouhisha juyou bunseki (Consumer demand analysis). In *Ouyou keiryou keizaigaku handobukku (Handbook of applied econometrics)*, ed. C. Minotani, and A. Maki, 39–78. Tokyo: Asakura Publishing.

Matsuda, T. 2014. Hiteijou dēta ni yoru kokusan yunyū nikurui juyou no keiryou bunseki (An analysis of Japanese demand for domestic and imported meats using nonstationary time series data). *Journal of the Japanese Society of Agricultural Technology Management* 20 (4):127–138.

Ministry of Agriculture, Forestry and Fisheries. 2015. Hinmoku goto no nourin suisan butsu eno eikyou ni tsuite (About the impact on each item of agricultural, forest and fishery products). http://www.maff.go.jp/j/kanbo/tpp/pdf/151224_bunseki.pdf. Accessed 6 Jan 2016.

Mori, H., and B.H. Lin. 1990. Japanese demand for beef by class: Results of the almost ideal demand system estimation and implications for trade liberalization. *Journal of Rural Economics* 61 (4): 195–203.

Pantula, S.G., G. Gonzalez-Farias, and W.A. Fuller. 1994. A comparison of unit-root test criteria. *Journal of Business and Economic Statistics* 12(4):449–459. https://doi.org/10.1080/07350015.1994.10524567.

Park, H.J., and W.A. Fuller. 1995. Alternative estimators and unit root tests for the autoregressive process. *Journal of Time Series Analysis* 16(4):415-429. https://doi.org/10.1111/j.1467-9892.1995.tb00243.x.

Phillips, P.C.B., and P. Perron. 1988. Testing for a unit root in time series regression. *Biometrika* 75(2):335–346. https://doi.org/10.1093/biomet/75.2.335.

Policy Research Institute, Ministry of Agriculture, Forestry and Fisheries. 2013. Nikurui ni kansuru sapuraichēn no bunseki: Kokusan gyūniku, butaniku, toriniku wo hikaku shite (Analysis of the meat supply chain: Comparing domestically produced beef, pork and chicken), Sapuraichēn purojekuto kenkyū shiryou dai ni gou (Material for supply chain project, No.2).

Wahl, T.I., D.J. Hayes, and G.W. Williams. 1991. Dynamic adjustment in the Japanese livestock industry under beef import liberalization. *American Journal of Agricultural Economics* 73(1):118–132. https://doi.org/10.2307/1242888.

Yen, S.T., and W.S. Chern. 1992. Flexible demand systems with serially correlated errors: Fat and oil consumption in the United States. *American Journal of Agricultural Economics* 74(3):689–697. https://doi.org/10.2307/1242582.

# Chapter 10
# Effects of Tariff Reduction on Economic Growth

**Katsufumi Fukuda**

## 10.1 Introduction

Relationship between tariff level and growth rate has been vastly researched empirically and theoretically by international economics and economic growth literature. See Vamvakidis (2002) and Clemens and Williamson (2004), and Wacziarg and Welch (2008) for empirical results.

Baldwin and Forslid (1999) examine effects of three kinds of trade liberalization on economic growth in a variety expansion growth model with identical firms. They show that there is an inverted U-shaped relationship between specific tariff and growth rate, no relationship between iceberg cost and growth, and U-shaped relationship between specific tariff and growth rate.

Recently, many papers pay attention to the role of firm heterogeneity in the international trade literature. Melitz (2003) constructs a new monopolistically competitive model with firm heterogeneity and show that non-exporting firms' productivities is strictly lower than that of exporting firms and decreases in iceberg cost leads to reallocation from non-exporting firms to exporting firms. Thus, productivities in an industry increase. Moreover, Baldwin and Robert-Nicoud (2008) examines effects of decreases in iceberg cost on economic growth. But these papers do not analyze effect of decreases in tariff on economic growth.

Motivated by these things, this paper examines effect of increases in tariff on economic growth in a model with firm heterogeneity. This paper show that increases in the *ad valorem* tariff on growth rate because expenditure minus tariff revenue decreases more compared with asset income. This result is different from Baldwin and Forslid (1999).

K. Fukuda (✉)
Hiroshima University, Higashihiroshima, Japan
e-mail: 2katsufumi.fukuda@gmail.com



M. Hosoe et al. (eds.), *Applied Analysis of Growth, Trade, and Public Policy*,
https://doi.org/10.1007/978-981-13-1876-4_10

### *10.1.1 The Model*

There are structurally symmetry two countries. Each worker supplies one unit labor inelastically in each time. Wage rate is normalized to be one. There are monopolistically competitive goods sector and perfectly competitive R&D sector with free entry and exit. In the former sector, each firm has a different productivity drawn from a Pareto distribution by incurring the sunk cost. Comparing the value of entering each market with sunk entry costs, each firm decide entering or not each market. In the R&D sector,

### *10.1.2 Consumer/Worker*

Each worker/consumer supplies one unit of labor inelastically each time. So, population must be identical with labor supply which given by $L_t$ Consumer earns asset and labor incomes. Each consumer chooses time path of expenditure so as to maximizes intertemporal utility. Intertemporal utility function is

$$u\left(D_t\right) = \int_0^\infty e^{-\rho t} \log D_t \mathrm{d}t, \tag{10.1}$$

where $D_t$ is consumption index which is defined as

$$D_t = \left(\int_{i\in\Theta} x_{Lt}\left(i\right)^{\frac{\sigma-1}{\sigma}} + \int_{i\in\Theta} x_{Et}\left(i\right)^{\frac{\sigma-1}{\sigma}} \mathrm{d}i\right)^{\frac{\sigma}{\sigma-1}}, \sigma > 1, \tag{10.2}$$

where $\Theta$ is the set of varieties we can consume.$x_{Lt}\left(i\right)\left(x_{Et}\left(i\right)\right)$ is the $i$th domestically produced (exported) varieties consumption, $\rho$ is subjective discount factor. Flow budget constraint is

$$\dot{s}_t = r_t s_t + w_t L_t + TR - e_t, \tag{10.3}$$

where $s_t$ is asset stock, $r_t$ is rat of return of firms' share, $w_t$ is wage rate where which is normalized to be one, $TR$ is tariff revenue which is redistributed by government, $e_t$ is consumption expenditure for (exported) produced varieties, $\rho$ is subjective discount factor. Consumer's optimization problem consists of dynamic optimization and static problem.

Solving dynamic optimization problem, we derive following Euler equation:

$$\frac{\dot{e}_t}{e_t} = r_t - \rho. \tag{10.4}$$

We turn to static utility maximization problem. Static budget constraint is

$$e_t = \int_\Theta p_{Lt}(i)x_{Lt}(i)\mathrm{d}i + \int_\Theta p_{Et}(i)x_{Et}(i)\mathrm{d}i \tag{10.5}$$

where $p_L(i)\,(p_E(i))$ is the price of $x_L(i)(x_E(i))$. Demand function for each variety is derived as follows:

$$x_t(i) = \frac{p_j(i)^{-\sigma}}{(P_t)^{1-\sigma}} e_t, \; j = LE \tag{10.6}$$

where

$$P_t = \left( \int_{i\in\Theta} [p_L(i)]^{1-\sigma} \mathrm{d}i + \int_{i\in\Theta} [p_E(i)]^{1-\sigma} \mathrm{d}i \right)^{\frac{1}{1-\sigma}} \tag{10.7}$$

is the price index of consumption index. We finished explanation of consumer activity. We turn to explanation of manufacturing firm activity.

### *10.1.3 Manufacturing Firm*

For each manufacturing firms to start production their manufacturing goods, each faces two-step decision making. In the first stage, he/she decides whether drawing a productivity of manufacturing good, $\phi$ from a Pareto distribution, $G(\phi) = 1 - \phi^{-k}$ for $\phi \in [1, \infty]$ by creating $F_I$ units of knowledge which costs $b_{It}F_I$ where $b_{It} = \frac{1}{(1+\lambda)m_t}$ is marginal cost of creating knowledge with $1 > \lambda > 0$ is international spillover and $m_t$ is the number of varieties. Associated benefit of drawing a marginals cost is expected excess profits from serving the market. In the second stage, each firm to serve the domestic (foreign) market needs create $b_{It}F_L(F_E)$ units of knowledge. Depending on values supplying each market, $V_i(\phi)$, $i = L, E$, each firm decides to enter each market or not. Due to iceberg cost and tariff which are measured by $\tau$ and $T$ respectively, the value of serving the foreign market is strictly below of that of domestic market. Baldwin and Robert-Nicoud (2008) considered a decreasing effect of iceberg costs as trade liberalization, but they do not examine effects of falling in tariff.

### *10.1.4 Cut-off conditions*

Non-exporting firm activity is identical with Baldwin and Robert-Nicoud (2008). Profits of non-exporting firm with productivity $\phi$ is given by

$$\pi_{Lt}(\phi) = p_{Lt}(\phi)\, q_{Lt}(\phi) - \frac{q_{Lt}(\phi)}{\phi}$$

By solving profit-maximizing problem, following profit-maximizing price and profit function are derived as follows:

$$p_{Lt}(\phi) = \frac{\sigma}{(\sigma-1)\phi} \quad \text{and}$$
$$\pi_{Lt}(\phi) = \frac{\sigma^{-\sigma}(\sigma-1)^{\sigma-1}\phi^{\sigma-1}e_t}{P^{1-\sigma}} \tag{10.8}$$

As in Melitz (2003), holding other endogenous variables like expenditure and price index, profit function is monotonically increasing function of productivity.

We turn to exporting firms. Exporting firms face two types of trade barriers. The first is iceberg cost as in Baldwin and Robert-Nicoud (2008) examined. The second is ad-valorem tariffs is denoted with $T$. So, profit from exporting with productivity $\phi$ is given by

$$\pi_{Et}(\phi) = \frac{p_{xt}(\phi)\,q_{xt}(\phi)}{1+T} - \tau\frac{q_{xt}(\phi)}{\phi}$$

Profit-maximizing price and profit function for exporting are given by

$$p_{Et}(\phi) = \frac{\sigma\tau(1+T)}{(\sigma-1)\phi} \; and \; \pi_{Et}(\phi) = \sigma^{-\sigma}(\sigma-1)^{\sigma-1}(1+T)^{-\sigma}\left(\frac{\tau}{P\phi}\right)^{1-\sigma}e \tag{10.9}$$

Consumer can save in two ways: investment in bond and firms' share. Return on firms' share consists of dividend and capital gain (loss). The former is given by $\frac{\pi_{jt}(\phi)}{V_{jt}(\phi)}$, $j = L, E$, and the latter is $\frac{\dot{V}_{jt}(\phi)}{V_{jt}(\phi)}$, $j = L, E$, where $V_{jt}(\phi)$, $j = L, E$, denotes the value of serving the market. On the other hand, the rate of return on bond is given by interest rate, $r_t$. We consider an equilibrium in which consumer invest both in them. Thus, rate of returns must be identical. This condition called as no-arbitrage condition is given by

$$\frac{\pi_{jt}(\phi)}{V_{jt}(\phi)} + \frac{\dot{V}_{jt}(\phi)}{V_{jt}(\phi)} = r_t, \quad j = L, E. \tag{10.10}$$

Because serving each market costs $b_{It}F_i$, $i = L, E$, The cutoff level of productivity in each market is determined as follows:

$$V_{jt}\left(\phi_j\right) = b_{It}F_j, \; j = L, E. \tag{10.11}$$

Using (10.11) in both markets, we derive ratio of cutoff points which is given by

$$\frac{\phi_E}{\phi_L} = \left(\frac{F_E}{\tau^{1-\sigma}F_L(1+T)^{-\sigma}}\right)^{\frac{1}{\sigma-1}} \tag{10.12}$$

We assume a sufficient condition that exporting firms are more productive compared with non-exporting firms, and it is given by

$$\frac{F_E}{\tau^{1-\sigma}F_L(1+T)^{-\sigma}} > 1 \tag{10.13}$$

### 10.1.5 R&D Sector

R&D sector is perfectly competitive and free entry and exit. Thus, expected value of entry must be same with sunk cost for drawing a productivity. Free condition is

$$\int_{\phi_L}^{\infty} [V_L(\phi) - b_{It} F_L] g(\phi) d\phi + \int_{\phi_E}^{\infty} [V_E(\phi) - b_{It} F_E] g(\phi) d\phi = b_{It} F_I$$

Rewriting free entry condition yields

$$E[V] \equiv \frac{\sigma^{-\sigma}(\sigma-1)^{\sigma-1} \Delta e_t}{(P_t)^{1-\sigma}\left(r_t - \frac{\dot{b}_{It}}{b_{It}}\right)} = b_{It} \bar{F} \tag{10.14}$$

where

$$\bar{F} \equiv \frac{F_I}{1-G(\phi_L)} + \int_{\phi_L}^{\infty} F_L \frac{g(\phi)\, d\phi}{1-G(\phi_L)} + \int_{\phi_E}^{\infty} F_E \frac{g(\phi)\, d\phi}{1-G(\phi_L)} \tag{10.15}$$

is the expected number of creating knowledge for production firms and

$$\Delta \equiv \int_{\phi_L}^{\infty} \phi^{\sigma-1} \frac{g(\phi)\, d\phi}{1-G(\phi_L)} + \tau^{1-\sigma}(1+T)^{-\sigma} \int_{\phi_E}^{\infty} \phi^{\sigma-1} \frac{g(\phi)\, d\phi}{1-G(\phi_L)} \tag{10.16}$$

is the weighted average of productivities among production firms.

### 10.1.6 Creating New Varieties

Production function of new varieties is given by

$$\dot{m}_t = \frac{L_R}{b_{It}\bar{F}} = \frac{(1+\lambda) m_t L_R}{\bar{F}} \tag{10.17}$$

In this paper, $g \equiv \frac{\dot{m}_t}{m_t} = \frac{(1+\lambda)L_R}{\bar{F}}$ is growth rate.

### 10.1.7 Steady State

Using a Pareto distribution, cutoff condition for the local market, and free entry condition yields the cutoff level of productivity for domestic market, and it is given by

$$\phi_L = \left\{ \frac{(\sigma - 1)\, F_L}{(1 + k - \sigma)\, F_I} \left[ 1 + \tau^{-k} (1 + T)^{\frac{-\sigma k}{\sigma - 1}} \left[ \frac{F_E}{F_L} \right]^{\frac{\sigma - k - 1}{\sigma - 1}} \right] \right\}^{\frac{1}{k}} \tag{10.18}$$

Price index (10.7) in terms of a Pareto distribution is

$$P^{1-\sigma} = \int_{\phi_L}^{\infty} p_L(\phi)^{1-\sigma} m(t) \frac{g(\phi) d\phi}{1 - G(\phi_L)} + \int_{\phi_E}^{\infty} p_E(\phi)^{1-\sigma} m(t) \frac{g(\phi) d\phi}{1 - G(\phi_L)}$$

Moreover, using profit-maximizing prices for domestic and foreign markets, a Pareto distribution, ratio of cutoff points, we derive price index as follows:

$$P^{1-\sigma} = \left( \frac{\sigma}{\sigma - 1} \right)^{1-\sigma} \frac{km\,(t)\,(\phi_L)^{\sigma-1}}{1 + k - \sigma} \left[ 1 + \tau^{-k} (1 + T)^{\frac{\sigma - (1 + \sigma k)}{\sigma - 1}} (\frac{F_E}{F_L})^{\frac{\sigma - (1 + k)}{\sigma - 1}} \right] \tag{10.19}$$

Substituting the expected number of creating knowledge for production firms, weighted average of productivities among production firms, cutoff point for domestic market, rewritten price index into free entry condition derive aggregate expenditure as a function of growth rate, and it is

$$\frac{e}{\sigma(\rho + g)} = \frac{kF_L \left[ 1 + \tau^{-k} (1 + T)^{\frac{\sigma - (1 + k\sigma)}{\sigma - 1}} \left( \frac{F_E}{F_L} \right)^{\frac{\sigma - (k + 1)}{\sigma - 1}} \right]}{(1 + \lambda)(1 + k - \sigma)} \tag{10.20}$$

We turn to rewrite the flow budget constraint to derive the other relationship between aggregate expenditure and growth rate. From the flow budget constraint, aggregate expenditure depends on wage income, asset income, and tariff revenue redistributed by government. First, wage income is given by number of worker due to normalization of wage. Second, asset income is given by aggregate value of production firms. Finally, tariff revenue is given by

$$TR = \int_{\phi_E}^{\infty} m\,(t)\, x_{Et}(\phi) \frac{T}{1 + T} p_x\,(\phi)\, \frac{g\,(\phi)\, d\phi}{1 - G\,(\phi_L)}$$

Moreover, a Pareto distribution and profit-maximizing price for exporting derives tariff revenue as follows.

$$TR = \frac{T(t + \tau)^{-k} (1 + T)^{-\frac{\sigma k}{\sigma - 1}} \left( \frac{F_E}{F_L} \right)^{\frac{\sigma - (1 + k)}{\sigma - 1}} e}{1 + (t + \tau)^{-k}\, (1 + T)^{\frac{\sigma - (1 + k)}{\sigma - 1}} \left( \frac{F_E}{F_L} \right)^{\frac{\sigma - (1 + k)}{\sigma - 1}}}$$

Summing these three incomes, aggregate consumption expenditure becomes a function of parameters, and it is

$$e = L + \frac{\rho k F_L \left[ 1 + \tau^{-k} (1+T)^{\frac{\sigma-(1+k\sigma)}{\sigma-1}} \left( \frac{F_E}{F_L} \right)^{\frac{\sigma-(1+k)}{\sigma-1}} \right]}{(1+\lambda)(1+k-\sigma)} + \frac{\tau^{-k}(1+T)^{-\frac{\sigma k}{\sigma-1}} \left( \frac{F_E}{F_L} \right)^{\frac{\sigma-(1+k)}{\sigma-1}} T}{1 + \tau^{-k}(1+T)^{\frac{\sigma-(1+k)}{\sigma-1}} \left( \frac{F_E}{F_L} \right)^{\frac{\sigma-(1+k)}{\sigma-1}}} e \tag{10.21}$$

Following Baldwin and Forslid (1999) we consider effects of change of *ad valorem* tariff on growth rate with zero iceberg cost and sunk costs for domestic and foreign markets. Combining (10.19) and (10.21) yields following growth determination equation as follows:

$$\left[ \frac{1 + (1+T)^{\frac{\sigma-(1+k)}{\sigma-1}} - (1+T)^{-\frac{\sigma k}{\sigma-1}} T}{1 + (1+T)^{\frac{\sigma-(1+k)}{\sigma-1}}} \right] \frac{\sigma k F_L (\rho + g) \left[ 1 + (1+T)^{\frac{\sigma-(1+k\sigma)}{\sigma-1}} \right]}{(1+\lambda)(1+k-\sigma)} = L + \frac{\rho k F_L [1 + (1+T)^{\frac{\sigma-(1+k\sigma)}{\sigma-1}}]}{(1+\lambda)(1+k-\sigma)} \tag{10.22}$$

The LHS of (10.22) means expenditure minus tariff revenue while RHS of (10.22) means wage income plus asset income.

We turn to derive a sufficient condition for existence and uniqueness of steady state.

$$\begin{gathered} 1 + (1+T)x^{\frac{\sigma-(1+k)}{\sigma-1}} > (1+T)^{-\frac{\sigma k}{\sigma-1}} T. \\ \left\{ (\sigma - 1)[1 + (1+T)^{\frac{\sigma-(1+k)}{\sigma-1}}] - \sigma (1+T)^{-\frac{\sigma k}{\sigma-1}} T \right\} \\ \frac{k F_L \rho \left[ 1 + (1+T)^{\frac{\sigma-(1+k\sigma)}{\sigma-1}} \right]}{(1+\lambda)(1+k-\sigma)} < \left[ 1 + (1+T)^{\frac{\sigma-(1+k)}{\sigma-1}} \right] L. \end{gathered} \tag{10.23}$$

The first means the slope of LHS of (10.22) is positive. The second condition means the value of LHS of (10.22) at $g = 0$ is higher than that of RHS at $g = 0$. From these conditions, the unique steady state exists when the level of *ad valorem* tariff is low and population size is large.

We turn to examine effects of incremental increases in the ad valorem tariff on growth rate as follows:

$$\frac{d}{dT} \left\{ \frac{1 + (1+T)^{\frac{\sigma-(1+k)}{\sigma-1}} - (1+T)^{-\frac{\sigma k}{\sigma-1}} T}{1 + (1+T)^{\frac{\sigma-(1+k)}{\sigma-1}}} \right|_{\frac{F_E}{F_L}=1,\, \tau=1} = sign\{ -(1+T)^{-\frac{\sigma k}{\sigma-1}} [1 + (1+T)^{\frac{\sigma-(1+k)}{\sigma-1}}]^{-1} \} < 0. \tag{10.24}$$

This means incremental increases in *ad valorem* tariff from zero with no iceberg cost and identical sunk costs for domestic and foreign markets leads to lower expenditure minus tariff revenue and asset income. But the former effect dominates the latter one, and growth rate decreases. This result is contrast with identical firms model by Baldwin and Forslid (1999) because they show that effect on *ad valorem* tariff on economic growth is the U-shaped. Moreover, Baldwin and Robert-Nicoud (2008) examines the growth effects of incrementally liberalizing iceberg costs but does not examine effects of incremental increases in *ad valorem* tariff on economic growth.

## 10.2 Conclusion

In this chapter we examines the effects of *ad valorem* tariffs on economic growth in a growth and trade model with firm heterogeneity. We show that *ad valorem* tariffs from zero tariffs with no iceberg cost and identical sunk costs for domestic and foreign markets leads to lower growth rate. This result is contrast with symmetry firm model by Baldwin and Forslid (1999).

## References

Baldwin, Richard E., and Frédéric Robert-Nicoud. 2008. Trade and Growth with Heterogeneous Firms. *Journal of International Economics* 74(1): 21–34.
Baldwin, Richard E., and Rikard Forslid. 1999. Incremental Trade Policy and Endogenous Growth?: A q-Theory Approach. *Journal of Economic Dynamics and Control* 23(5–6): 797–822.
Clemens, Michael A., and Jeffrey G. Williamson. 2004. Why Did the Tariff-Growth Correlation Change after 1950?. *Journal of Economic Growth* 9(1): 5–46.
Melitz, Marc J. 2003. The Impact of Trade on Aggregate Industry Productivity and Intra-Industry Reallocation. *Econometrica* 71(6): 1695–1725.
Vamvakidis, Athanasios. 2002. How Robust is the Growth-Openness Connection? Historical Evidence. *Journal of Economic Growth* 7(1): 57–80.
Wacziarg, Romain, and Karen Horn Welch. 2008. Trade Liberalization and Growth: New Evidence. *The World Bank Economic Review* 22(2): 187–231.

# Part III
# Public Activity and Roles of Government

# Chapter 11
# Tax Shelter and Tax Administration

**Keisuke Morita**

## 11.1 Introduction

Tax shelter, which allows taxpayers to avoid tax through complicated transactions, has become a serious problem for the tax administration since the 1990s. Slemrod (2004) mentioned that tax revenue loss from abusive tax shelter was estimated to be between \$14.5 billion and \$18.4 billion in 1999 and increased by 50% in 1993. Wilson (2009) showed that the mean federal tax deficiency associated with use of tax shelter is over \$375 million. Bankman (2004) pointed out that tax shelter makes fiscal planning difficult and hinders the efficient distribution of resources.

This paper aims to clarify the structure of the tax shelter market from the economic theory viewpoint and to determine which type of strategy reduces tax shelter activities more effectively. We set up a model of the tax shelter market by considering two characteristics of tax shelter: variety of schemes and compatibility between scheme and taxpayer. According to Bankman (2004), various schemes of tax shelters such as high-basis, low-value shelter and COBRA shelter have developed and have been marketed in recent years. Matsuda (2009) pointed out that promoters tend to prevent a scheme from becoming common so that it does not attract the attention of tax authorities. Because each promoter provides the specific scheme with the own skill, it may be not compatible with a customer. However, customers have only limited knowledge about specialized fields like law and accounting or strong point that a promoter has. Therefore, a customer can have a contract with a promoter who is not the best for him/her.

We construct a model of the tax shelter market by combining the tax evasion models of Allingham and Sandmo (1972) and Yitzhaki (1974) with the production differentiation model of Perloff and Salop (1986). First, we show that a harder crack-down by the audit and penalty rates does not always reduce the size of tax shelter

K. Morita (✉)
Kanagawa University, Yokohama, Japan
e-mail: kmorita@kanagawa-u.ac.jp



M. Hosoe et al. (eds.), *Applied Analysis of Growth, Trade, and Public Policy*,
https://doi.org/10.1007/978-981-13-1876-4_11

market due to price effect. Second, policy instruments acting on the marginal cost and fixed cost for promoters reduces tax shelter activities more steadily than an increase of the audit and penalty rates, in the current scenario wherein tax shelter is used by only certain taxpayers. Third, we explain conditions to use countermeasures to tax shelter more effectively.

The next section describes the framework of our analysis. In Sect. 11.3, we discuss the results for the short period wherein the number of promoters is given exogenously. In Sect. 11.3, we investigate the case of long period wherein free entry is possible. Finally, in Sect. 11.5, we present some concluding remarks.

## 11.2 Model

We consider an economy that there are some taxpayers with income $y$ and $n$ promoters who provide tax shelters.[1] We assume that the total number of taxpayers is unity. Each promoter develops an original tax shelter scheme using his/her own skills and provides taxpayers with the opportunity to reduce tax burden. We represent the possible proportion of tax that an taxpayer can reduce using a scheme $i$ $(i = 1, \ldots, n)$, which is provided by promoter $i$, as $\beta_i$. taxpayers have different circumstances and different income-earning processes. Therefore, scheme $i$ does not always give taxpayers the same opportunity to reduce tax burden. The better the compatibility between the taxpayer and scheme $i$ is, the larger the possible proportion of tax relief $\beta_i$ is. taxpayers' distribution for $\beta_i$ is according to the cumulative distribution function $G_i(\beta_i)$. To simplify our discussion, we assume that the configuration of the distribution function is identical for all promoters: $G_i(\hat{\beta}) = G_j(\hat{\beta}) \equiv G(\hat{\beta})$, $g_i(\hat{\beta}) = g_j(\hat{\beta}) \equiv g(\hat{\beta})$, and $g_i'(\hat{\beta}) = g_j'(\hat{\beta}) \equiv g'(\hat{\beta})$ for any $\hat{\beta}$ $(i \neq j,\ i, j = 1, \ldots, n)$.[2]

The taxpayer pays a fee $p_i$ to promoter $i$ who provides the scheme $i$. We assume that the taxpayer closes a contract only with a promoter. A scheme is rejected by the tax authority at a probability $\pi$ $(0 \leq \pi \leq 1)$. If a scheme is rejected, the taxpayer must pay the corrected taxes $t(y)$ and the penalty. We assume that the penalty is the amount obtained by multiplying the taxes avoided with the tax shelter $\beta_i t(y)$ by the penalty rate $\phi \geq 0$: i.e., the amount of penalty is $\phi\beta_i t(y)$.[3]

When a risk-neutral taxpayer enters into a contract with promoter $i$, the expected utility is represented as

[1]This paper develops an argument on a supposition that users of tax shelters is individuals as individual investors and high income earners. However, our discussion does not exclude the case that firms use tax shelters, as long as they consult an outside expert on how to avoide their taxes. In our setting, the taxable income is exogenous. This is the same setting as Crocker and Slemrod (2005), who assume that the firm's taxable income has been realized before it makes decision on tax avoidance behavior.

[2]The dash symbol denotes the differentiation.

[3]Our setting of the penalty structure is taken from Yitzhaki (1974).

$$EU_i = (1-\pi)\,U\,[y - t\,(y) + \beta_i t\,(y) - p_i] + \pi U\,[y - t\,(y) - \phi\beta_i t\,(y) - p_i]$$
$$= y - t\,(y) + [1 - (1+\phi)\,\pi]\,\beta_i t\,(y) - p_i.$$

Since $y$ is exogenous, the maximizing the expected utility is equal to maximize the net expected benefit $EB_i$ as

$$EB_i = \gamma\beta_i t\,(y) - p_i, \tag{11.1}$$

where $\gamma \equiv [1 - (1+\phi)\pi]$.

We derive the demand function of promoter $i$ using (11.1). By performing mathematical manipulation in Appendix A, we obtain the demand function of promoter $i$ as

$$D_i = \int_{\beta_i^*}^{1} \Pi_{j\neq i} G\left[\frac{p_j - p_i}{\gamma t\,(y)} + \beta_i\right] g\,(\beta_i)\,d\beta_i, \tag{11.2}$$

where $\beta_i^* \equiv p_i/\gamma t\,(y)$ represents the lowest value of $\beta_i$ among taxpayers who have a contract with promoter $i$.

Promoter $i$ determines the price of tax shelter $p_i$ in order to maximize his/her own profit. This is represented mathematically as

$$\max_{p_i} \quad (p_i - c)\,D_i - K,$$

where $c$ is the marginal cost (for example, the filing cost), and $K$ is the fixed cost (for example, the licensing cost). The first order condition of this problem is

$$D_i + (p_i - c)\,\frac{\partial D}{\partial p_i} = 0. \tag{11.3}$$

Each promoter in the market determines his/her own price under the Nash conjecture.

## 11.3 Symmetric Equilibrium

In what follows, we focus on the symmetric equilibrium in order to simplify our discussion. In the symmetric equilibrium, (11.2) is represented as

$$D = \int_{\beta^*}^{1} G\,(\beta)^{n-1}\,g\,(\beta)\,d\beta. \tag{11.4}$$

Rewriting (11.4) using partial integration, we have

$$D = \frac{1}{n}\left\{1 - G\left(\beta^{*}\right)^{n}\right\}. \tag{11.5}$$

From (11.3) using (11.5), we have

$$\gamma t\left(y\right)\left\{1 - G\left(\beta^{*}\right)^{n}\right\} = n\left(p - c\right)G\left(\beta^{*}\right)^{n-1} g\left(\beta^{*}\right) \tag{11.6}$$

In the symmetric equilibrium, the twice differentiation of price on profit is

$$H \equiv -2nG\left(\beta^{*}\right)^{n-1} g\left(\beta^{*}\right) - \frac{n\left(p - c\right)}{\gamma t\left(y\right)} G\left(\beta^{*}\right)^{n-1} L,$$

where $L \equiv (n-1)\,G\left(\beta^{*}\right)^{-1} g\left(\beta^{*}\right)^{2} + g'\left(\beta^{*}\right) \lesseqgtr 0$. We assume that the second order condition is satisfied: $H < 0$.

Differentiating (11.6) with respect to $\gamma$, we have

$$\frac{\partial p}{\partial \gamma} = -\frac{1}{H}\left\langle \frac{n\left(p - c\right)p}{\gamma^{2} t\left(y\right)} G\left(\beta^{*}\right)^{n-1} L + t\left(y\right)\left\{1 - G\left(\beta^{*}\right)^{n}\right\} + \frac{np}{\gamma} G\left(\beta^{*}\right)^{n-1} g\left(\beta^{*}\right)\right\rangle. \tag{11.7}$$

Equation (11.7) is ambiguous because the first term depends on the ambiguous $L$ while the second and third terms are positive. When $\gamma$ decreases with the audit rate $\pi$ or penalty rate $\phi$, the total demand of tax shelter decrease because the expected benefits of taxpayers decreases: consequently, the promoter decreases the price of tax shelter. This effect is represented by the second and third terms in (11.7). However, the decrease in the total demand changes the price elasticity of demand. The change in the price elasticity of demand can increase the net marginal benefits of the promoter, and the price of tax shelter is likely to then increase. The latter effect is represented by the first term in (11.7). Therefore, the price of tax shelter does not always decrease with the audit rate or the penalty rate.

Differentiating (11.6) with respect to $n$, we have

$$\frac{\partial p}{\partial n} = \frac{1}{H}\left\langle \left(p - c\right)G\left(\beta^{*}\right)^{n-1} g\left(\beta^{*}\right) + G\left(\beta^{*}\right)^{n} \log G\left(\beta^{*}\right)\left[\gamma t\left(y\right) + n\left(p - c\right)\frac{g\left(\beta^{*}\right)}{G\left(\beta^{*}\right)}\right]\right\rangle. \tag{11.8}$$

Equation (11.8) is ambiguous since the first term is positive while the second term is negative. This shows that the price of tax shelter does not always decrease with the number of promoters $n$. Increasing the number of promoters $n$ has two effects on the price of tax shelter. First, the number of clients per promoter decreases with $n$ if the total demand is constant. This decreases the net marginal benefits of the promoter, and then the promoter decreases the price of tax shelter. This effect is represented by the first term in (11.8). Second, taxpayers interested in new promoters enter into the market when the number of promoters increases. Therefore, the net marginal benefits of promoters increase, and thus, the price of tax shelter rises. This effect is represented by the second term in (11.8). The ambiguous effect of the number of promoters on the price of tax shelter is owing to these conflicting effects.

Differentiating (11.6) with respect to $c$, we have

$$\frac{\partial p}{\partial c} = -\frac{nG\left(\beta^*\right)^{n-1} g\left(\beta^*\right)}{H} > 0. \tag{11.9}$$

Equation (11.9) shows that promoters intend to increase the price of tax shelter when the marginal cost $c$ increases.

From (11.5), the total demand of tax shelter *TD* is represented as $1 - G\left(\beta^*\right)^n$ in a symmetric equilibrium. By differentiating *TD* with respect to $\gamma$, we have

$$\frac{\partial TD}{\partial \gamma} = \frac{nG\left(\beta^*\right)^{n-1} g\left(\beta^*\right)}{\gamma t\left(y\right)} \left[\frac{p}{\gamma} - \frac{\partial p}{\partial \gamma}\right] \gtrless 0. \tag{11.10}$$

Equation (11.10) shows that the total demand of tax shelter does not always decrease with the audit rate $\pi$ and penalty rate $\phi$ because of two effects. First, decreasing $\gamma$ is likely to increase the total demand of tax shelter through a change in the price as (11.7). This effect is represented by the first term in (11.10). Second, decreasing $\gamma$ decreases the expected benefit *EB* and then increases the lowest value of $\beta$ among taxpayers who utilize the tax shelter, $\beta^*$. Therefore, the total demand of tax shelter decreases. This effect is represented by the second term in (11.10).

Differentiating *TD* with respect to $c$, we have

$$\frac{\partial TD}{\partial c} = -\frac{nG\left(\beta^*\right)^{n-1} g\left(\beta^*\right)}{\gamma t\left(y\right)} \frac{\partial p}{\partial c} < 0. \tag{11.11}$$

As shown in (11.9), the price of tax shelter increases with the marginal cost $c$. Since increasing the price of tax shelter decreases the attraction of tax shelter, the demand of tax shelter decreases.

**Proposition 11.1** *In the short period wherein the number of promoters is given exogenously, increasing the audit rate or penalty rate does not always decrease the total demand of tax shelter. Rather, it decreases when increasing the marginal cost of the promoter.*

Differentiating *TD* with respect to $n$, we have

$$\frac{\partial TD}{\partial n} = -G\left(\beta^*\right) \left\{\log G\left(\beta^*\right) + \frac{n}{\gamma t\left(y\right)} \frac{g\left(\beta^*\right)}{G\left(\beta^*\right)} \frac{\partial p}{\partial n}\right\} \gtrless 0. \tag{11.12}$$

When the number of promoters $n$ increases, taxpayers interested in new promoters enter into the market, and then, the total demand of tax shelter increases. This effect is represented by the first term in (11.12). However, increasing the number of promoters $n$ can decrease the total demand of tax shelter through a change in price, which is represented by the second term in (11.12). Therefore, the total demand of tax shelter does not always increase when the number of promoters increases.

**Proposition 11.2** *In the short period, increasing the exogenous number of promoters $n$ does not always increase the total demand of tax shelter.*

We consider a particular case in order to investigate the effect of $\gamma$ and $n$ on the total demand of tax shelter in depth. In the current scenario, tax shelter is used only by a small number of taxpayers, although the problem of tax shelter has developed rapidly.[4] Considering this, we focus on the case of $G(\beta^*) \to 1$ wherein tax shelters are not used by most taxpayers. In this case, (11.7) and (11.8) is rewritten as

$$\frac{\partial p}{\partial \gamma} = -\frac{1}{H}\left\{\frac{n(p-c)p}{\gamma^2 t(y)}\left[(n-1)g(\beta^*)^2 + g'(\beta^*)\right] + \frac{np}{\gamma}g(\beta^*)\right\} \gtrless 0, \quad (11.13)$$

$$\frac{\partial p}{\partial n} = \frac{(p-c)g(\beta^*)}{H} < 0. \quad (11.14)$$

(11.13) shows that the price of tax shelter does not always decrease with the audit rate or the penalty rate in the case of $G(\beta^*) \to 1$. On the other hand, (11.14) shows that the price of tax shelter increases with a decrease in the number of promoters in the case of $G(\beta^*) \to 1$.

When $G(\beta^*) \to 1$, (11.10) and (11.12) can be rewritten as

$$\frac{\partial TD}{\partial \gamma} = \frac{ng(\beta^*)}{\gamma t(y)}\left[\frac{p}{\gamma} - \frac{\partial p}{\partial \gamma}\right] \gtrless 0, \quad (11.15)$$

$$\frac{\partial TD}{\partial n} = -\frac{ng(\beta^*)}{\gamma t(y)}\frac{\partial p}{\partial n} > 0. \quad (11.16)$$

From (11.15) and (11.16), we have the following result.

**Proposition 11.3** *We consider a case wherein tax shelter is used only by a small number of taxpayers. In the short period, the total demand of tax shelter decreases when the number of promoters decreases, but this result is not always brought about by increasing the audit and penalty rates.*

Many studies on tax evasion, such as Allingham and Sandmo (1972) and Yitzhaki (1974), pointed out that increasing the audit rate and penalty rate is useful to deter tax evasion. Proposition 11.3 suggests that these strategies are not always useful to deter tax avoidance through tax shelter in the short period, wherein the number of promoters is exogenous, if only few taxpayers use tax shelter.

## 11.4 Free Entry Symmetric Equilibrium

In this section, we focus on the free entry symmetric equilibrium and investigate how certain strategies of tax administration influence the size of the tax shelter market in

[4] See Savino (2005).

the long period, wherein the number of promoters is determined endogenously. The number of promoters in the free entry symmetric equilibrium $\tilde{n}$ satisfies

$$(\tilde{p} - c)\left[1 - G\left(\beta^*\right)^{\tilde{n}}\right] = \tilde{n}K, \tag{11.17}$$

where $\tilde{p}$ is the price of tax shelter in the free entry symmetric equilibrium. From (11.17), we have

$$\frac{\partial \tilde{n}}{\partial \gamma} = -\frac{(\tilde{p} - c)\, \tilde{n} G\left(\beta^*\right)^{\tilde{n}-1} g\left(\beta^*\right) \tilde{p} t\left(y\right)}{\mu \left\{\gamma t\left(y\right)\right\}^2} \gtrless 0, \tag{11.18}$$

$$\frac{\partial \tilde{n}}{\partial c} = \frac{1 - G\left(\beta^*\right)}{\mu} \gtrless 0, \tag{11.19}$$

$$\frac{\partial \tilde{n}}{\partial K} = \frac{\tilde{n}}{\mu} \gtrless 0, \tag{11.20}$$

where $\mu \equiv -[(\tilde{p} - c)G(\beta^*)^{\tilde{n}} \log G(\beta^*) + K] \gtrless 0$. When $\gamma$ decreases with the audit rate $\pi$ or the penalty rate $\phi$, the total demand of tax shelter decreases because of increasing $\beta^*$, and then, the left-hand side is smaller than right hand side in (11.17). Similarly, increasing the marginal cost $c$ or the fixed cost $K$ makes the left-hand side smaller than right-hand side in (11.17). The number of promoters arranged as (11.17) is satisfied again by two effects when entry and exit are free. First, since attraction for the market decreases with a decrease in the total demand of tax shelter, some firms exit from the market. Second, since the number of clients per promoter increases as rival promoters exit, new promoters enter into the market. Consequently, decreasing $\gamma$ and increasing $c$ or $K$ does not always decrease the number of promoters.

We denote $-(\tilde{p} - c)G(\beta^*)^{\tilde{n}} \log G(\beta^*)$ as $\eta$. When $K$ is sufficiently large (small) such that $K > \eta$ ($K < \eta$) holds, (11.18) becomes positive (negative), and (11.19) and (11.20) become negative (positive). We thus derive the following proposition.

**Proposition 11.4** *We consider the free entry symmetric equilibrium. When fixed cost is larger (smaller) than a threshold level* $\eta \equiv -(\tilde{p} - c)G(\beta^*)^{\tilde{n}} \log G(\beta^*)$, *the number of promoters decreases (increases) with the audit rate, penalty rate, marginal cost, or fixed cost.*

The results that the number of promoters increases with an increase in $c$ and $K$, which decrease the net benefits of promoters directly, are seemingly paradoxical. These results are obtained because the effect attracting new promoters into the market works more strongly than the effect causing the exit of the existing promoters from the market.

Differentiating $\widetilde{TD}$, which is the total demand of tax shelter in free entry symmetric equilibrium, with respect $a = \{\gamma, c, K\}$, we have

$$\frac{\partial \widetilde{TD}}{\partial a} = \frac{\partial \widetilde{TD}}{\partial a} + \frac{\partial \widetilde{TD}}{\partial n}\frac{\partial \tilde{n}}{\partial a}.$$

The first term is the direct effect and the second term is the indirect effect in this expression. From (11.12), it is not clear whether the total demand of tax shelter increases or not with $\gamma$, $c$ or $K$.

**Proposition 11.5** *We consider the free entry symmetric equilibrium. The size of the tax shelter market does not always decrease with the audit rate and penalty rate. Similarly, it does not always decrease with the marginal cost and fixed cost of promoters.*

We focus again on the case of $G(\beta^*) \to 1$ considering the current scenario wherein tax shelter is used only by some taxpayers. In this case, $\partial\widetilde{TD}/\partial\gamma$ is ambiguous from Propositions 11.3 and 11.4. On the other hand, $\partial\widetilde{TD}/\partial c$ is negative if $K$ is over $\eta$, while it is ambiguous if $K$ is under $\eta$. Furthermore, $\partial\widetilde{TD}/\partial K$ is positive if $K$ is over $\eta$, and negative if $K$ is under $\eta$.[5]

**Proposition 11.6** *We consider a case wherein tax shelter is used only by a small number of taxpayers in the free entry symmetric equilibrium. When the fixed cost is higher than a threshold level* $\eta \equiv -(\tilde{p} - c)G(\beta^*)^{\tilde{n}} \log G(\beta^*)$*, increasing the fixed cost and marginal cost decreases the size of the tax shelter market, although it does not always decrease by increasing the audit rate and penalty rate. On the other hand, when the fixed cost is lower than* $\eta$*, decreasing the fixed cost decreases the size of the tax shelter market, although the influence of the audit rate, penalty rate, and marginal cost on the size of the tax shelter market is ambiguous.*

Proposition 11.6 gives us two interesting suggestions for countermeasures to tax shelter in a case wherein the number of taxpayers with tax shelter is small. First, increasing the audit rate and penalty rate does not have a stable effect in both the short and long periods. Rather, policy instruments acting on fixed cost and marginal cost are useful in decreasing the size of the tax shelter market steadily in the long period. Second, it is important to pay attention to the current level of fixed cost when utilizing policy instruments acting on fixed cost and marginal cost; if it is sufficiently high, the size of the tax shelter market decreases by increasing the fixed cost and marginal cost. However, if the current level of fixed cost is sufficiently low, policy instruments acting on fixed cost are more useful than those that regulate marginal cost, because the latter does not have a stable effect unlike the former.

## 11.5 Concluding Remarks

In this paper, we constructed a model of tax shelter by focusing on different tax shelter schemes and compatibility between schemes and taxpayers. We investigated theoretically which policy instruments reduce the size of tax shelter market. We showed that a harder crackdown on the audit rate or penalty rate does not always

[5]We note that the direct effect of $K$ is not observed.

reduce that size. A major reason for this result is that promoters intend to arrange the price in order to increase the demand of tax shelter when the audit rate or penalty rate increases. Rather, policy instruments that regulate the marginal cost and fixed cost are more useful in reducing the size of tax shelter market steadily as long as we consider the current scenario wherein tax shelter is used by only certain taxpayers, because they do not directly lead to a fall in price. However, we must note the level of fixed cost when we implement policy instruments acting on marginal cost and fixed cost, because they can decrease the price indirectly, depending on the level of fixed cost.

As Savino (2005) and Bankman (2004) have shown, certain policy instruments to increase the marginal cost and fixed cost have been put in place already. For example, amending tax laws to plug loopholes implies increasing fixed cost, because it increases costs to develop the basic scheme. Making promoters register transactions and lists of investors corresponds to increasing marginal cost. Furthermore, tightening the restrictions on acquiring a license is another example of increasing fixed cost. Our results provide some suggestions of more effective methods to use these policy instruments.

Our results are based on some assumptions in order to simplify our discussion. First, we assume that the shape of the cumulative distribution function for compatibility between taxpayers and a tax shelter scheme is identical for all schemes. Second, we assume that taxpayers are risk neutral, although many studies on tax evasion consider taxpayers risk averse. Third, our discussion is based on the symmetric equilibrium, and we do not provide any policy implications for cases other than the symmetric equilibrium. Fourth, we consider the case wherein the number of promoters is exogenous as the short period and that wherein promoters enter and exit freely into the market as the long period. It is interesting to capture the notion of time more accurately from the viewpoint of dynamics. These issues are left for future research.

# Appendix A

When an taxpayer prefers promoter $i$ to promoter $j$, the relation of $EB_i \geq EB_j$ holds. By rewriting this relation, we have

$$\beta_j \leq \frac{p_j - p_i}{\gamma t(y)} + \beta_i. \tag{A.1}$$

From (A.1), we can represent the probability that the taxpayer with $\beta_i$ will select promoter $i$ rather than promoter $j$ as follows.

$$\Pr\left[EB_i \geq EB_j\right] = G\left[\frac{p_j - p_i}{\gamma t(y)} + \beta_i\right]. \tag{A.2}$$

From (A.2), the probability that the taxpayer will select promoter $i$ from among all promoters is represented as

$$\Pr\left[EB_i \geq \max_{j \neq i} EB_j\right] = \Pi_{j \neq i} G\left[\frac{p_j - p_i}{\gamma t(y)} + \beta_i\right]. \tag{A.3}$$

However, the taxpayer does not consult with promoter $i$ even if (A.3) is satisfied when $EB_i < 0$. Rewriting $EB_i < 0$ yields

$$\beta_i < \frac{p_i}{\gamma t(y)} \equiv \beta_i^*. \tag{A.4}$$

From (A.3) and (A.4), the demand of promoter $i$ is (11.2).

# References


Allingham, M.G., and A. Sandmo. 1972. Income tax evasion: A theoretical analysis. *Journal of Public Economics* 1: 323–338.

Bankman, J. 2004. The tax shelter problem. *National Tax Journal* 57: 925–936.

Beeman, E.R. 2005. Keeping the faith: the permanent campaign against tax shelters. *National Tax Journal* 58: 449–470.

Crocker, K.J., and J. Slemrod. 2005. Corporate tax evasion with agency costs. *Journal of Public Economics* 89: 1593–1610.

Hanlon, M., and J. Slemrod. 2009. What does tax aggressiveness signal? evidence from stock price reactions to news about tax shelter involvement. *Journal of Public Economics* 93: 126–141.

Matsuda, N. 2009. *Tax avoidance versus counter-measures*. Tokyo: Gyousei Co.

Perloff, J.M., and A.C. Salop. 1986. Firm-specific information, product differentiation, and industry equilibrium. *Oxford Economics Papers* 38: 184–202.

Savino, K.O. 2005. Changing calculus: making tax shelters unprofitable. *National Tax Journal* 58: 471–482.

Slemrod, J. 2004. The economics of corporate tax selfishness. *National Tax Journal* 57: 877–899.

Wilson, R.J. 2009. An examination of corporate tax shelter participants. *The Accounting Review* 84: 969–999.

Yitzhaki, S. 1974. A note on income tax evasion: a theoretical analysis. *Journal of Public Economics* 3: 201–202.

# Chapter 12
# Effect of CSR Promotion on the Market and the Role of Government

**Woohyung Lee and Chongung Kim**

## 12.1 Introduction

For the bigger part of the 20th century, most countries have placed much value on economic growth. Only in the late 20th century they began to pay attention to environmental and social issues. In response to these issues, many US and European NGOs and other organizations have strengthened their oversight of multinational corporations that are causing problems. Social interest in corporate social responsibility (hereinafter, CSR) has also heightened. Modern society emphasizes social concerns in the conduct of business. For instance, the KPMG survey (2017) points out that CSR activities are perceived as an important factor in corporate global management. Nevertheless, it is true that many corporations are burdened by CSR activities because such an activity can lead to higher costs.

CSR research in the field of economics has been relatively recent and most previous studies have focused on explaining the phenomenon of how corporations are actively participating in CSR by using an oligopoly model. Liu et al. (2017) mention that most of the CSR literature is on a voluntary basis. Lambertini and Tampieri (2015) investigate how the presence of a CSR firm influences a profit-maximizing (PM) oligopoly with pollution. They conclude that a CSR firm has higher profit than a PM firm and its presence improves social welfare when a first-best Pigouvian tax is introduced. Flores and García (2016) consider a mixed oligopoly market with a for-profit firm and a non-profit organization (NPO) and insist that technical efficiency at the margin is crucial in determining whether more social responsibility of the NPO increases or reduces welfare. Moreover, Bian (2016) investigate the strategic design

W. Lee
Keimyung University, Daegu, South Korea
e-mail: iuh1231@kmu.ac.kr

C. Kim (✉)
Daegu Hanny University, Gyeongsan, South Korea
e-mail: kimcu59@hanmail.net



M. Hosoe et al. (eds.), *Applied Analysis of Growth, Trade, and Public Policy*,
https://doi.org/10.1007/978-981-13-1876-4_12

of CSR-related managerial incentives in a duopoly and examine both Bertrand and Cournot competition models. They suggest that the firms are CSR-friendly under Cournot competition and CSR-unfriendly under Bertrand competition.

On the other hand, some literature addresses CSR promotion through consumers' behavior, e.g., Aurora and Georgantzís (2009), Alves and Santos-Pinto (2008), Manasaki et al. (2013). Especially, Alves and Santos-Pinto (2008) introduce the duopoly market with differentiated goods and find that firms commit CSR when products are complements but not necessarily when products are substitutes.

The motivation behind our research is that, in reality, voluntary basis may not be the only reason why corporations adopt CSR. For instance, as we can see in green consumerism, consumers are more actively responding to corporate activities as the economy grows. Therefore, we assume that consumers can affect the market by increasing the demand for CSR-friendly products. While the literature on CSR promotion through the behavior of consumers we have mentioned above assumes consumer heterogeneity, we assume that consumers accurately monitor the degree of corporate CSR and reflect this in their consumption behavior. This assumption is similar to the advertising competition model, which is very common in the field of industrial organization. In reality, many corporations are trying to advertise their CSR activities to society through various channels. Furthermore, consumers change their perception of these enterprises through firm and government advertising.

Basically, our model is similar to Fanti and and Buccella (2017). They investigate the firms' strategic choice whether to adopt CSR or not under a duopoly market. They find that in a game situation where firms' strategies are CSR or non-CSR, various Nash equilibria may arise due to the degree of product differentiation and firms' social concerns. These results, however, come from situations where consumers' behavior is not taken into account. In this paper, we analyze how consumers' active behavior changes the market and how this affects firms' CSR strategies.

The remainder of the paper is organized as follows. Section 12.2 presents the basic model. In this paper, we consider a two-stage game. At stage 1, firms decide the degree of social responsibility and at stage 2 firms engage in a Cournot competition. The equilibria in both stages are investigated in Sects. 12.3 and 12.4, respectively. In Sect. 12.5, we explore which strategy, CSR or non-CSR, is realized as a Nash equilibrium. Section 12.6 contains some concluding remarks.

## 12.2 The Model

Consider a duopoly market with two firms, firm 1 and firm 2. Both firms produce differentiated goods $q_i$, $(i = 1,\ 2)$, respectively. Consumers in the market obtain their utility by consuming both goods. The utility function is assumed to be quadric and strictly concave, as is usual in an oligopoly model, for instance, Bian (2016), and Lee and Lee (2018).

$$U = \alpha_i q_i + \alpha_j q_j - \frac{1}{2}\left(q_i^2 + q_j^2\right) - \beta q_i q_j,\ i,\ j = 1,\ 2,\ i \neq j \tag{12.1}$$

where $\beta \in (-1,\ 1)$ measures product differentiation. $\beta \in (-1,\ 0), 0, (0,1)$ represents complementary, independent, substitutable, respectively. In this paper, we assume both goods are substitutes and set $\beta = 1/2$.

We assume that consumers prefer the CSR firm's goods over those of the other firm, an assumption different from most previous CSR literature. If consumers know that firm $i$ is a CSR firm, they consume more of the firm's goods. Green consumerism could be an example. People who value the environment consume more eco-friendly goods and this leads firms to produce goods with eco-friendly technology.

In previous studies, a firm's CSR activity is defined as the objective function that takes into account not only its profit but also a share of the consumer surplus. Following the traditional CSR model, such as Liu et al. (2017), Flores and García (2016), and Bian (2016), we define the CSR firm's objective function of CSR firm as follows.

$$V_i = \pi_i + k_i CS, \tag{12.2}$$

where $\pi_i$ is the firm's profit and $CS$ is consumer surplus. Assuming constant marginal cost, $c$, firm $i$'s profit function is $\pi_i = (p_i - c_i)q_i$. For simplicity, we assume $c_i = 0$.[1] Since both goods are differentiated, consumer surplus is given as follows.

$$CS = \frac{1}{2}\left(q_i^2 + 2\beta q_i q_j + q_j^2\right) \tag{12.3}$$

The parameter $k_i \in [0,\ 1]$ measures the firm's degree of social responsibility. Based on the assumption of consumer behavior, we assume that the higher the $k$, the more goods will be consumed. Therefore, we define $\alpha$ in the utility function as a function of $k$: $\alpha_i = \alpha(k_i)$, $\alpha(0) = \alpha$. Without loss of generality, we redefine $\alpha$ as $\alpha(k_i) = \alpha + \theta(k_i)$, $\theta(0) = 0,\ d\theta/dk_i > 0$.

From utility maximization, we can obtain the following demand functions.

$$p_i = \alpha_i(k_i) - q_i - \beta q_j \tag{12.4}$$

In this paper, we consider a two-stage game. At stage 1, both firms decide the degree of social responsibility, $k_i$, simultaneously, and all consumers and firms in the market observe it. At stage 2, both firms engage in a Cournot competition.

[1] While most CSR literature considers a quadric cost function like $c_i(q_i) = \frac{1}{2}q_i^2$, the assumption of constant marginal cost does not significantly affect our analysis.

## 12.3 Stage 2: Cournot Competition

To analyze the firms' CSR strategies, we consider three cases. In the first case only one firm chooses a positive CSR strategy: $k_i > 0,\ k_j = 0$. In the second case both firms choose to adopt CSR strategies: $k_i > 0$. In the last case both firms choose not to adopt CSR strategies: $k_i = 0,\ (i = 1,\ 2)$.

### 12.3.1 *Case 1: $k_i > 0,\ k_j = 0$*

In this case, we assume that firm 1 takes into account CSR in its production while firm 2 does not. Let $k_1 = k > 0$. From the objective function in Eq. (12.2) and demand function in Eq. (12.4), the reaction function of each firm is given as

$$q_1 = \frac{2\alpha_1 - (1-k)q_2}{2(2-k)},\ q_2 = \frac{2\alpha - q_1}{4}.$$

Based on the firms' reaction functions, each firm's output in equilibrium is obtained as follows.

$$q_1 = \frac{2\,(4\alpha_1 - (1-k)\alpha)}{15 - 7k} \tag{12.5}$$

$$q_2 = \frac{2\,(2(2-k)\alpha - \alpha_1)}{15 - 7k} \tag{12.6}$$

It is necessary to check the market participation condition for both firms, i.e., the condition for $q_i > 0$. Based on Eqs. (12.5) and (12.6), the condition should be $4\alpha_1 > (1-k)\alpha$ for $q_1 > 0$ and $2(2-k)\alpha > \alpha_1$ for $q_2 > 0$. Since we assume $\alpha_i = \alpha + \theta(k_i),\ \theta(0) = 0$, we can summarize the condition as $0 \le \theta(k) < (3-2k)\alpha$. If $k$ approaches zero, it should be $0 \le \theta(k) < 3\alpha$, and if $k$approaches unity, it should be $0 \le \theta(k) < \alpha$. This means that if firm 1 is very CSR- active ($k \to 1$) and consumers prefer firm 1's goods so that the market size gap doubles, firm 2's best response is to exit the market ($q_2 = 0$).

Equations (12.5) and (12.6) indicate that firm $i$'s output is a function of $k$: $q_i = q_i(\alpha_1, k)$. The effect of $k$ on the firms' outputs consists of direct and indirect effects.

$$\frac{\partial q_i}{\partial k} = \left.\frac{\partial q_i}{\partial k}\right|_{\alpha_1} + \frac{\partial q_i}{\partial \alpha_1}\frac{\partial \alpha_1}{\partial k}$$

A large $k$ means that firm 1 is more interested in CSR. The increase in $k$ means that the CS weight is larger, so the firm 1's output increases. Accordingly, the first term on the R.H.S. is positive (negative) for firm 1 (firm 2). It means that an increase in $k$ directly leads to an increase in $q_1$. On the other hand, the increase in $k$ indirectly leads to an increase in $q_1$ due to the increase in demand: $d\alpha_1/dk > 0$. Comparative statics show these effects below.

$$\frac{\partial q_1}{\partial k} = \frac{8(2\alpha + 7\alpha_1)}{(15 - 7k)^2} + \frac{8}{15 - 7k}\frac{\partial \alpha_1}{\partial k} > 0 \tag{12.7}$$

$$\frac{\partial q_2}{\partial k} = -\frac{2(2\alpha + 7\alpha_1)}{(15 - 7k)^2} - \frac{1}{15 - 7k}\frac{\partial \alpha_1}{\partial k} < 0 \tag{12.8}$$

Substituting Eqs. (12.5) and (12.6) into (12.4), the price of firm $i$, $p_i$, is given as

$$p_1 = \frac{(8 - 7k)\alpha_1 - 2\alpha}{15 - 7k}, \tag{12.9}$$

$$p_2 = \frac{2(2(2 - k)\alpha - \alpha_1)}{15 - 7k}. \tag{12.10}$$

The price of firm $i$ is also a function of $k$: $p_i = p_i(\alpha_1, k)$. Therefore, the effect of $k$ on $p_i$ is divided into a direct and indirect effect too.

$$\frac{\partial p_i}{\partial k} = \left.\frac{\partial p_i}{\partial k}\right|_{\alpha_1} + \frac{\partial p_i}{\partial \alpha_1}\frac{\partial \alpha_1}{\partial k}$$

Equations (12.7) and (12.8) indicate that a larger value for $k$ leads to an increase in $q_1$ and a decrease in $q_2$. Equation (12.4) also indicates that the price of firm 1, $p_1$, is a decreasing function of $q_1$ and $q_2$. The direct effect depends on these two effects. Equation (12.4) shows that the former is larger than the latter, so the direct effect is negative.

The indirect effect becomes positive since the demand for firm 1's goods increases as $k$ rises. Consequently, the total effect of $k$ on $p_1$ is ambiguous. Equation (12.11) implies that if a firm is involved in CSR activities, the equilibrium price is determined by the magnitude of the two opposing effects- the output effect and the demand effect. The former lowers the price and the latter raises the price.

$$\frac{\partial p_1}{\partial k} = -\frac{7(2\alpha + 7\alpha_1)}{(15 - 7k)^2} + \frac{8 - 7k}{15 - 7k}\frac{\partial \alpha_1}{\partial k} \tag{12.11}$$

$$\frac{\partial p_2}{\partial k} = -\frac{2(2\alpha + 7\alpha_1)}{(15 - 7k)^2} - \frac{2}{15 - 7k}\frac{\partial \alpha_1}{\partial k} < 0 \tag{12.12}$$

Meanwhile, the effect of $k$ on $p_2$ is obvious. Equation (12.12) shows that the direct and indirect effects are both negative so the total effect is negative. Since firm 2 chooses $k = 0$, the direct effect by consumers does not occur.

### 12.3.2 Case 2: $k_1 > 0,\ k_2 > 0$

In this case, both firms take into account CSR in their production: $k_i > 0,\ (i = 1,\ 2)$. Similar to case 1, we can obtain each firm's reaction function using the objective function from Eq. (12.2) and the demand function from Eq. (12.4).

$$q_i = \frac{2\alpha_i - (1 - k_i)q_j}{2(2 - k_i)},\ i,\ j = 1,\ 2,\quad i \neq j \tag{12.13}$$

Both firms' output in equilibrium is obtained as follows.

$$q_i = \frac{4(2 - k_j)\alpha_i - 2(1 - k_i)\alpha_j}{15 - 7k_2 - (7 - 3k_2)k_1} \tag{12.14}$$

Unlike case 1, both firms engage in CSR behavior in this case and their output in equilibrium depends on $\alpha_i$and $k_i$ $(i = 1,\ 2)$, that is, $q_i = q_i(\alpha_i, \alpha_j, k_i, k_j)$. Since we set $k \in [0,\ 1]$, the denominator in Eq. (12.14) is positive. The market participation condition must satisfy the following.

$$\frac{\alpha_i}{\alpha_j} = \frac{1 - k_i}{2(2 - k_j)} \tag{12.15}$$

When the difference in demand expansion becomes larger than the critical point, the less expansionary firm will exit the market. Equation (12.15) derives the critical point.

The effect of $k_i$ and $k_j$ on $q_i$ comprises of a direct and indirect effect.

$$\frac{\partial q_i}{\partial k_i} = \left.\frac{\partial q_i}{\partial k_i}\right|_{\alpha_i} + \frac{\partial q_i}{\partial \alpha_i}\frac{\partial \alpha_i}{\partial k_i} \text{and} \frac{\partial q_i}{\partial k_j} = \left.\frac{\partial q_i}{\partial k_j}\right|_{\alpha_j} + \frac{\partial q_i}{\partial \alpha_j}\frac{\partial \alpha_j}{\partial k_j}.$$

From Eq. (12.14), we can obtain

$$\left.\frac{\partial q_i}{\partial k_i}\right|_{\alpha_i} = \frac{4(2 - k_j)\left((7 - 3k_j)\alpha_i - 2\alpha_j\right)}{(15 - 7k_2 - (7 - 3k_2)k_1)^2} > 0. \quad (12.12.1)$$

Eq. (12.12.1) is positive if $\alpha_i/\alpha_j > 2/(7 - 3k_j)$. Comparing the market participation condition, we know that $\alpha_i/\alpha_j > (1 - k_i)/2(2 - k_j) > 2/(7 - 3k_j)$. Therefore, Eq. (12.12.1) is positive. The indirect effect of $k_i$ on $q_i$ is also positive.

$$\frac{\partial q_i}{\partial k_i} = \frac{8 - 4k_j}{15 - 7k_2 - (7 - 3k_2)k_1}\frac{\partial \alpha_i}{\partial k_i} > 0 \quad (12.12.2)$$

On the other hand, the effect of $k_j$ on $q_i$ is given as

$$\left.\frac{\partial q_i}{\partial k_j}\right|_{\alpha_j} = -\frac{2(1-k_i)\left(2\alpha_i + (7-3k_i)\alpha_j\right)}{(15-7k_2-(7-3k_2)k_1)^2} < 0, \quad (12.12.3)$$

$$\frac{\partial q_i}{\partial k_j} = -\frac{2(1-k_i)}{15-7k_2-(7-3k_2)k_1}\frac{\partial \alpha_j}{\partial k_j} < 0. \quad (12.12.4)$$

These results are similar to Eqs. (12.7) and (12.8). Firm $i$ needs to increase its output ($q_i$) to increase the consumer surplus (higher $k_i$) directly. If the firm raises $k_i$, the demand for its goods will increase (higher $\alpha_i$). This increase in demand leads to an increase in output.

Next, we should check the effect of $k_i$ and $k_j$ on $p_i$. Using Eqs. (12.4) and (12.14), the equilibrium price can be obtained as

$$p_i = \frac{\left(8-4k_j-(7-3k_j)k_i\right)\alpha_i - 2\alpha_j}{15-7k_2-(7-3k_2)k_1}. \quad (12.16)$$

As with the effects on $q_i$, the effects on $p_i$ can be divided into direct and indirect effects

$$\frac{\partial p_i}{\partial k_i} = \left.\frac{\partial p_i}{\partial k_i}\right|_{\alpha_i} + \frac{\partial p_i}{\partial \alpha_i}\frac{\partial \alpha_i}{\partial k_i} = -\frac{(7-3k_j)\left((7-3k_j)\alpha_i + 2\alpha_j\right)}{(15-7k_2-(7-3k_2)k_1)^2} + \frac{8-4k_j-(7-3k_j)k_i}{15-7k_2-(7-3k_2)k_1}\frac{\partial \alpha_i}{\partial k_i} \quad (12.17)$$

For the same reason as in case 1, the direct effect is negative. The indirect effect becomes positive since the demand for firm $i$'s goods increases as $k_i$ rises. Consequently, as in case 1, the total effect on $p_i$ is ambiguous.

On the other hand, the effect of $k_j$ on $p_i$ is clear. Both the direct and indirect effect are negative, so the total effect is negative as well.

$$\frac{\partial p_i}{\partial k_j} = \left.\frac{\partial p_i}{\partial k_j}\right|_{\alpha_j} + \frac{\partial p_i}{\partial \alpha_j}\frac{\partial \alpha_j}{\partial k_j} = -\frac{2\left((7-3k_i)\alpha_j + 2\alpha_i\right)}{(15-7k_2-(7-3k_2)k_1)^2} - \frac{2}{15-7k_2-(7-3k_2)k_1}\frac{\partial \alpha_j}{\partial k_j} < 0 \quad (12.18)$$

### 12.3.3 Case 3: $k_1 = k_2 = 0$

In case 3 both firms are not interested in CSR: $k_1 = k_2 = 0$. Unlike the previous cases, the market is a pure profit-maximizing duopoly. Let $\alpha_1 = \alpha_2 = \alpha$, then the reaction function is given as

$$q_i = \frac{2\alpha - q_j}{4}.$$

From this equation, both firms' output and prices are

$$q_1 = q_2 = \frac{2\alpha}{5} \tag{12.19}$$

$$p_1 = p_2 = \frac{2\alpha}{5}. \tag{12.20}$$

## 12.4 Stage 1: CSR Degree Determination

At stage 1, each firm chooses the degree of social responsibility, $k_i$ $(i = 1,\ 2)$. In case 1, we assume only firm 1 chooses to adopt CSR $(k_1 = k > 0)$. Firm 2 chooses a pure profit-maximizing behavior $(k_2 = 0)$. In the previous section we assumed $\alpha_i = \alpha + \theta(k_i)$. To clarify the analysis here, we specify $\theta(k_i)$ as $\gamma k_i$, where $\gamma \in (0,\ 1)$.[2] Thus, we have $\alpha_i = \alpha + \gamma k_i$.

Using $p_i$ and $q_i$ obtained at stage 1 under case 1, we can rewrite the variables in equilibrium as follows.[3]

$$p_1^1 = \frac{(8-7k)(\alpha+\gamma k) - 2\alpha}{15-7k} \tag{12.18.1}$$

$$p_2^1 = \frac{2\left((3-2k)\alpha - \gamma k\right)}{15-7k} \tag{12.18.2}$$

$$q_1^1 = \frac{2(3+k)\alpha + 8\gamma k}{15-7k} \tag{12.18.3}$$

$$q_2^1 = \frac{2\left((3-2k)\alpha - \gamma k\right)}{15-7k} \tag{12.18.4}$$

$$\pi_1^1 = \frac{2\left((3+k)\alpha + 4\gamma k\right)\left((6-7k)\alpha + (8-7k)\gamma k\right)}{(15-7k)^2} \tag{12.18.5}$$

$$\pi_2^1 = \frac{4\left(\gamma k - (3-2k)\alpha\right)^2}{(15-7k)^2} \tag{12.18.6}$$

Firm 1 determines $k$ to maximize its profit. Even though it is difficult to derive the value of $k$ explicitly, it is possible to compare both firms' profit. Let $k^*$ be the

[2] To satisfy the market participant condition in Eqs. (12.1) and (12.2), $0 \leq \theta(k) < \alpha$ must hold. It means that $\gamma$ should be less than unity. If $\gamma = 0$, the consumers do not respond to CSR at all. Accordingly, it is necessary to set $\gamma \in (0,\ 1)$.

[3] Henceforth the superscript $i$ indicates case $i$ for $(i = 1,\ 2,\ 3)$.

equilibrium value of $k$, then the following can be obtained.

$$\pi_1^1(k^*) - \pi_2^1(k^*) = \frac{2k^*\left\{3(3-5k^*)\alpha^2 + (60-49k^*-(7k^*)^2)\alpha\gamma + 2k^*(15-14k^*)\gamma^2\right\}}{(15-7k^*)^2} > 0 \tag{12.21}$$

From Eqs. (12.18.3) and (12.18.4), we can find that the CSR firm's output (firm 1) is higher than the non-CSR firm's output (firm 2).

$$q_1^1(k^*) - q_2^1(k^*) = \frac{2k^*(3\alpha+5\gamma)}{15-7k^*} > 0 \tag{12.22}$$

The intuition is straightforward. Equation (12.3) indicates that the consumer surplus is an increasing function of output. Since the CSR firm accounts for consumer surplus in its objective function, it has an incentive to increase output before the CSR introduction. Accordingly, the price of the CSR firm is lower than that of the non-CSR firm.

$$p_1^1(k^*) - p_2^1(k^*) = \frac{k^*\left((10-7k^*)\gamma - 3\alpha\right)}{15-7k^*} < 0 \tag{12.23}$$

As the profit is determined by the product of the price and output, Eq. (12.21) implies that the CSR firm is more profitable because it increases output beyond the price decline. We can summarize these results as Lemma 12.1.

**Lemma 12.1** *If consumers increase their demand for the CSR firm's goods, the CSR firm chooses to produce more output at a lower price than the non-CSR firm in a duopoly market. In equilibrium, the CSR firm's profit is larger than that of the non-CSR firm.*

On the other hand, both firms decide to produce the same amount of output under case 2 because we assume that both firms are symmetric. Similar to case 1, we can rewrite the variables in equilibrium as follows.

$$p_i^2 = \frac{\left\{8-4k_j-(7-3k_j)k_i\right\}(\alpha+\gamma k_i) - 2(\alpha+\gamma k_j)}{15-7k_2-(7-3k_2)k_1} \tag{12.24}$$

$$q_i^2 = \frac{2(3+k_i-2k_j)\alpha + 2\gamma\left\{(4-k_j)k_i - k_j\right\}}{15-7k_2-(7-3k_2)k_1} \tag{12.25}$$

$$i,\ j = 1,\ 2,\ i \neq j$$

Similar to case 1, it is difficult to obtain an explicit value for $k$ in this case. We use numerical analysis to get clear results.[4] Since $k_i \in [0,\ 1]$, we can obtain
$k_i|_{k_j=0} = 0.096$ and $k_i|_{k_j=1} = 0.004$

[4] The values of each parameter are the same as in Fig. 12.1, i.e., $\alpha = 100$ and $\gamma = 0.5$.

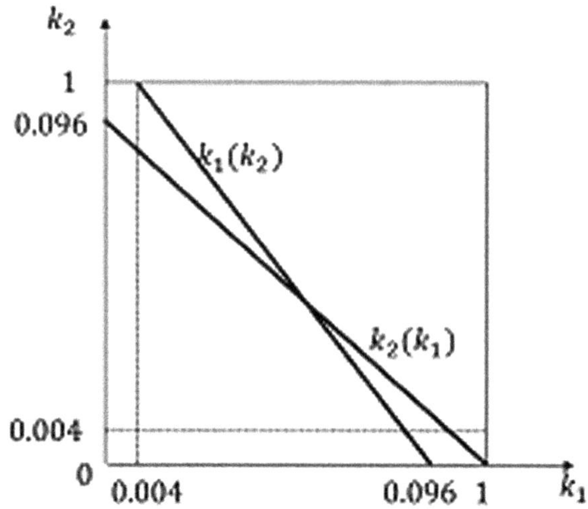


**Fig. 12.1** Reaction curves for both firms under case 2

Subsequently, we can deduce the reaction curve in this analysis. Figure 12.1 shows that CSR is a strategic substitute for both firms.

Since both firms are symmetric, they will choose the same degree of CSR, i.e., $k_1 = k_2$. Let $k^{**}$ be the equilibrium value of $k$. Firm $i$'s profit function is given by

$$\pi_i^2(k^{**}) = \frac{2(2 - 3k^{**})(\alpha + \gamma k^{**})^2}{(5 - 3k^{**})^2}. \tag{12.26}$$

In case 3, the equilibrium values of the variables are quite simple because $k_1 = k_2 = 0$ and there is no consumer response to firms' behavior in the market.

$$p_i^3 = q_i^3 = \frac{2\alpha}{5}, \; i = 1, \; 2 \tag{12.27}$$

$$\pi_i^3 = \left(\frac{2\alpha}{5}\right)^2 \tag{12.28}$$

## 12.5 Firms' Strategic Behavior for CSR

In the previous section, we explored how consumers' response to firms' CSR activities affects the market and looked at the degree of CSR if firms decide to engage in CSR activities.

In this section, we investigate whether both firms have incentives to pursue CSR. This problem can be expressed as a simultaneous game situation. This game is summarized in Table 12.1. Both firms have the same strategies, that is, non-CSR and

**Table 12.1** CSR game

| | | Firm 2 | |
|---|---|---|---|
| | | Non-CSR ($k_2 = 0$) | CSR ($k_2 > 0$) |
| Firm 1 | Non-CSR ($k_1 = 0$) | $\pi_1^3, \pi_2^3$ | $\pi_2^1, \pi_1^1$ |
| | CSR ($k_1 > 0$) | $\pi_1^1, \pi_2^1$ | $\pi_1^2, \pi_2^2$ |

CSR. If a firm adopts CSR, it decides the degree of CSR according to process in the previous section.

To see the existence of Nash equilibrium, it is necessary to compare the profits in each case. At first, we can obtain the following relationship derived from Eqs. (12.18.5) and (12.27).

$$\pi_1^3 - \pi_1^1 = -\frac{2k^*\left\{(45 - 273k^*)\alpha^2 + (1200 - 1025k^* - 175(k^*)^2)\alpha\gamma + (800 - 700k^*)k^*\gamma^2\right\}}{25(15 - 7k^*)^2} \tag{12.29}$$

It is difficult to know the sign of the above equation directly, but it can be deduced indirectly. If $k$ approaches zero, even if the firms engage in CSR activities, there is a little change in demand due to consumer behavior. Therefore, Eq. (12.29) approaches zero. In this case, the firms do not have any incentives to participate in CSR activities. On the other hand, if $k$approaches unity, consumers increase their demand so much that the profit of the firm that adopts CSR increases only if $k = k^* = 1$. If $k^* < 1$, then $\pi_1^1$ is smaller than $\pi_1^3$. Therefore, the sign of Eq. (12.29) becomes positive when $k \to 1$.

$$\left(\pi_1^3 - \pi_1^1\right)\Big|_{k\to 1} = \frac{27\alpha^2 - 25\gamma^2}{200} > 0$$

Figure 12.2 illustrates this point.[5] The degree of CSR that maximizes profits ($k^*$) is where $(\pi_1^3 - \pi_1^1)$ is minimized because $\pi_1^3$ does not depend on $k$. Consequently, it can be said that $\pi_1^3 < \pi_1^1$ when $k = k^*$.

Meanwhile, based on Eqs. (12.18.6) and (12.27), we can obtain the following.

$$\pi_2^1 - \pi_1^2 = \frac{4\left(\gamma k^* - (3 - 2k^*)\right)^2}{(15 - 7k^*)^2} - \frac{2(2 - 3k^{**})(\alpha - \gamma k^{**})^2}{(5 - 3k^{**})^2}$$

As we can see from the above equation, the comparison between $\pi_2^1$ and $\pi_1^2$ is complicated and difficult to identify directly. A numerical analysis gives us concrete values to compare. Table 12.2 shows the results of the analysis.[6]

We can find some interesting insights from Table 12.2. First, $k^*$ is larger than $k^{**}$ at the profit maximization point. Higher $k$ means that the firm increases the weight of consumer surplus in its' objective function, which negatively affects the firm's

[5] We set $\alpha = 100$.

[6] The profit values are rounded to the first decimal point.

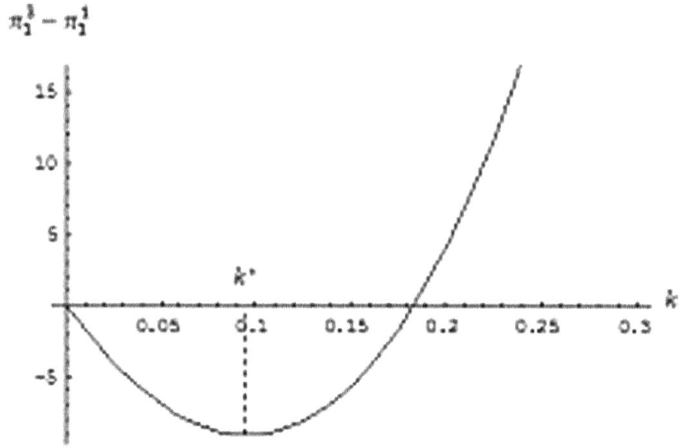


**Fig. 12.2** Comparison between $\pi_1^1$ and $\pi_1^3$

**Table 12.2** Results from the numerical analysis

| $\gamma$ | $k^*$ | $k^{**}$ | $\pi_1^1$ | $\pi_2^1$ | $\pi_i^2$ | $\pi_i^3$ |
|---|---|---|---|---|---|---|
| 0.1 | 0.088 | 0.082 | 1608 | 1542 | 1553 | 1600 |
| 0.5 | 0.096 | 0.089 | 1609 | 1536 | 1549 | 1600 |
| 0.9 | 0.104 | 0.096 | 1611 | 1530 | 1545 | 1600 |

profit. In case 1, the CSR firm benefits from the higher demand alone, while in case 2 the benefits are divided because both firms adopt the same degree of CSR. That is the reason why $k^* > k^{**}$. For the same reason, the CSR firm will take higher $k$ as $\gamma$ rises. A change in the profit of both firms due to the rise of $\gamma$ means that, unless the non-CSR firm participates in CSR, the benefit of higher demand is greater than the negative effect due to the higher value of $k$. That is, as $\gamma$ rises, the CSR firm raises $k$, and the CSR firm's profit ($\pi_1^1$) increases while that of the non-CSR firm ($\pi_2^1$) decreases.

**Lemma 12.2** *In a duopoly market, the degree of CSR when only one firm adopts it is greater than that when both firms adopt it,* $k^* > k^{**}$.

Second, Table 12.2 indicates that in case 2 $k^{**}$ rises and both firms' profit decreases as $\gamma$ rises. Case 2 is quite different from case 1. In case 1, firm 1 unilaterally decides the degree of CSR, but both firms decide it through competition in the second case.

The higher the $\gamma$, the greater the market demand. This moves the reaction curves in Fig. 12.1 outward. For instance, the intersection point of the reaction curves is higher when $\gamma = 0.9$ such as $k_i|_{k_j=0} = 0.104$ and $k_i|_{k_j=1} = 0.008$. It means that both firms increase $k$ competitively as $\gamma$ rises, $\partial k^{**}/\partial\gamma > 0$. From Eq. (12.27), the effect of a larger $\gamma$ on profit is divided into a direct and indirect one.

$$\frac{\partial \pi_i^2}{\partial \gamma} = \left.\frac{\partial \pi_i^2}{\partial \gamma}\right|_{k^{**}} + \frac{\partial \pi_i^2}{\partial k^{**}} \frac{\partial k^{**}}{\partial \gamma}, \quad (12.28.1)$$

where

$$\left.\frac{\partial \pi_i^2}{\partial \gamma}\right|_{k^{**}} = \frac{4k^{**}(2-3k^{**})(\alpha+\gamma k^{**})}{(5-3k^{**})^2} > 0, \quad (12.28.2)$$

$$\frac{\partial \pi_i^2}{\partial k^{**}} \frac{\partial k^{**}}{\partial \gamma} = -\frac{2\left\{(3+9k^{**})\alpha^2 - 4(5-12k^{**})\alpha\gamma - (20-45k^{**}-(9k^{**})^2)\gamma^2 k^{**}\right\}}{(5-3k^{**})^3} < 0. \quad (12.28.3)$$

Equation (12.28.2) shows that the direct effect is positive. The increase in $\gamma$ positively affects the firm's profit by increasing the market demand. Equation (12.28.3), however, indicates that the indirect effect is negative. As we see above, higher $k$ means that the firm increases the weight of consumer surplus, which negatively affects the firm's profit. Although we cannot compare these two opposing effects explicitly, Table 12.2 proves that the negative effect dominates the positive effect.

**Lemma 12.3** *In a duopoly market with two CSR firms, as consumers increase their demand for the CSR firm's goods, their profits decrease in equilibrium.*

Finally, the Nash equilibrium in the game shown in Table 12.1. is (CSR, CSR). That is, both firms will engage in CSR even though their profits are lower than in the non-participation case. Adopting CSR is a dominant strategy for both firms. If both firms do not participate in CSR through cooperation, they can receive higher profits. Nonetheless, they choose to participate in CSR. This can be a kind of a prisoner's dilemma. This result is different from Fanti and and Buccella (2017) that suggest multiple equilibria. They show that (CSR, CSR), (CSR, non-CSR) and (non-CSR, non-CSR) can be realized as Nash equilibria. This difference in results seems to be due to two differences in both models. One is the firms' social concern, $k$. The authors consider $k$ as an exogenous variable, but our model treated it as endogenous. The other difference is that they did not take into account the consumer response to corporate CSR activities while we emphasized this point.

**Proposition 12.1** *If consumers increase their demand for the CSR firm's goods, both firms face the prisoner's dilemma. That is, both firms adopt CSR despite the decline in profit compared to the case where they did not adopt CSR cooperatively.*

Why do firms face a prisoner's dilemma where they can get more profit if they cooperate with each other and avoid CSR? This paper explains the reason for this in terms of consumers' reactions to the firm's CSR activities. The consumers' CSR-friendly behavior provides an incentive to non-CSR firms to deviate from cooperation. It means that consumers drive this game to be a non-cooperative game between the firms.

**Table 12.3** Welfare analysis

| $\gamma$ | $CS^1$ | $CS^2$ | $CS^3$ | $SW^1$ | $SW^2$ | $SW^3$ |
|---|---|---|---|---|---|---|
| 0.1 | 2535.5 | 2654.2 | 2400 | 5684.9 | 5759.5 | 5600 |
| 0.5 | 2549.8 | 2680.3 | 2400 | 5694.8 | 5777.7 | 5600 |
| 0.9 | 2564.1 | 2706.4 | 2400 | 5705 | 5796.3 | 5600 |

Next, it is also important to compare the social welfare in each case. Social welfare can be defined as the sum of consumer surplus and both firms' profits. The results of numerical analysis are summarized in Table 12.3.

*CS* is the largest in case 2. It is obvious that the more firms participate in CSR, the lower the firms' profits, but the greater the *CS*. In addition, the greater the consumers' response to CSR, the greater the *CS*. Social welfare (SW) is also the largest in case 2. This means that the increase in consumer surplus through CSR outweighs the decline in the firms' profits.

**Proposition 12.2** *1. Firms' CSR activities improve social welfare even though their profits are lower.*

*2. Consumers' response to CSR promotes firms' CSR activities and leads to an increase in social welfare. That is, higher* $\gamma$ *causes higher k and consequently SW is improved.*

The policy implication is straightforward. While Liu et al. (2017) suggest that the government needs to promote CSR, this paper insists that consumers promote CSR. The authors also consider the degree of CSR as a policy variable and find the optimal degree which maximizes social welfare. Our paper, however, considers the degree of CSR as an endogenous variable for the firms. According to our results, the government's direct role in promoting CSR is relatively less important. If consumers are able to be proactive in the market and influence firms' CSR activities, social welfare can be improved without government intervention. For this structure to be established, information is important. Although firms are trying to communicate information about their CSR activities to consumers, information asymmetry may distort the market. Therefore, it may be better if the government tries to provide information rather than intervene directly in the market so that consumers can make the right decisions.

## 12.6 Concluding Remarks

Modern society emphasizes social concerns in the conduct of business activities by adding social problems that occur in the stage of economic development. Many CSR studies have focused on firms' voluntary participation through market competition, e.g., a duopoly market. However, it is not enough to explain firms' CSR activities in the real world. In this paper, we assume that consumers respond more actively to corporate activities. Green consumerism is a good example. Consumers who care for the environment try to consume eco-friendly products, even though they may be more expensive. Therefore, we assume that consumers can influence the market by increasing their demand for CSR-friendly products.

The main results are as follows. First, in a duopoly market the CSR firm chooses to supply more output at a lower price than the non-CSR firm. In equilibrium, the CSR firm's profit is larger than that of the non-CSR firm. Second, the degree of CSR when only one firm adopts it is greater than that when both firms adopt it. Third, in a duopoly market with two CSR firms, as consumers increase their demand for the CSR firm's goods, both firms' profits decrease in equilibrium. Fourth, both firms adopt CSR despite the decline in profit compared to the case when they do not adopt CSR cooperatively. Finally, consumers' response to CSR promotes firms' CSR activities and leads to an increase in social welfare.

We also consider the government's role and conclude that it may be better for the government to try to provide information so that consumers can make the right decision rather than intervene directly in the market.

Our model has some limitations. One of them is that we exclude the cost of CSR activities. Actually, it is costly for firms to promote CSR activities and to inform consumers about their CSR efforts. Further research must reflect this cost and investigate how it affects the results. We leave this issue for further studies.

## References


Alves, C., and L. Santos-Pinto. 2008. A theory of corporate social responsibility in oligopolistic markets, *DEEP 09.04*, Universite de Lausanne, Faculte des HEC, DEEP.

Aurora, G., and N. Georgantzís. 2009. Market effects of changes in consumer's social responsibility. *Journal of Economics & Management Strategy* 18 (1): 235–262.

Bian, J.K., W. Li, and X. Guo. 2016. A strategic analysis of incorporating CSR into managerial incentive design. *Transportation Research Part E* 86: 83–93.

Fanti, L., and D. Buccella. 2017. Corporate social responsibility in a game-theoric context. *Economia e Politica Industriale* 44: 371–390.

Flores, D., and A. García. 2016. On the output and welfare effects of a non-profit firm in a mixed duopoly: A generalization. *Economic Systems* 40: 631–637.

KPMG. 2017. *The KPMG survey of corporate responsibility reporting 2017*.

Lambertini, L., and A. Tampieri. 2015. Incentives, performance and desirability of socially responsible firms in a Cournot oligopoly. *Economic Modelling* 50: 40–48.

Lee, W., and K. Lee. 2018. Strategic behaviors on privatization between regions. *Asia-Pacific Journal of Regional Science* 2: 227–242.

Liu, Q., L.F.S. Wang, and C.L. Chen. 2017. CSR in an oligopoly with foreign competition: policy and welfare implication, *Economic Modelling*, 1–7.

Manasakis, C., M. Evangelos, and E. Petrakis. 2013. Certification of CSR activities in oligopolistic markets. *Canadian Journal of Economics* 46 (1): 282–309.

# Chapter 13
# Will Abenomics Expand Employment?–Interpreting Abenomics Through DSGE Modeling

**Minoru Hayashida, Masaya Yasuoka, Ryoichi Nanba and Hiroyuki Ohno**

## 13.1 Introduction

The economic policy known as Abenomics comprises three "policy arrows"[1]: (1) bold monetary easing by the Bank of Japan ("BOJ"), (2) flexible fiscal policy, and (3) growth strategy that brings about private investment.

Of these, "flexible fiscal policy" and "growth strategy" are based on conventional Keynesian economic theory, and they do not attract attention inside academic circles as being anything new. The main reason why Abenomics basks in the world spotlight can be said to be (1) bold monetary easing by the BOJ, and the effects thereof.

As most readers know, the BOJ established an inflation target of 2% in January 2013, and implemented mass-scale purchasing of open-market Japanese government bonds. The BOJ aims to achieve this inflation target at an early stage by supplying the private sector with the ample funds this policy provides. Originally, the BOJ set this inflation target intending for there to be brisk financing activity in the private sector. The actual effect, however, was to rapidly correct the excessively strong yen. The yen-dollar exchange rate temporarily exceeded 125 yen, and it is now stable around 110 yen. This leaves us wondering how many experts were there, at the time when

[1] https://www.japan.go.jp/abenomics/about/

M. Hayashida (✉)
The University of Kitakyushu, Kitakyushu, Japan
e-mail: kazetatinu@kme.biglobe.ne.jp

M. Yasuoka
Kwansei Gakuin University, Nishinomiya, Japan
e-mail: yasuoka@kwansei.ac.jp

R. Nanba
Research Department, Chubu Region Institute for Social Economic Research, Nagoya, Japan

H. Ohno
Toyo University, Tokyo, Japan
e-mail: hiroono@toyo.jp



M. Hosoe et al. (eds.), *Applied Analysis of Growth, Trade, and Public Policy*,
https://doi.org/10.1007/978-981-13-1876-4_13

Abenomics was launched, who were able to recognize that economic policy had the potential to change the yen-dollar rate on the foreign exchange market. *Trusting the yen-dollar exchange to the market is the only approach* —that is what we remember as the mainstream opinion, despite governments repeatedly intervening in the foreign currency markets, and despite the strong yen. When people raise the achievements of Abenomics, this point is also included as an achievement worthy of praise. By any measurement, the recovery of the Japanese economy through yen depreciation was remarkable with the Nikkei average exceeding 20,000 yen in April 2015 and exceeding 24,000 yen in January 2018.

Although the effective opening-to-application ratio is surging these days, Abenomics' effect on employment, however, had attracted very little discussion in Japan compared with the discussion about yen depreciation as a consequence of Abenomics. In particular, it is barely possible to find the type of dynamic stochastic general equilibrium ("DSGE") modeling used in this paper, which incorporates structural unemployment components including labor unions. In this paper, we use DSGE modeling to analyze Abenomic's effect on employment. The fundamental model is based on the models used by Christiano et al. (2005), and Smets and Wouters (2003, 2007) as general tools to evaluate monetary policy by contemporary central banks and the like.[2]

To summarize, the conclusion of this paper is as follows. We performed Bayesian estimation of DSGE models comprising 10 endogenous variables using data from the first quarter of 1990 until the second quarter of 2013. When we introduced productivity shock, monetary easing shock and preference shock to these estimated DSGE models, we obtained results that were mostly consistent with economic theory. We then analyzed these results to observe what kind of effect the shock of the inflation target, a primal policy of Abenomics, has on the major economic variables such as employment and the like. To do this, we defined the inflation target's shock as a shock that leads to the inflation rate deviating in the minus direction from the steady state of expected inflation rate, and calculated the impulse response function. As a result of this analysis, we found that inflation target shock leads to expanded production volume, and higher wage rates and inflation rates. Employment, our subject of focus, also improved. Excluding some parts, these results were also consistent with the trend of the real economy that followed after the start of Abenomics. We also learned that the inflation target's effect was far more sustainable than monetary easing's effect.

[2]Sugo and Ueda (2008) and others cite the model of Christiano et al. (2005) as an example of a model applicable to the Japanese economy. See Kato (2007) and Eguchi (2011) for Japanese language texts on DSGE models. Fujiwara and Watanabe (2011) also provide a useful and comprehensive explanatory guide. Iwata (2009, 2012) uses DSGE modeling to analyze Japanese national fiscal policies.

## 13.2 Model

There are four economic agents in the model economy in this chapter: households, firms, government, and labor unions. Below, we describe the optimization behavior of each, in the order of household, firm, government, and labor union.

### 13.2.1 Households

Households survive for an infinite period, and utility is obtained from consumption and real money holdings. In this paper the utility function is assumed to be the following constant relative risk aversion ("CRRA") type of utility function $U_t$. The population size of households is 1.

$$U_t = E_t \sum_{s=t}^{\infty} \beta^{s-t} \left[ \frac{c_s^{1-\theta}}{1-\theta} + \frac{m_s^{1-\mu}}{1-\mu} \right] \tag{13.1}$$

where:
$c_s$ = consumption
$m_s$ = real money holdings
$E_t$ = expected value operator
$\beta$ = discount factor (assuming $0 < \beta < 1$)
$\theta$ and $\mu$ = parameters expressing relative risk aversion (assuming $0 < \theta,\ 0 < \mu$)

Households can earn labor income by doing labor. On the other hand, it is assumed that a certain percentage inside households is in a state of being unable to work, in other words, an unemployed state. While in an unemployed state, unemployment benefits can be obtained from the government.

In addition, households own assets. There are three methods of asset ownership for households: safe assets, rental of capital to firms, and monetary holdings. The instantaneous budget constraint equation that expresses the real value of households at this time can be expressed as follows.

$$\begin{aligned} m_t + b_t + c_t + I_t = & \frac{1}{1+\pi_t} \left[ (1+i_t)\, b_{t-1} + m_{t-1} \right] + \varphi_t + N_t w_t + r_t K_{t-1} \\ & + (1-N_t)\, u_t - T_t \end{aligned} \tag{13.2}$$

where:
$N_t$ = employment rate
$1 - N_t$ = unemployment rate
$w_t$ = real wages that can be obtained through employment
$u_t$ = real unemployment benefits that can be obtained by being unemployed
$T_t$ = collective tax to provide unemployment benefit
$b_t$ = holdings of safe assets

$i_t$ = nominal interest rate of interest income received from holding these assets

$r_t$ = real interest rate of income that households can obtain by renting capital to firms

$\varphi_t$ = excess profits generated by firms owned by households that households can obtain

$\pi_t$ = inflation rate

$I_t$ = Investment

$K_{t-1}$ = Capital stock

By making $p_t$ the price level, $1 + \pi_t = \frac{p_t}{p_{t-1}}$ is established.

The capital stock $K_t$ can be accumulated through investment $I_t$, and the capital stock accumulation equation is expressed as follows.

$$K_t = I_t + (1 - \delta) K_{t-1} - S\left(\frac{I_t}{I_{t-1}}\right) I_t \tag{13.3}$$

where:

$\delta$ = depreciation rate

$S$ = adjustment function where the following properties hold:

$$S' > 0,\ S(1) = S'(1) = 0$$

In other words, the adjustment cost will increase as the amount of investment in this period increases compared with the investment amount in the previous period.

Using the budget constraint equation (13.2) for each period and the capital stock accumulation equation (13.3) as constraints, we obtain the distribution that achieves maximization of the utility function (13.1). The Lagrangian function $L$ can be expressed as follows.

$$\begin{aligned} L = {} & E_0 \sum_{t=0}^{\infty} \beta^t \left[\frac{c_t^{1-\theta}}{1-\theta} + \frac{m_t^{1-\mu}}{1-\mu}\right] \\ & + E_0 \sum_{t=0}^{\infty} \lambda_t \left[m_t + b_t + c_t + I_t - \frac{1}{1+\pi_t}\left[(1+i_t) b_{t-1} + m_{t-1}\right]\right. \\ & \left. - \varphi_t - N_t w_t - r_t K_{t-1} - (1 - N_t) u_t + T_t\right] \\ & + E_0 \sum_{t=0}^{\infty} \gamma_t \left[K_t - I_t - (1-\delta) K_{t-1} + S\left(\frac{I_t}{I_{t-1}}\right) I_t\right] \end{aligned}$$

$\lambda_t$ and $\gamma_t$ are the respective Lagrangian multipliers. If we derive these for $c_t$, $c_{t+1}$, $m_t$, $I_t$, $K_{t-1}$ and $b_t$, the required conditions for optimization are formed as follows.

$$\beta^t c_t^{-\theta} + \lambda_t = 0 \tag{13.A.1}$$

$$\beta^{t+1} E_t c_{t+1}^{-\theta} + \lambda_{t+1} = 0 \tag{13.A.2}$$

$$\beta^t m_t^{-\mu} + \lambda_t - E_t \frac{\lambda_{t+1}}{1+\pi_{t+1}} = 0 \tag{13.A.3}$$

$$1 = q_t \left(1 - S\left(\frac{I_t}{I_{t-1}}\right) - S'\left(\frac{I_t}{I_{t-1}}\right)\left(\frac{I_t}{I_{t-1}}\right)\right) + E_t q_{t+1} \frac{1+\pi_{t+1}}{1+i_{t+1}} S'\left(\frac{I_{t+1}}{I_t}\right)\left(\frac{I_{t+1}}{I_t}\right)^2 \tag{13.A.4}$$

$$-\lambda_t r_t - \gamma_t (1-\delta) + \gamma_{t-1} = 0 \tag{13.A.5}$$

$$\lambda_t - E_t \lambda_{t+1} \frac{1+i_{t+1}}{1+\pi_{t+1}} = 0 \tag{13.A.6}$$

$$\frac{\partial L}{\partial \lambda_t} = 0 \tag{13.A.7}$$

$$\frac{\partial L}{\partial \gamma_t} = 0 \tag{13.A.8}$$

In the above, $q_t \equiv \frac{\gamma_t}{\lambda_t}$.

We can obtain Euler's equation from (13.A.1), (13.A.2), and (13.A.6) as follows.

$$c_t^{-\theta} = \beta E_t c_{t+1}^{-\theta} \frac{1+i_{t+1}}{1+\pi_{t+1}} \tag{13.B.1}$$

Next, we can obtain the marginal rate of substitution of money holdings and consumption from (13.A.1), (13.A.3), and (13.A.6) as follows.

$$m_t^{-\mu} = c_t^{-\theta} E_t \frac{2+i_{t+1}}{1+i_{t+1}} \tag{13.B.2}$$

Then, we can obtain the relational expression for the relationship between real interest rate, nominal interest rate and inflation rate from (13.A.5) and (13.A.6) as follows.

$$E_t \left(r_{t+1} + q_{t+1}(1-\delta)\right) = q_t E_t \frac{1+i_{t+1}}{1+\pi_{t+1}} \tag{13.B.3}$$

### *13.2.2 Firms*

Among firms, there are final-good firms purchasing intermediate goods from intermediategood firms to produce final goods, and there are intermediategood firms producing intermediate goods.

## Final-Good Firms

Here we assume that the market in which final goods are produced is perfectly competitive. We assume the production function of the firm producing the final good $Y_t$ is as follows; where, $Y_{it}$ is the intermediate good, and $\varepsilon$ is the elasticity of substitution of the intermediate good ($\varepsilon > 1$).

$$Y_t = \left( \int_0^1 Y_{it}^{\frac{\varepsilon-1}{\varepsilon}} di \right)^{\frac{\varepsilon}{\varepsilon-1}} \tag{13.4}$$

At this time, the profit function $\pi_t^f$ of the final good firm is shown as follows; where, $p_{it}$ is the price of the ith intermediate good and $p_t$ is the price of the final goods.

$$\pi_t^f = p_t Y_t - \int_0^1 p_{it} Y_{it} di \tag{13.5}$$

We can obtain the demand function of intermediate goods from the final good firms faced by the intermediate good firms by maximizing the firm's profit equation (13.5) for $Y_{it}$ under the constraint of Eq. (13.4) as follows ($p_{it}$ is given).

$$Y_{it} = \left( \frac{p_{it}}{p_t} \right)^{-\varepsilon} Y_t \tag{13.6}$$

Note that at this time, the following relationship is formed.

$$p_t = \left( \int_0^1 p_{it}^{1-\varepsilon} di \right)^{\frac{1}{1-\varepsilon}} \tag{13.7}$$

$$p_t Y_t = \int_0^1 p_{it} Y_{it} di \tag{13.8}$$

## Intermediate-Good Firms

By inputting capital stock and labor, we can express that intermediategood firms produce intermediate goods based on the technology using a production function, as follows.

$$Y_{it} = K_{it}^{\alpha} N_{it}^{1-\alpha} \quad (0 < \alpha < 1) \tag{13.9}$$

where:

$K_{it}$ = capital stock that was inputted into production of the ith good
$N_{it}$ = labor that was inputted into production of the ith good

To determine the price of factors of production, we consider the optimization condition for cost minimization. At this time, we can define the Lagrangian function as follows, where $\omega_{it}$ is the Lagrangian multiplier.

$$M = w_{it} N_{it} + r_{it} K_{it} + \omega_{it} \left( Y_{it} - K_{it}^{\alpha} N_{it}^{1-\alpha} \right) \tag{13.10}$$

By minimizing the costs for $N_{it}$ and $K_{it}$, we can obtain the relationship between the price of factors of production and marginal productivity of factors of production as follows.

$$w_{it} = \omega_{it}(1-\alpha)\left(\frac{K_{it}}{N_{it}}\right)^{\alpha} \tag{13.11}$$

$$r_{it} = \omega_{it}\alpha\left(\frac{K_{it}}{N_{it}}\right)^{\alpha-1} \tag{13.12}$$

If wages are different between firms, workers will move to seek higher wages and wages will be equal among firms. If the interest rate differs between firms, it is possible to invest in a place with a higher interest rate, so it is considered that the interest rate will also be equal among firms. Accordingly, we can consider that the capital labor ratio $\frac{K_{it}}{N_{it}}$ becomes equal from (13.11) and (13.12), and that $\omega_{it}$ is also equal.

As the production function is linear homogeneous, we can express the equation for total cost $C$ from (13.11) and (13.12) as follows.

$$C = w_t N_{it} + r_t K_{it} = \omega_t Y_{it} \tag{13.13}$$

Note that in this equation, the Lagrangian multiplier $\omega_t$ can be considered to be the marginal cost of $Y_{it}$.

Next, we obtain the equation for the intermediate-good firms' profit function, which takes into account demand, from (13.6) and (13.13), as follows.

$$\pi_{it} = \frac{p_{it}}{p_t}\left(\frac{p_{it}}{p_t}\right)^{-\varepsilon} Y_t - \omega_t\left(\frac{p_{it}}{p_t}\right)^{-\varepsilon} Y_t \tag{13.14}$$

Therefore, we can set $p_{it}$ so that intermediate-good firms maximize the profit of (13.14). The resulting equation is as follows. This equation becomes the starting point for Calvo-type price setting.

$$\omega_t = \frac{\varepsilon-1}{\varepsilon}\frac{p_{it}}{p_t} \tag{13.15}$$

Accordingly, we can form the following equation if we consider firms are indiscrete for price-setting purposes.

$$\omega = \frac{\varepsilon-1}{\varepsilon} \tag{13.16}$$

Because of monopolistic competition, $\omega$ is generally not 1. At this time, as shown in (13.13), the total cost will be a fixed percentage of production output, and the rest will be distributed as excess profit. In this paper, we consider this excess profit as part of household receipts. If $\varepsilon$ is infinite, it becomes perfect competition, $\omega = 1$, excess profit does not occur, and all income is distributed to labor income and capital income.

### 13.2.3 Government

In this paper, the government pays unemployment benefit. The political budget constraints of unemployment benefits are as follows, with unemployment benefits being paid based on a balanced budget.

$$T_t = (1 - N_t)\, u_t \tag{13.17}$$

We assume that the collective tax $T_t$ is constant over time $T_t = T$.

### 13.2.4 Labor Unions

The existence of labor unions is a notable feature of this paper's model economy. The purpose of the labor unions is to decide the wage rate and employment rate using a method that maximizes total income $V_t$ in each given time $t$.

$$V_t = N_t w_t + (1 - N_t)\, u_t \tag{13.18}$$

Households supply one unit of labor inflexibly while firms decide labor demand based on the labor demand function (13.11). As (13.11) shows, labor demand declines with the rise in wage rate, and the employment rate declines. Labor unions consider the labor demand from firms, and in other words, by using Eq. (13.18) with (13.11) substituted into it, the wage rate that maximizes for $N_t$ is decided. The wage rate $w_t^u$ that is required by labor union at that time is as follows.

$$w_t^u = \frac{u_t}{1 - \alpha} \tag{13.19}$$

The following graph shows the wage rate and employment rate when labor unions exist.

As Fig. 13.1 shows, if labor unions exist, wage rate is decided by the level of $\bar{w}_t$ where labor demand matches labor supply. Note that population size has been standardized to 1 in this paper, and population growth does not exist. As one unit of labor time is supplied inflexibly, labor supply is 1, and, therefore, $1 - N_t$ becomes the unemployment rate.

We can show the wage rate required by labor unions from (13.17) and (13.19) as follows.

$$w_t^u = \frac{T}{(1 - \alpha)(1 - N_t)} \tag{13.20}$$

In this chapter, we consider the wage rate level required by labor unions requires a fixed adjustment period rather than as something that is adopted instantaneously. Therefore, we determine the wage rate based on the following equation.

$$w_t = \sigma w_t^u + (1 - \sigma)\, w_{t-1} = \sigma \frac{T}{(1 - \alpha)(1 - N_t)} + (1 - \sigma)\, w_{t-1} \tag{13.21}$$

where $\sigma$ denotes the adjustment level of wage rate.

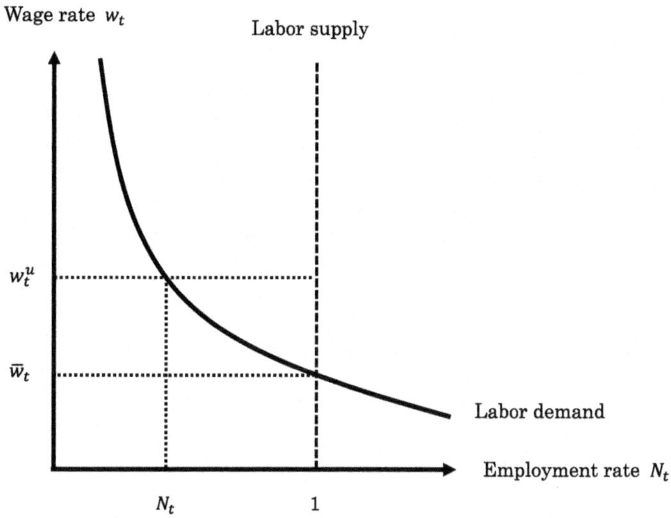


**Fig. 13.1** Relationship between real wage rate and employment rate

### 13.2.5 Introduction of Price Rigidity

Calvo (1983) assumes that each firm in monopolistic competition cannot set optimum prices in each period for certain reasons. In other words, when each firm sets prices, it considers the probability that the price can be changed and the probability that the price cannot be changed. Because prices are found through this determination, the price initially departs from the optimum price $p_t^*$. We can express an optimum price that satisfies (13.15) as follows.

$$\ln p_t^* = \ln \frac{\varepsilon}{\varepsilon - 1} + \ln \omega_t + \ln p_t \tag{13.22}$$

For the convenience of later calculations, we show (13.22) logarithmically. Among the entire population of firms, if the ratio $\rho$ can set the price to the optimum price, and the ratio $1 - \rho$ cannot set the optimum price, firms are able to change the price to the optimum price with a probability of $\rho$, and they are unable to change the price to the optimum price with a probability of $1 - \rho$. Assuming this, we can express the set price determined by the firm as follows.

$$\begin{aligned} \ln x_t &= \rho \ln p_t^* + \rho (1 - \rho)\, E_t \ln p_t^* + \cdots \\ &= \rho \ln p_t^* + (1 - \rho)\, E_t \ln x_{t+1} \end{aligned} \tag{13.23}$$

If we define $\ln \Delta x_{t+1} = \ln x_{t+1} - \ln x_t$, and substitute (13.22) into (13.23), we get the following equation.

$$E_t \ln \Delta x_{t+1} = \rho E_t \ln x_{t+1} - \rho \left( \ln \frac{\varepsilon}{\varepsilon - 1} + \ln \omega_t + \ln p_t \right) \tag{13.24}$$

On the other hand, as the price level $p_t$ is a weighted average of $x_t$, set by a firm that is able to change the price in the period $t$, and $p_{t-1}$, set by a firm that is unable to change the in the period $t-1$, we can form an equation as follows.

$$\ln p_t = \rho \ln x_t + (1 - \rho) \ln p_{t-1} \tag{13.25}$$

If we consider $1 + \pi_t = \frac{p_t}{p_{t-1}}$, we can show the relationship between $\rho \ln x_t$ and the inflation rate as follows.

$$\rho \ln x_t = \ln (1 + \pi_t) + \rho \ln p_{t-1} \tag{13.26}$$

$$\rho E_t \ln x_{t+1} = E_t \ln (1 + \pi_{t+1}) + \rho \ln p_t \tag{13.27}$$

By subtracting from both sides of (13.26) and (13.27), we obtain the following equation.

$$\rho E_t \ln \Delta x_{t+1} = E_t \ln (1 + \pi_{t+1}) - (1 - \rho) \ln (1 + \pi_t) \tag{13.28}$$

Then, by substituting (13.27) and (13.28) into (13.24), we obtain the following equation.

$$\ln (1 + \pi_t) = E_t \ln (1 + \pi_{t+1}) + \frac{\rho^2}{1 - \rho} \left( \ln \frac{\varepsilon}{\varepsilon - 1} + \ln \omega_t \right) \tag{13.29}$$

By finding a linear approximation of this equation with a steady state, we obtain the following equation.

$$\tilde{\pi}_t = E_t \tilde{\pi}_{t+1} + \frac{\rho^2}{1 - \rho} \hat{\omega}_t \tag{13.30}$$

where
$\tilde{\pi}_t$ = the change level of $\pi_t$
$\hat{\omega}_t$ = the change rate of $\omega_t$

### 13.2.6 Monetary Policy

We form equations for monetary policy based on Taylor's rule, as follows.

$$\tilde{i}_t = \chi \tilde{i}_{t-1} + (1 - \chi) \left\{ \phi_1 E_t \tilde{\pi}_{t+1} + \phi_2 \hat{Y}_t \right\}, \ 0 < \chi < 1, \ 0 < \phi_1, \ 0 < \phi_2 \tag{13.31}$$

$\tilde{i}_t$ = the change level of $i_t$
$\hat{Y}_t$ = the change rate of $Y_t$

The model derivation in the above can clearly be seen. The DSGE modeling actually used in this paper is summarized in the Appendix, for the reader's convenience.

## 13.3 Preparations

### *13.3.1 Data*

The data used in the estimations comprised the 7 variables of GDP, consumption, investment, wage rate, employment rate, inflation rate, and interest rate, which were taken from the period from first quarter of 1990 until the second quarter of 2013. Of these variables, we used residuals obtained using the Prescott filter for GDP, consumption, investment, wage rate, and employment rate. We defined the employment rate as (1 – unemployment rate) and used a real wage index as the wage rate for which we set 2010 as 100. For both inflation rate and interest rate, we used the respective deviations from the period averages. Taking into account that Abenomics was put into effect substantively from the beginning of 2013, we considered that time to be the appropriate end point for the data period. Also, we excluded the data from before 1990 to avoid the effect of the so-called bubble economy on model estimation.

### *13.3.2 Prior Distribution of Parameters*

We set up the prior distribution of parameters as shown in Table 13.1. Generally, the values we used were similar to prior research. With respect to convergence relationships, however, we assume that the values $\delta$, $\alpha$, $N$ and $S$"(1) followed a uniform distribution. We consider this to be in line with the spirit of Bayesian statistics, i.e. if the parameters are known to be in the vicinity of certain value, this should be actively taken advantage of. As shown in Table 13.2, we performed calibration for the steady state of variables. Please refer to the Appendix for other parameter settings.

## 13.4 Estimation Results

### *13.4.1 Posterior Distribution of Parameters*

The posterior distribution parameter averages and credible intervals are listed in Table 13.3. From this, we learn that reasonable estimates have been obtained for

**Table 13.1** Settings for prior distribution of parameters

| | Init. value | Min value | Max | Distribution | Average | Std. dev. |
|---|---|---|---|---|---|---|
| $\theta$ | 1 | | 10 | Normal distribution | 1 | 4 |
| $\delta$ | 0.05 | 0.01 | 0.1 | Uniform distribution | | |
| $\alpha$ | 0.33 | 0.23 | 0.43 | Uniform distribution | | |
| $\rho$ | 0.25 | | 0.9999 | Normal distribution | 0.25 | 0.2 |
| $\chi$ | 0.7 | | 0.9999 | $\beta$ distribution | 0.6 | 0.25 |
| $\phi_1$ | 2 | | 10 | Normal distribution | 2 | 4 |
| $\phi_2$ | 0.2 | | 10 | Normal distribution | 0.2 | 0.25 |
| $N$ | 0.95 | 0.9 | 0.98 | Uniform distribution | | |
| $S''(1)$ | 0.13 | | 10 | Normal distribution | 0.13 | 3 |
| $\sigma$ | 0.05 | | 0.5 | Uniform distribution | | |
| Std. dev: NKPC shock | 1.5 | | 10 | Inverse gamma distribution | 1.5 | 4 |
| Std. dev: Technology shock | 1.5 | | 10 | Inverse gamma distribution | 1.5 | 4 |
| Std. dev: Preference shock | 1.5 | | 10 | Inverse gamma distribution | 1.5 | 4 |
| Std. dev: Monetary policy (tightening) shock | 1.5 | | 10 | Inverse gamma distribution | 1.5 | 4 |
| Std. dev: Employment shock | 1.5 | | 10 | Inverse gamma distribution | 1.5 | 4 |
| Std. dev: Investment adjustment cost shock | 1.5 | | 10 | Inverse gamma distribution | 1.5 | 4 |
| AR(1) coeff: NKPC shock | 0.5 | | 0.9999 | $\beta$ distribution | 0.6 | 0.25 |
| AR(1) coeff: Technology shock | 0.5 | | 0.9999 | $\beta$ distribution | 0.6 | 0.25 |
| AR(1) coeff: Preference shock | 0.5 | | 0.9999 | $\beta$ distribution | 0.6 | 0.25 |
| AR(1) coeff: Monetary policy (tightening) shock | 0.5 | | 0.9999 | $\beta$ distribution | 0.6 | 0.25 |
| AR(1) coeff: Employment shock | 0.5 | | 0.9999 | $\beta$ distribution | 0.6 | 0.25 |
| AR(1) coeff: Investment adjustment cost shock | 0.5 | | 0.9999 | $\beta$ distribution | 0.6 | 0.25 |

**Table 13.2** Calibrated parameters

| | | |
|---|---|---|
| $\frac{C}{Y}$ | Steady state consumption calculation ratio | 0.8 |
| $\frac{I}{Y}$ | Steady state investment calculation ratio | 0.2 |
| $\pi$ | Steady state inflation ratio | 0 |
| $q$ | Steady state $q$ | 1 |

most parameters. However, the value of 9.02 as the posterior average of $S''(1)$ is a large value compared with the same value of Eguchi (2011). Moreover, the value of 0.44 as the posterior average of $\sigma$ suggests that the effect of past wage rates has a

**Table 13.3** Posterior parameter distribution

| | Posterior distribution ave. | Posterior distribution credible interval | |
|---|---|---|---|
| $\theta$ | 1.1982 | 0.9042 | 1.4981 |
| $\delta$ | 0.0849 | 0.0675 | 0.1 |
| $\alpha$ | 0.2485 | 0.23 | 0.2732 |
| $\rho$ | 0.2252 | 0.1762 | 0.2713 |
| $\chi$ | 0.3673 | 0.1914 | 0.5367 |
| $\phi_1$ | 8.8722 | 7.7406 | 9.9998 |
| $\phi_2$ | 0.1848 | 0.0002 | 0.3547 |
| $N$ | 0.9651 | 0.9506 | 0.98 |
| $S''(1)$ | 9.02 | 7.8557 | 9.9999 |
| $\sigma$ | 0.4438 | 0.3762 | 0.5 |
| Std. dev: NKPC shock | 0.0091 | 0.0001 | 0.018 |
| Std. dev: Technology shock | 0.9877 | 0.9758 | 0.9998 |
| Std. dev: Preference shock | 0.9697 | 0.9537 | 0.9863 |
| Std. dev: Monetary policy (tightening) shock | 0.4014 | 0.176 | 0.5982 |
| Std. dev: Employment shock | 0.8405 | 0.7493 | 0.9332 |
| Std. dev: Investment adjustment cost shock | 0.2041 | 0.1456 | 0.2625 |
| AR(1) coeff: NKPC shock | 6.2438 | 3.5853 | 9.6155 |
| AR(1) coeff: Technology shock | 1.0611 | 0.9352 | 1.1843 |
| AR(1) coeff: Preference shock | 5.7652 | 3.355 | 8.4509 |
| AR(1) coeff: Monetary policy (tightening) shock | 0.5087 | 0.3438 | 0.6679 |
| AR(1) coeff: Employment shock | 1.6875 | 0.8514 | 2.4917 |
| AR(1) coeff: Investment adjustment cost shock | 5.5303 | 4.8293 | 6.281 |

controlling influence. This is a suitable result, however, considering how the current wage rates are determined.

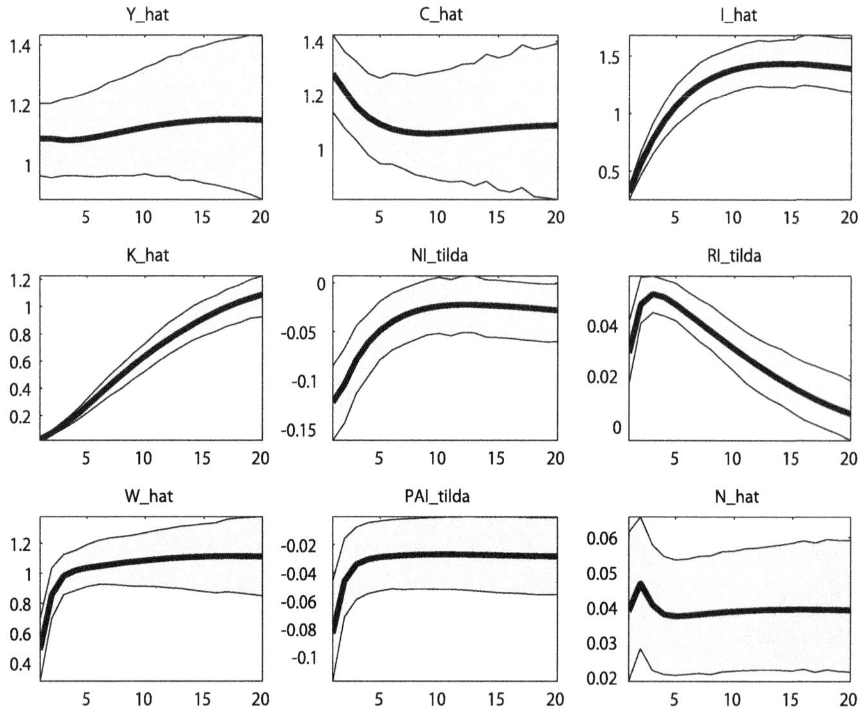


**Fig. 13.2** Impulses in response to productivity shock. Note: From top left: production output(Y_hat, $\hat{Y}_t$), consumption(C_hat, $\hat{c}_t$), investment(I_hat, $\hat{I}_t$), capital stock(K_hat, $\hat{K}_t$), nominal interest rate(NI_tilda, $\tilde{i}_t$), real interest rate(RI_tilda, $\tilde{r}_t$), wage rate(W_hat, $\hat{w}_t$), inflation rate(PAI_tilda, $\tilde{\pi}_t$), and employment rate(N_hat, $\hat{N}_t$).[3]

## 13.4.2 Impulses

To examine model validity, let's check the impulse response functions of the productivity shock, preference shock, and monetary easing shock.

First, Fig. 13.2 shows the impulse response functions for productivity shock. Based on these results, we see that if the productivity shock is positive, production, consumption and investment all rise. At the same time, nominal interest rate, real interest rate and inflation rate are also rising. Wage rate and employment rate are expanding and sustainability can be observed. Overall, we see suitable curves in line with economic theory.

Next let's look at the impulses of the preference shocks (Fig. 13.3). Based on these shocks, a growth in consumption can be observed due to the expansion of the utility of the current period's consumption. As prices rise as a result of this, inflation advances, and nominal and real interest rates also rise. Rising interest rates, however, lowers

[3]"hat" and "tilda" show the change rate and the change level of the variable, respectively.

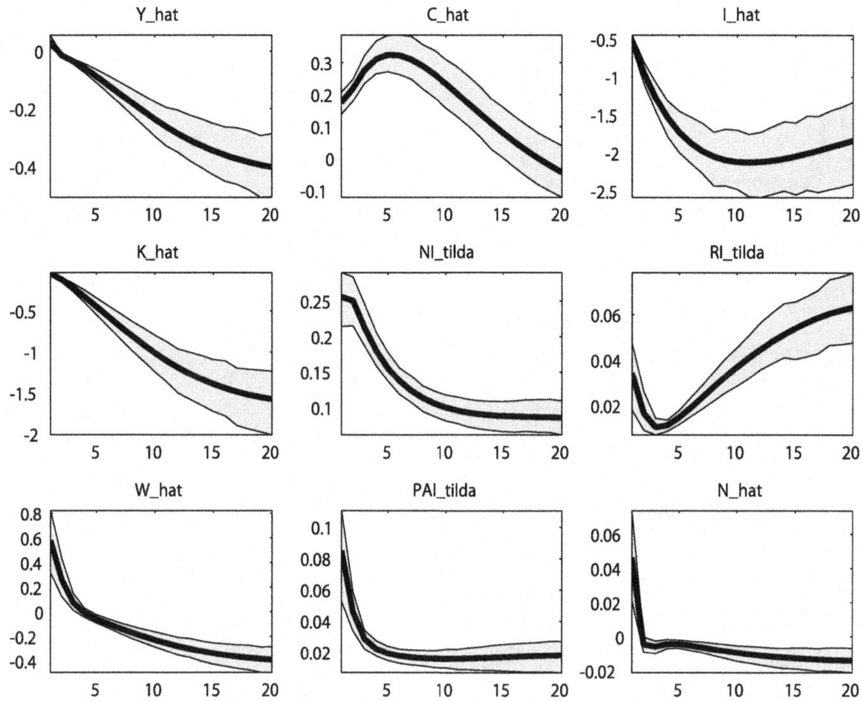


**Fig. 13.3** Impulses in response to preferential shock. Note: From top left: production output, consumption, investment, capital stock, nominal interest rate, real interest rate, wage rate, inflation rate, and employment rate

investment, and as a result, we see a decline in production output. Employment is also positive in the initial period, reflecting the expansion of consumption, but then as time passes, it will be brought back down in the negative direction by the drop in production output. From the above, the phenomenon that can be reproduced from the impulse of the preferential shock is almost the same as the one predicted by theory.

Lastly, the impulses of monetary easing shock are shown below (Fig. 13.4). As a response to monetary easing, production, consumption and investment are all expanding. Wages rise, and employment also improves. Naturally, inflation is also occurring. Unfortunately, nominal interest rate rises slightly, and the real interest rate also turns positive. Although the movement in interest rates in response to monetary easing shock is inexplicable, we can say that overall, the obtained results are natural.

The shapes of the impulse response functions above provide us with decent basis for our judgment that this paper's model is estimating parameters whose results mostly replicate the theory. In the next section, we at last turn our analysis to employment.

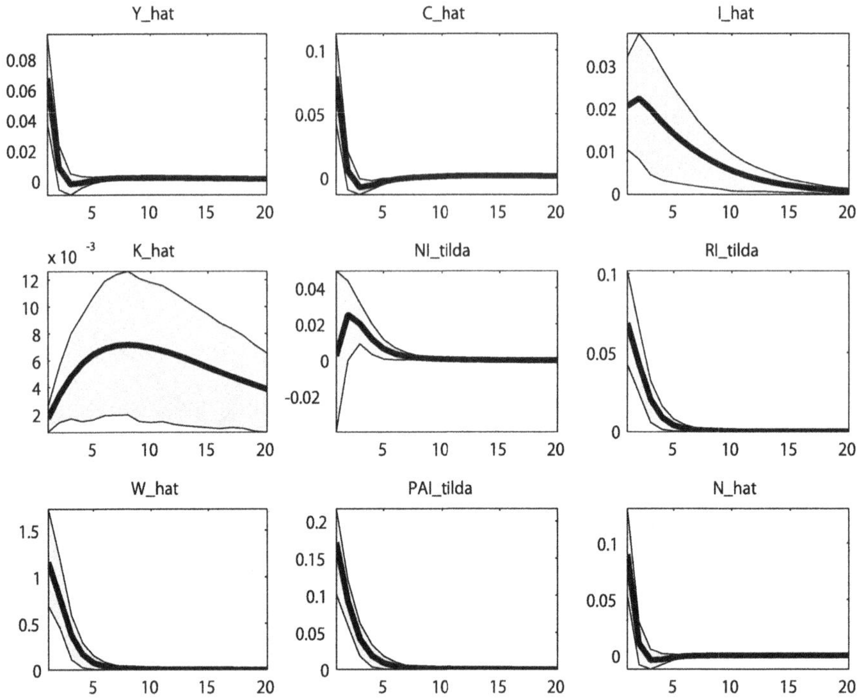


**Fig. 13.4** Impulses in response to monetary easing shock. Note: From top left: production output, consumption, investment, capital stock, nominal interest rate, real interest rate, wage rate, inflation rate, and employment rate

## 13.5 Abenomics and Employment

### *13.5.1 Inflation Target Shock*

It goes without saying that the most pressing economic policy in Japan under Abenomics is the setting of a 2% inflation target. However, as we have next to no idea on what kinds of things should be incorporated as the shock of the inflation target, we decided on the following approach.

First of all, in terms of related variables, there naturally exists $E_t\tilde{\pi}_{t+1} = E_t(\pi_{t+1} - \pi)$. Even before inflation targets were explicitly introduced, it would be safe to assume that common perceptions were held regarding $\pi$ among officials in charge of economic policy. We should bear in mind Japan's lost decade when considering $\pi$. It probably was at 0 or in some cases even negative. The significance of setting a 2% inflation target in the context of such an economy is really the fact that $\pi$ will rise. In the end, you could say it is about $E_t\tilde{\pi}_{t+1}$ taking on a negative value. So we decided to treat a shock from inflation target the same as the shock of $E_t\tilde{\pi}_{t+1}$ taking on a negative value, and we incorporated this into the model.

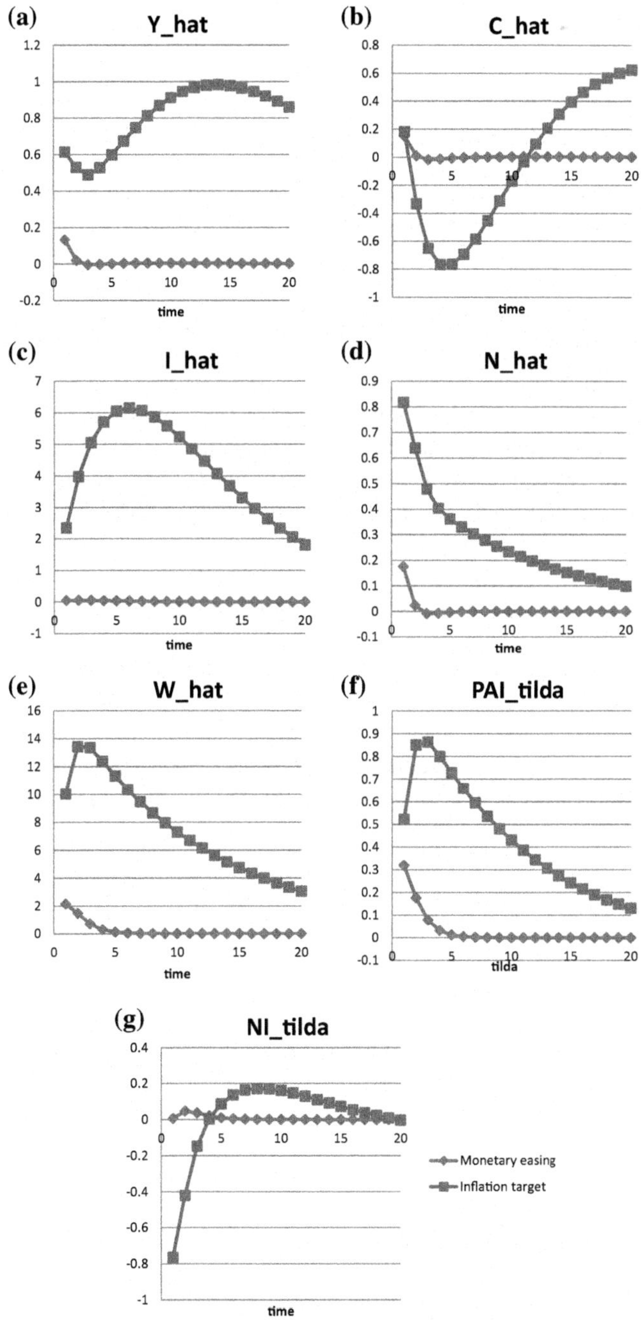


**Fig. 13.5** **a** Production output, **b** Consumption, **c** Investment, **d** Employment rate, **e** Wage rate, **f** Inflation rate, **g** Nominal interest rate

### *13.5.2 Inflation Target Shock and Employment*

The following figure shows the impulse response function for inflation target shock. We also show the impulse response function for monetary easing shock from the previous section for comparison (Fig. 13.5).

Under the impact of inflation target shock, investment is increasing due to confidence in future inflation, and consumption has also turned positive for the first period at least. As a result, production output is expanding. Along with this, the wage rate is rising and employment is improving as well. The inflation rate, of course, is rising. Especially interesting is that the discrepancy of the nominal interest rate from the steady state has turned negative.

Comparing this with the monetary easing shock, our attention is attracted to the trend of production output. In the first period, production output's impulse in response to the inflation target shock is four times that of monetary easing shock. This clearly indicates that the effect of inflation target outperforms that of monetary easing shock. In terms of sustainability, also, the effect of the inflation target shock has a much longer impact.

It is worthwhile to compare the above simulation results with the trends of actual data. Figure 13.6 shows graphs of the major statistical data up until the first quarter of 2018.

According to the graphs of Fig. 13.6, the unemployment rate is falling (employment rate is rising), and the GDP deflator is also on an upward trend. Also, the nominal wage rate is rising slightly. These are consistent with the results of the impulse response functions of the inflation target shock. However, as real wage rate is falling, so in this regard, the simulation results do not reflect the reality.

## 13.6 Conclusion

In this chapter, we performed Bayesian estimation through DSGE modeling and analyzed the effect of the shock of inflation target on the economy. According to our analysis, we predicted that the inflation target has the effect of increasing production output, improving employment and advancing inflation. We also showed that compared with the shock of monetary easing, this effect was larger and more sustainable.

This investigation is a milestone toward our major goal of analyzing real-life economic problems using DSGE modeling, which has become a mainstream method in Europe and the United States. Various issues still remain, of course, on our path toward dealing with these big issues. For example, the modeling we use in this paper does not take into account foreign currency exchange and its effect on the Japanese economy. We are therefore unable to analyze the effect of yen depreciation, one of the effects of Abenomics, on the domestic economy. Our modeling also does not include the mechanism for following the tax reforms implemented to achieve the

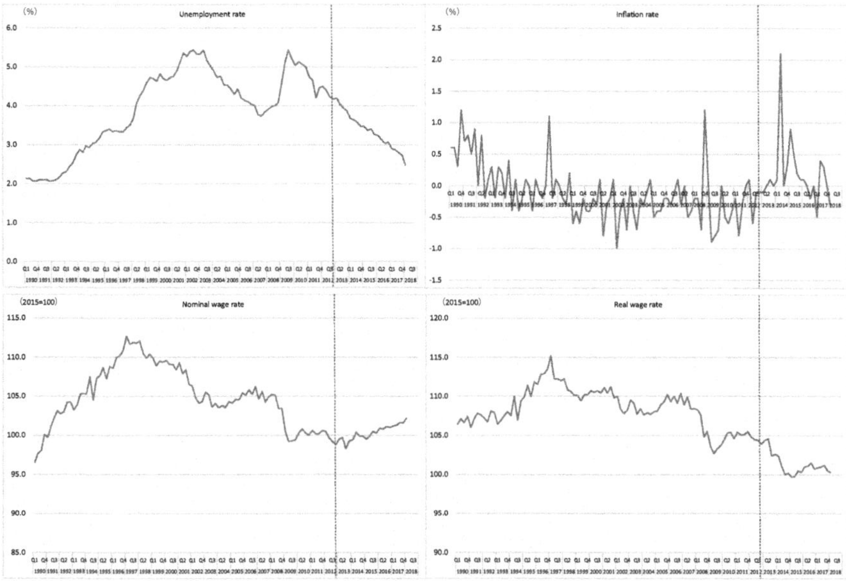


**Fig. 13.6** Trends of major statistics

growth that has become the symbolic promise of corporate tax cuts. We consider these issues to be important research challenges for the future. We would like to continue to develop our research so that it may play its role in full-scale empirical analysis utilizing DSGE modeling.

**Acknowledgements** We would like to thank seminar participants for helpful comments. Research for this paper was supported financially by JSPS KAKENHI Grant Numbers 26380367. Nevertheless, any remaining errors are the authors' responsibility.

## 13.7 Appendix

**Structure of log-linear approximation model**

Here, we clearly show the relationship between the model developed in this paper and the DSGE model used for the simulation. The following equations (13.C.1) through (13.C.10) are, respectively, goods market equilibrium equations of (13.3), (13.9), (13.30), log-linear approximated terms or actual terms of (13.B.3), (13.B.1), (13.12), (13.21), (13.31), (13.A.4), (13.B.1) and (13.B.3). Through this process, $\omega$ appears, but this is erased using (13.11).

$$\tilde{\pi}_t = \mathrm{E_t}\tilde{\pi}_{t+1} + \frac{\rho^2}{1-\rho}\left(\hat{w}_\mathrm{t} - \alpha\hat{K}_\mathrm{t} + \alpha\hat{N}_\mathrm{t}\right) \tag{13.C.1}$$

$$\hat{Y}_\mathrm{t} = \hat{K}_\mathrm{t} + (1-\alpha)\,\hat{N}_\mathrm{t} \tag{13.C.2}$$

$$\hat{K}_{t+1} = \delta \hat{I}_t + (1 - \delta)\, \hat{K}_t \tag{13.C.3}$$

$$\hat{Y}_{t+1} = \frac{C}{Y}\hat{C}_t + \frac{I}{Y}\hat{I}_t \tag{13.C.4}$$

$$E_t\hat{q}_{t+1} = \frac{1}{1-\delta}\left(\frac{1+i}{1+\pi}\left(\hat{q}_t + E_t(\tilde{i}_{t+1} - \tilde{\pi}_{t+1})\right) - \frac{r}{q}\hat{r}_t\right) \tag{13.C.5}$$

$$\hat{c}_t = E_t\hat{c}_{t+1} - \frac{1}{\theta}E_t\tilde{i}_{t+1} + \frac{1}{\theta}E_t\tilde{\pi}_{t+1} \tag{13.C.6}$$

$$\tilde{i}_t = \chi\tilde{i}_{t-1} + (1-\chi)\left\{\phi_1 E_t\tilde{\pi}_{t+1} + \phi_2\hat{Y}_t\right\} \tag{13.C.7}$$

$$\hat{w}_t = \frac{\sigma}{1-N}\tilde{N}_t + (1-\sigma)\,\hat{w}_{t-1} \tag{13.C.8}$$

$$\hat{r}_t = \left(\hat{w}_t - \alpha\hat{K}_t + \alpha\hat{N}_t\right) + (\alpha - 1)\,\hat{K}_t - (\alpha - 1)\,\hat{N}_t \tag{13.C.9}$$

$$\hat{I}_t = \frac{1+i}{2+i+\pi}\hat{I}_{t-1} + \frac{1+\pi}{2+i+\pi}E_t\hat{I}_{t+1} + \frac{1+i}{(2+i+\pi)\,S''(1)}\hat{q}_t \tag{13.C.10}$$

Note, however, that the estimation was further set as follows:

$$\frac{C}{Y} = \text{Steady state consumption calculation ratio} = 0.8$$

$$\frac{I}{Y} = \text{Steady state investment calculation ratio} = 0.2$$

$$\frac{1+i}{1+\pi} = \frac{1}{\beta} = \frac{1}{0.995}$$

$$\frac{r}{q}\hat{r}_t = \frac{1}{q}r\hat{r}_t = \frac{1}{1}\tilde{r}_t = \tilde{r}_t$$

$$\frac{\sigma}{1-N} = \frac{\sigma}{1-0.95}$$

$$\hat{r}_t = \frac{\tilde{r}_t}{r} = \frac{\tilde{r}_t}{r} = \frac{\tilde{r}_t}{\left\{\frac{1}{\beta} - (1-\delta)\right\}q} = \frac{\tilde{r}_t}{\left\{\frac{1}{0.995} - (1-\delta)\right\}1}$$

$$\frac{1+i}{2+i+\pi} = \frac{1}{1+\beta}$$

$$\frac{1+\pi}{2+i+\pi} = \frac{\beta}{1+\beta}$$

## References


Calvo, G. 1983. Staggered Prices in A Utility-Maximizing Framework. *Journal of Monetary Economics* 12: 383–398.

Eguchi, M. 2011. *Dogakuteki ippan kinko moderu ni yoru zaisei seisaku no bunseki* (Analysis of Fiscal Policy Through Dynamic General Equilibrium Modeling), in Japanese, Mitsubishi Economic Research Institute.

Kato, R. 2007. *Gendai makurokeizaigaku kōgi* (Lecture on Modern Macroeconomics), in Japanese, Toyo Keizai Inc.

Fujiwara, I., and T. Watanabe. 2011. Makuro dōgaku ippan kinkō moderu – sābei to Nihon no makurodēta e no ōyō –, (Dynamic General Equilibrium Model–A Survey with the Application to the Japanese Macroeconomic Date–), in Japanese, *Keizai Kenkyu* 62 (1): 66–93.

Christiano, L.J., M. Eichenbaum, and C. Evans. 2005. Nominal Rigidities and the Dynamic Effects of a Shock to Monetary Policy. *Journal of Political Economy* 113 (1): 1–45.

Iwata, Y. 2009. Fiscal Policy in an Estimated DSGE Model of the Japanese Economy: Do Non-Ricardian Households Explain All, *ESRI Discussion Paper Series* No. 216.

Iwata, Y. 2012. Non-Wasteful Government Spending in an Estimated Open Economy DSGE Model: Two Fiscal Policy Puzzles Revisited, *ESRI Discussion Paper Series* No. 285.

Smets, F., and R. Wouters. 2003. An Estimated Dynamic Stochastic General Equilibrium Models of the Euro Area. *Journal of the European Economic Association* 1 (5): 1123–1175.

Smets, F., and R. Wouters. 2007. Shocks and Frictions in US Business Cycles: A Bayesian DSGE Approach. *The American Economic Review* 97 (3): 586–606.

Sugo, T., and K. Ueda. 2008. Estimating a Dynamic Stochastic General Equilibrium Model for Japan. *Journal of the Japanese and International Economies* 22 (4): 476–502.

# Chapter 14
# The Impacts of Public Spending by Function on Regional Economic Growth and Interregional Income Disparities: Evidence from Korea

**Ki-Dong Lee, Sijin Moon and Jiah Choi**

## 14.1 Introduction

Although the demand for government assistance is rapidly increasing in Korea, it has become increasingly more difficult for the government to secure available financial resources. Amidst stagnant economic growth with considerable unemployment, the working age population in Korea is decreasing owing to the rapid process of fertility declines and population aging, while demand for social welfare and related government spending is increasing continuously. Considering that local governments account for 60% of total government spending in Korea, it is important to investigate the effects of government spending on economic growth from a regional perspective. In addition, as different types of government spending have different effects on output, the analysis should be conducted by distinguishing between the different components of government spending.

Meanwhile, government spending can be used to provide infrastructure, especially for underdeveloped regions from the perspective of regional development. Government spending also can be used to correct income inequalities. Many countries have adopted policies in which government spending aims to reduce inequality, measured as income inequality. This is also true for Korea. Korea has several social spending programs that affect poverty and the income distribution. Direct spending programs include old age pensions, veteran' grants, child grants, foster parent grants, and

K.-D. Lee (✉)
Keimyung University, Daegu, South Korea
e-mail: kdlee@kmu.ac.kr

S. Moon
Pusan National University, Busan, South Korea
e-mail: liebemoon@hanmail.net

J. Choi
Bank of Korea, Seoul, South Korea
e-mail: jachoi@bok.or.kr



M. Hosoe et al. (eds.), *Applied Analysis of Growth, Trade, and Public Policy*,
https://doi.org/10.1007/978-981-13-1876-4_14

disability grants for adults and children. Indirect or in-kind transfers include those for education and health.

In this context, the objective of this paper is twofold. First, we examine the effects of local government expenditures on regional economic growth by exploiting a rich dataset of sectoral regional government expenditures by 16 provinces in Korea during the 1986–2014 period. The dataset includes detailed data on the different components of local government expenditures as well as the private capital stock of 16 provinces in Korea. Regarding the empirical analysis, we estimate the output elasticity of each component of government spending, and we then calculate fiscal multipliers at the provincial level, which help us identify the policy implications for regional government spending.

Second, we examine the impacts of regional government spending on income disparities among regions in Korea for the 1986–2014 period. We test for absolute and conditional $\beta$-convergence on Korean regional provinces to determine whether local fiscal spending reduces the income inequality between regions. The $\beta$-convergence is obtained by a regression analysis that estimates the growth in per capita income for a certain period of time on the initial level of per capita income.

The key differences of this paper from the existing literature are twofold. First, using regional data, this paper presents estimates of the fiscal multiplier of each type of local government expenditure by distinguishing between the different components of government spending. Several studies have also examined the multiplier effects of government spending in Korea (Oh 2006; Kim 2009; Lee and Choe 2015); however, they have examined only the multiplier effects based on country-level data on government expenditures or the effects of a specific sector. The use of regional data enables us to compare the multiplier effects of government spending between provincial regions, which may have implications for regional government spending policy. Second, this paper aims to link regional government spending by function and income inequality between provincial regions. With respect to Korea, many previous studies on government expenditures have mainly addressed the impact of government spending on economic growth; hence, the relationship with income inequality has been neglected. In this paper, we explore the effects of regional government spending on income inequality, with a particular focus on type of government spending.

This paper is organized as follows. Section 14.2 provides a theoretical background on the relationship between government expenditures by function and regional economic growth and offers a review of the literature on the effectiveness of local government expenditures. Using panel data for the 1986–2014 period, Sect. 14.3 investigates the effects of government spending by function on regional economic growth. In addition, this Section derives fiscal multipliers by region and by sector based on the output elasticities of government expenditures. Section 14.4 examines the income convergence hypothesis for Korean regional provinces to determine whether regional government spending reduces the income inequality between regions. Finally, in Sect. 14.5, we summarize the main results of our study and provide concluding remarks.

## 14.2 Background and Literature Review

Local government expenditures in Korea have been classified by a new functional category system since 2008. This categorization increased the number of categories from five to thirteen, following the UN COFOG (Classification of the Functions of Government) in order to merge the classification of functions of local governments with that of the central government. The fourteen categories include (1) general administration, (2) public safety, (3) education, (4) culture and tourism, (5) environmental protection, (6) social welfare, (7) health, (8) agriculture, sea and fishery, (9) industry and small business, (10) logistics and transportation, (11) land and local development, (12) science technology, (13) reserves, and (14) miscellaneous. Except for general administration and public safety of the above-mentioned categories, most categories have characteristics belonging to either social development or economic development.

This study examines the impacts of local government expenditures of four major sectors, which account for a large part of total government expenditures or are classified as productive government expenditure: (1) education and culture, (2) social welfare, (3) regional economy, and (4) transportation and water resources. Of the fourteen categories based on the new categorization system since 2008, the first sector (i.e., education and culture) includes the categories of education, culture, and tourism; the second sector (i.e., social welfare) includes only the social welfare; the third sector (i.e., regional economy) includes industry and small business and science technology; and the last sector (i.e., transportation and water resources) includes logistics and transportation and water resources and industrial complex, which are sub-categories of land and local development. The data are collected for the period 1986–2014, during which the categorization system was revised several times, and we match the codes between the revisions in line with Choe and Lee (2014).

Of the abovementioned four sectors, government expenditure both on education and culture and on social welfare can be captured as social development expenditures, while expenditures both on regional economy and on transportation and water resources corresponds to economic development expenditures. Figure 14.1 shows the time trends of the total magnitude of regional government expenditures on both social development and economic development since 1986. As can be seen in the figure, spending on regional economic development exceeded that on regional social development before 2000. However, this pattern reversed in 2000: regional government spending on social development exceeds that on economic development in most provinces after 2000. In other words, since 2000, reflecting the large demand for social welfare services, regional government spending on public welfare programs has increased rapidly compared with other expenditure items.

Different types of government spending may have a very different effects on output. Regional government expenditure on education and culture can be an effective tool in accumulating human capital in society, which leads to improved efficiency and strengthened production capacity. Consequently, it might have a positive impact on regional economic growth. In fact, some empirical studies have shown that

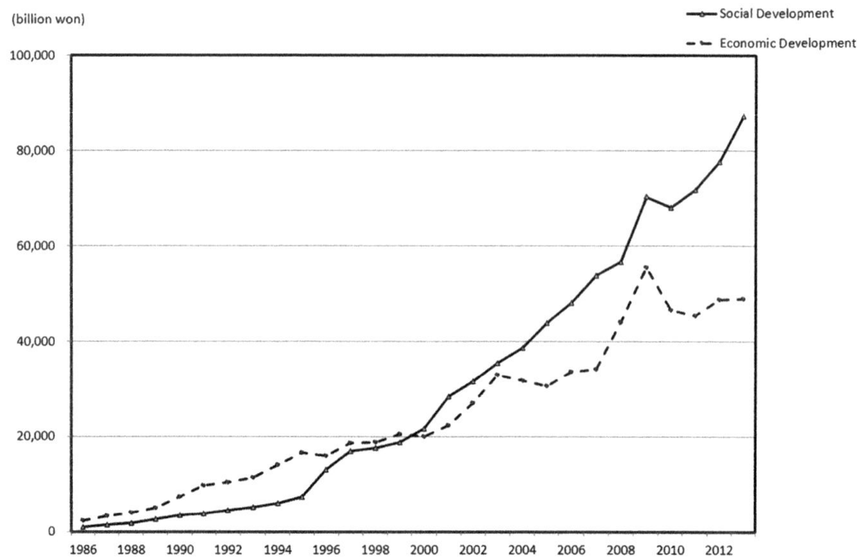


**Fig. 14.1** Trends in government expenditure

education fosters human capital, which increases labor productivity, and thus increases economic growth (Fleisher et al. 2011; Lucas 1988; Mankiw et al. 1992; Oketch 2006; Teixeira and Fortuna 2004).

On the other hand, the literature on the relationship between regional government expenditures on social welfare and regional economic growth offers mixed results. One group of scholars argue that government spending on welfare-related programs promotes economic growth. For instance, Wolfe (2002) contends that welfare improves growth because welfare recipients who achieve higher levels of education undertake employment at higher wages, providing a return of taxation and higher levels of investment (see also McCallum and Blais 1987; McDonald and Miller 2010). Similarly, Brooks and Manza (2007) finds a positive association between welfare expenditures and economic productivity.

In contrast, regional government expenditure on social welfare can hinder regional economic growth (Persson and Tabellini 1994). A main assertion of this view is on the relationship between government expenditures and incentives to work, whereby welfare programs by the regional government tend to encourage recipients to remain unemployed. As Lindbeck et al. (1993) note, welfare incentives can limit growth by creating an overburdened economy. Lichter and Jayakody (2002) find that while welfare expenditures help reduce poverty, they provide no positive return on investment to the economy because they may "crowd out" economic activity in the private sector.

Government spending on the regional economy implies indirect support to industry and firms, and it specifically includes the support for industry technology, trade, and investment attraction; the development of energy and resources; support for industry and small and medium-sized firms; and research and development in the science technology sector. Government spending on transportation and water resources includes spending on roads, railways, ports, maritime transport, airports, logistics, and the development of water resources. This type of government spending contributes to setting up infrastructure, which facilitates the movement of goods and creates a productive economic environment. According to Aschauer (1989), Garcia-Milà et al. (1996), and Moon et al. (2015), government spending on the regional economy and infrastructure leads to an accumulation of public capital, which in turn increases the marginal product of factor of production and promotes regional economic growth.

## 14.3 Methodology and Estimation

### *14.3.1 Model and Data*

In this section, we investigate the effects of regional government spending by function on GRDP for the period 1986–2014. To test the effects, we use the modified equation suggested by Bruckner and Tuladhar (2010), which estimates the output elasticity of government spending. The basic model is as follows:

$$\ln y_{i,t} = const. + \alpha_1 \ln c_{i,t} + \alpha_2 \ln s_{i,t} + \alpha_3 \ln e_{i,t} + \alpha_4 \ln so_{i,t} + \beta \ln tx_{i,t} + \varepsilon_{i,t}, \tag{14.1}$$

where dependent variable $y_{i,t}$ represents per-capita GRDP in province $i$ at time $t$, and for the explanatory variables, $c_{i,t}$ is regional government spending on education and culture, $s_{i,t}$ is that on social welfare, $e_{i,t}$ is that on regional economy, $so_{i,t}$ is that on transportation and water resources, $tx_{i,t}$ is the share of local tax in per-capita GDP, and $\varepsilon_{i,t}$ is the error term. All variables of interest are measured in per-capita terms.

In addition, to confirm the robustness of the estimated output elasticity of government spending, we add a Cobb-Douglas production function in the estimation. According to Oh (2014), compared with other regions, firms show higher productivity in specific regions where expenditures by local governments are implemented effectively. This provides the justification of including not only labor and capital but also variables associated with public investment as inputs in the production function. For example, Aschauer (1989), Barro (1990), Barro and Sala-i-Martin (1995), Roh et al. (1995), and Oh (2014) explicitly incorporate the government sector in the production function. The following Eq. (14.2) represents the per-capita production function, where $pk_{i,t}$, private capital stock in the region, is newly entered in the explanatory variables. All the variables are measured in per-capita terms.

$$\ln y_{i,t} = \text{constant} + \alpha_1 \ln c_{i,t} + \alpha_2 \ln s_{i,t} + \alpha_3 \ln e_{i,t} + \alpha_4 \ln so_{i,t} + \beta \ln pk_{i,t} + \varepsilon_{i,t}. \tag{14.2}$$

Next, we examine the effects of structural changes on regional economic activities. To this end, we include interaction terms including dummy variable $d$ in the estimation model as in Eq. (14.3).

$$\ln y_{i,t} = \text{constant} + \alpha_{11} \ln c_{i,t} + \alpha_{12} \ln c_{i,t} \times d + \alpha_{21} \ln s_{i,t} + \alpha_{22} \ln s_{i,t} \times d \\ + \alpha_{31} \ln e_{i,t} + \alpha_{32} \ln e_{i,t} \times d + \alpha_{41} \ln so_{i,t} + \alpha_{42} \ln so_{i,t} \times d + \beta \ln tx_{i,t} + \varepsilon_{i,t} \tag{14.3}$$

With respect to Korea, it seems that a structural change occurred in 1996 and/or in 2000 in our sample period for the following reasons. The first structural change reflects the effects of the introduction of the local autonomous system in Korea. Korea initiated a full-fledged local autonomous system in the summer of 1995, which reinforced the decentralization of the Korean political system. This structural change may have affected not only the magnitude but also the composition of local government spending around 1996.

In addition, we conjecture that a structural break occurred in 2000, as social development expenditures exceed economic development expenditures in most provinces after this time point. As can be seen in Fig. 14.1, government expenditures on regional economic development exceed that on welfare programs before 2000; however, this pattern is reversed in 2000: that is, government spending on welfare programs exceeds that on regional economic development in most provinces after 2000. In other words, since 2000, local government spending on public welfare programs has rapidly increased compared with other expenditure items.

We include four interaction dummy variables, namely, $(\ln c_{i,t} \times d)$, $(\ln s_{i,t} \times d)$, $(\ln e_{i,t} \times d)$, and $(\ln so_{i,t} \times d)$, in the estimation model. If a structural change occurred in 1996, then dummy variable $d$ takes the value 1 if the observation units are after 1996 and zero otherwise. If the estimated coefficients on government spending for $c_{i,t}$(i.e., education and culture), $\alpha_{11}$and $\alpha_{12}$, are positive and statistically significant, then the output elasticity of government spending for education and culture is $\alpha_{11}$ for the period before 1996, while that of government spending for education and culture is $\alpha_{11} + \alpha_{12}$ for the period after 1996. On the other hand, if the estimated coefficient of $\alpha_{12}$ is statistically insignificant, then the output elasticity of government spending for education and culture is $\alpha_{11}$ for the entire sample period.

In this study, data from each of the 16 provinces in Korea are collected for the period 1986–2014, are outlaid in calendar years, and are expressed in 2010 constant values. Data for GRDP are collected from Statistics Korea, and data for both regional government spending decomposed by function and local tax are obtained from the Financial Yearbook of Local Government and Local Finance Integration Open System (Ministry of the Interior and Safety). Unfortunately, there is no official time series on regional capital stock; thus, we have measured the regional capital stock of 16 metropolitan or provincial regions using the polynomial benchmark year method. Furthermore, the dataset includes time-series on the population 15 years of age and over, which is obtained from Statistics Korea, to transform all variables to per capita terms. The summary statistics of the data are given in Table 14.1.

(Million won)

Table 14.1 Summary statistics of the data

| | Average | Standard deviation | Maximum | Minimum | No. of observations |
|---|---|---|---|---|---|
| GRDP | 54,470,302 | 60,848,495 | 314,626,356 | 2,780,768 | 448 |
| Education and culture | 582,664 | 773,922 | 4,100,531 | 19,593 | 448 |
| Social welfare | 1,105,691 | 1,423,820 | 10,704,210 | 29,856 | 448 |
| Industries and SMEs | 190,255 | 159,093 | 1,333,796 | 3,211 | 448 |
| Transportation and water resources | 1,144,492 | 979,458 | 5,800,029 | 83,436 | 448 |
| Local tax | 2,262,778 | 2,969,799 | 14,116,157 | 71,919 | 448 |
| Private capital stock | 151,165,288 | 167,218,473 | 945,196,782 | 3,272,109 | 448 |
| Population 15 years of age and over | 2,322,862 | 2,163,174 | 10,159,000 | 361,000 | 448 |

### *14.3.2 Government Expenditure and Regional Economic Growth*

Using regional panel data on the 16 metropolitan or provincial regions in Korea during the period 1986–2014, we investigate the effect of regional government spending on regional economic growth. If the time series of 29 years in the panel data shows some time trend, then the panel data are non-stationary. When non-stationary time series are used in a regression model, one may obtain significant relationships from unrelated variables; that is, a spurious regression problem occurs. To investigate the possibility of the non-stationarity of the panel, it is first necessary to determine whether a unit root exists in the data series. Augmented Dickey-Fuller (ADF) tests are conducted for these series at the variable level. We find that the null hypothesis of having a panel unit root is generally rejected in all series at the 1% level of significance, implying that the variables are stationary at the variable level.

Panel data models are usually estimated using either fixed or random effects techniques. To choose between a fixed effects and a random effects model, the Hausman specification test is conducted, and the results show that the fixed effect model is more appropriate for the data. Thus, a fixed effect model is used for the estimations. The results are summarized in Column (1) in Table 14.2.

According to Bruckner and Tuladhar (2010) and Choe and Lee (2014), if the government increases its expenditure during times of recession or decreases it during time of recovery, then there might be endogeneity problem owing to the fiscal policy responding to changes in the economic environment. We include both difference and

**Table 14.2** The impacts of regional government expenditures on GRDP

| | (1) | (2) | (3) |
|---|---|---|---|
| | Fixed Effects | Difference GMM | System GMM |
| Per-capita $GRDP_{t-1}$ | | 0.872*** | 0.879*** |
| | | (38.37) | (35.15) |
| Education and culture | 0.269*** | 0.024*** | 0.024*** |
| | (13.08) | (3.81) | (3.67) |
| Social welfare | 0.090*** | 0.011* | 0.009 |
| | (4.64) | (1.72) | (1.24) |
| Regional economy | 0.042*** | −0.008 | −0.009** |
| | (2.95) | (−1.59) | (−1.99) |
| Transportation and water resources | 0.092*** | 0.021** | 0.027** |
| | (3.69) | (2.29) | (2.05) |
| Share of local tax | −0.160*** | −0.038 | −0.033 |
| | (−3.81) | (−1.53) | (−1.3) |
| Constant | 3.233*** | 0.345*** | 0.342*** |
| | (24.33) | (4.90) | (4.10) |
| $R^2$ | 0.848 | | |
| F or $\chi^2$ | 474.8*** | 40427.3*** | 31120.4*** |

Note: *** is significant at 1% significance level, ** is at 5%, and * is at 10%

system GMM (generalized method of moments) estimation in our analysis to address the concerns of endogeneity bias mentioned above.

The parameter estimates of Eq. (14.2) are reported in Table 14.2. From the estimated coefficients of fixed effects (Column 1), difference GMM (Column 2) and system GMM (Column 3) estimation, we find that most of the estimated output elasticities of each variable are similar across the specifications in terms of both sign and significance.

In Column (2), which shows the estimation results by difference GMM, the coefficient of output elasticity of government spending on education and culture is 0.024, which is statistically significant at the 1% level, and that on transportation and water resources is 0.021, which is also statistically significant at the 1% level. These results indicate that both sectors have positive effects on GRDP. The coefficients of output elasticity of social welfare expenditure are estimated to be positive (0.090 in Column 1 and 0.011 in Column 2) and statistically significant in both Column (1) and Column (2). On the other hand, the estimated coefficients on regional economy vary depending on the estimation methodology. The coefficients on the ratio of local tax are estimated to be negative in all specifications. In particular, the estimated coefficient on this variable is −0.16 in Column (1), which is statistically significant at the 1% level, implying that an increase in local income tax reduces the amount of income that individuals have available to spend, save, or invest.

**Table 14.3** Estimates of the production function

| | (1) | (2) | (3) |
|---|---|---|---|
| | Fixed Effects | Difference GMM | System GMM |
| Per-capita $GRDP_{t-1}$ | | 0.838*** | 0.818*** |
| | | (20.74) | (16.61) |
| Education and culture | 0.149*** | 0.021*** | 0.019*** |
| | (7.97) | (3.34) | (3.05) |
| Social welfare | 0.024 | 0.005 | 0.003 |
| | (1.48) | (0.76) | (0.44) |
| Regional economy | 0.008 | −0.011** | −0.013*** |
| | (0.70) | (−2.018) | (−2.77) |
| Transportation and water resources | 0.054*** | 0.020** | 0.021* |
| | (2.61) | (2.25) | (1.70) |
| Share of local tax | −0.200*** | −0.048* | −0.041* |
| | (−5.81) | (−1.88) | (−1.70) |
| Private capital stock | 0.369*** | 0.043 | 0.068* |
| | (14.69) | (1.26) | (1.80) |
| Constant | 1.242*** | 0.222* | 0.195 |
| | (7.16) | (1.79) | (1.64) |
| $R^2$ | 0.899 | | |
| F or $\chi^2$ | 630.8*** | 19741.7*** | 20045.2*** |

Note: *** is significant at 1% significance level, ** is at 5%, and * is at 10%

However, notably, the above results are obtained on the assumption that per-capita GRDP can be explained only by government expenditure, and they cannot thus take into consideration the private sector factors that influence regional economic growth. To address this problem, we include, as an additional control variable, private capital stock in the estimation of the per-capita production function. Table 14.3 provides the estimation results for this production function.

The estimation results in Table 14.3 are similar to those in Table 14.2. The coefficients on education and culture and on transportation and water resources are estimated to be positive and statistically significant, which is similar to the results in Table 14.2. The elasticity estimates with respect to social welfare expenditures are positive in specifications (1) to (3), albeit insignificant. The coefficient on regional economy is estimated to be positive in Column 1 (fixed effects model) but insignificant, while it is estimated to be negative in both Column 2 (differential GMM) and Column 3 (system GMM) and statistically significant at the 5–10% level. Most of the estimated coefficients on regional economy reported in both Tables 14.3 and 14.4 are negative except for those in Column (1) in Table 14.3. This implies that local government fiscal policy aimed at developing the region's industrial complex and financial sector and to support industrial technology does not have a significant impact on regional economic growth.

Although the magnitude of the estimated coefficients on output elasticity of private capital stock vary across the specifications, the results in both Column (1) and Column (3) are positive and statistically significant, implying that capital stock in the private sector has a positive impact on regional economic growth. In addition, the estimated coefficients on the local tax ratio are negative and statistically significant across the specifications, suggesting that the results are robust.

Structural changes occur in many time series for a number of reasons, including economic crises, changes in institutional arrangements, policy changes, and regime shifts. To account for structural breaks, we include an interaction term involving dummy variables in the estimations. Column (1) of Table 14.4 shows the estimation results including the interaction term, which is introduced to account for the impacts of the local autonomous system in Korea. In this estimation, we regard the adoption of the local autonomous system as an important structural change. The estimate for education and culture is positive and significant (0.038 in Column (1)), while that for the interaction term, education and culture $\times d_{1996}$, is negative and insignificant (i.e., −0.021). This result indicates that the adoption of the local autonomous system in Korea has little relationship with the observed effects, implying that the adoption of the local autonomous system in Korea had little impact on the production efficiency of educational and cultural expenditures by local governments.

In addition, we find that social welfare expenditure has little impact on regional economic growth irrespective of the adoption of the local autonomous system in Korea. Although the estimated coefficient for regional economy is −0.022 and statistically significant for the period before 1996, the coefficient for this variable increases to 0.008 (i.e., −0.022+0.030) and is statistically significant after the introduction of the local autonomous system. However, the small value of the estimated coefficient on regional economy suggests that government expenditure on regional development plays a smaller role in per-capita GRDP. The coefficient on transportation and water resources is 0.052 for the period before 1996, but is reduced to 0.007 (i.e., 0.052–0.045) for the period after 1996.

The above discussion suggests that although the adoption of the local autonomous system in Korea has had little impact on the production efficiency of local government spending on social development (i.e., education and culture, social welfare), it has had a substantial impact on the production efficiency of government spending on economic development (i.e., regional economy, transportation and water resources): that is, the local autonomous system has improved the effectiveness of local government spending on regional economy but has reduced the effectiveness of government spending on transportation and water resources.

Another time-point of structural change that we assume is 2000. Social development expenditure by local governments has exceeded economic development expenditure in most regions after 2000, suggesting that a structural change occurred in about 2000. Column (2) of Table 14.4 shows the estimation results with the assumption that a structural break occurred in about 2000. Unlike the results in Column (1), all coefficients on the interaction terms in Column (2) are statistically significant. The output elasticity of education and culture is estimated to be 0.043 for the period before 2000 but is reduced to −0.007 (i.e., −0.050+0.043) for the period after 2000,

**Table 14.4** The impacts of regional government expenditures on GRDP for sub-periods

| | (1) | | (2) |
|---|---|---|---|
| *Time of structural change* | 1996 | *Time of structural change* | *2000* |
| Estimation Method | System GMM | Estimation Method | System GMM |
| Per-capita $GRDP_{t-1}$ | 0.880*** | Per-capita $GRDP_{t-1}$ | 0.860*** |
| | (36.93) | | (33.19) |
| Education and culture | 0.038*** | Education and culture | 0.043*** |
| | (2.59) | | (3.07) |
| (Education and culture) $\times d_{1996}$ | −0.021 | (Education and culture) $\times d_{2000}$ | −0.050*** |
| | (−1.40) | | (−3.52) |
| Social welfare | 0.0082 | Social Welfare | −0.013 |
| | (0.53) | | (−0.78) |
| (Social welfare) $\times d_{1996}$ | 0.001 | (Social welfare) $\times d_{2000}$ | 0.027* |
| | (0.06) | | (1.73) |
| Regional economy | −0.022*** | Regional economy | −0.015** |
| | (−3.34) | | (−2.03) |
| (Regional economy) $\times d_{1996}$ | 0.030*** | (Regional economy) $\times d_{2000}$ | 0.018** |
| | (4.71) | | (1.97) |
| Transportation and water resources (TWR) | 0.052* | Transportation and water resources (TWR) | 0.035* |
| | (1.96) | | (1.72) |
| (TWR) $\times$ $d_{1996}$ | −0.045** | (TWR) $\times$ $d_{2000}$ | −0.034* |
| | (−2.02) | | (−1.87) |
| Share of local tax | −0.055** | Share of local tax | −0.028 |
| | (−2.21) | | (−1.06) |
| Constant | 0.282*** | Constant | 0.400*** |
| | (3.95) | | (4.06) |
| $\chi^2$ | 101823.1*** | $\chi^2$ | 91010.2*** |

Note: *** is significant at 1% significance level, ** is at 5%, and * is at 10%

implying that the effectiveness of government spending on education and culture decreased sharply after 2000. The estimated coefficient on social welfare is negative and insignificant before 2000 but increases to 0.027 for the period after 2000, indicating that there has been an improvement in terms of the effectiveness of social welfare expenditure on regional economic growth. The estimated coefficients both on regional economy and on transportation and water resources in Column (2) are very similar to those in Column (1). The estimated coefficient on regional economy is −0.015 for the period before 2000 but is 0.003 (i.e., −0.015+0.018) after 2000 while that on transportation and water resources is 0.035 before 2000 but is 0.001 after 2000.

From the analysis, we can conclude that expenditure-reducing policies both on regional economy and on transportation and water resources, which have been widely used measures by the government since the mid1990s, have improved the effectiveness of government spending on regional economy but have reduced that of government spending on transportation and water resources.

### *14.3.3 Government Expenditure Multipliers*

Once the estimates on the output elasticity of each component of government expenditure are obtained, we can calculate the government investment multipliers using Eq. (14.4). That is, a multiplier effect of public investment on regional output is obtained by multiplying the elasticity estimate with the inverse of the average public investment to GDP ratio:

$$\frac{\partial y_{i,t}}{\partial g_{i,t}} = \alpha \times \frac{y_{i,t}}{g_{i,t}} \tag{14.4}$$

In Eq. (14.4), $y_{i,t}$ represents per-capita GRDP in region $i$ at time $t$ and $g_{i,t}$ stands for regional government expenditure by sector, such as education and culture, social welfare, regional economy, and transportation and water resources. In addition, $\alpha$ is the estimated output elasticity of regional government expenditure.

Table 14.5 presents the estimates of the fiscal multiplier for each type of local government expenditure. We calculate the government expenditure multiplier for 16 provinces by distinguishing between the different components, including education and culture, social welfare, and transportation and water resources. When we examine the sectoral multiplier of the country as a whole, the estimated multiplier is 3.2 for education and culture, which is the highest, 1.13 for transportation and water resources, and 0.83 for social welfare. A fiscal multiplier of 3.2 for education and culture implies that an additional dollar of government expenditure on education and culture increases real per-capita GRDP by 3.2 dollars. The multiplier value on government investment in education and culture is significantly larger than one in all regions, implying that expenditure on education and culture by local governments contributes to the regional economic growth.

The estimated multipliers on government investment on social welfare are larger than one for the Capital Region of Korea (that is, Seoul, Incheon, and Gyeonggi province) and Ulsan, while they are lower than one for the remaining regions. The average level of the multiplier for social welfare expenditure is 0.83 for the country as a whole, suggesting that government spending on social welfare has been inefficient. As for government spending on transportation and water resources, the multipliers are estimated to be greater than one for most of the metropolitan regions except Busan and Daegu and for Chungnam province. In addition, the average level of the multiplier without distinguishing by type of government spending is 1.13. This implies that government spending on transportation and water resources is more effective than spending on social welfare. Comparing the multipliers for expenditure

**Table 14.5** Estimates of government investment multiplier by sector and by region

| | Education and culture | Social welfare | Transportation and water resources |
|---|---|---|---|
| Seoul | 3.77 | 1.67 | 2.06 |
| Busan | 2.28 | 0.75 | 0.93 |
| Daegu | 3.15 | 0.75 | 0.94 |
| Incheon | 4.16 | 1.15 | 1.41 |
| Gwangju | 2.30 | 0.56 | 1.08 |
| Daejeon | 2.34 | 0.65 | 1.28 |
| Ulsan | 5.21 | 2.22 | 3.27 |
| Gyeonggi | 3.68 | 1.00 | 0.95 |
| Gangwon | 2.53 | 0.54 | 0.47 |
| Chungbuk | 3.32 | 0.53 | 0.70 |
| Chungnam | 3.48 | 0.64 | 1.18 |
| Jeonbuk | 2.62 | 0.38 | 0.72 |
| Jeonnam | 3.04 | 0.53 | 0.88 |
| Gyeongbuk | 3.20 | 0.58 | 0.79 |
| Gyeongnam | 4.24 | 0.78 | 0.78 |
| Jeju | 1.83 | 0.51 | 0.61 |
| Country | 3.20 | 0.83 | 1.13 |

on social welfare and those for expenditure on transportation and water resources, the latter are larger than the former for most provinces except Gangwon and Gyeonggi provinces, implying that government spending on transportation and water resources has a larger impact on regional economic growth than spending on social welfare.

## 14.4 Regional Convergence of Per-Capita Income

In this section, we test for $\beta$-convergence on Korean regional provinces to determine whether local fiscal spending reduces the income inequality between regions. The $\beta$-convergence is obtained by a regression analysis that estimates the growth of per-capita income for a certain period of time on the initial level of per capita income. Eq. (14.5) is the basic equation used to test for $\beta$-convergence (see, for example, Barro 1990; Barro and Sala-i-Martin 1991; Mankiw et al. 1992).

$$\frac{1}{T} \times \ln\left(\frac{y_{i,T}}{y_{i,0}}\right) = a + b\ln(y_{i,0}) + u_{i,0,T}. \tag{14.5}$$

In Eq. (14.5), $y_{i,0}$ and $y_{i,T}$ correspond to the per-capita income of region $i$ in the initial and final year, respectively; T is the time length in which the growth of per-capita income is measured; $u_{i,0,T}$ is the stochastic error of the equation; $a$ is the constant term, which (according to neo-classics) is influenced by the rate of technological progress and the steady-state growth rate of per-capita income; and $b(= -[1 - e^{-\beta T}]/T)$ is the parameter to be estimated. If a negative and statistically significant relationship is found between the initial per-capita income and the corresponding growth rate, we can assume the presence of absolute income $\beta$-convergence. That is, if the estimate of $b$ is less than zero (i.e., $b < 0$), then we say that the dataset (the economy) exhibits absolute $\beta$-convergence (Sala-i-Martin 1996). The above equation, which is proposed by Baumol (1986), describes a static model, but it is sufficient to detect the existence of absolute $\beta$-convergence.

However, the abovementioned convergence may be conditional on some region-specific variables. In such a case, Eq. (14.2) must be augmented by a set of conditioning independent variables that specify each region's steady state. If we control for the determinants of the steady state, the results are "conditional convergence"; that is, there is a relation between the growth rate and the initial conditions after controlling for some other variables. A conditional convergence regression equation can be presented as shown in Eq. (14.6):

$$\frac{1}{T} \times \ln\left(\frac{y_{i,T}}{y_{i,0}}\right) = a + b\ln(y_{i,0}) + \gamma Z_{i,t} + u_{i,0,T}, \tag{14.6}$$

where $Z_{i,t}$ is a set of structural exogenous variables that can influence the region's growth in per-capita income and is used as a control variable in the analysis. We examine the $\beta$convergence by distinguishing between absolute convergence and conditional convergence. In this context, Eq. (14.5) is an estimation formula for absolute convergence, whereas Eq. (14.6) is an estimation formula for conditional convergence that includes region-specific control variables. For the empirical analysis, Eq. (14.6) can be modified as follows:

$$\begin{aligned} \ln(\tfrac{y_{i,t+1}}{y_{i,t}}) &= a + b\ln(y_{i,0}) + \gamma_1 \ln(c_{i,t}) + \gamma_2 \ln(s_{i,t}) + \gamma_3 \ln(e_{i,t}) \\ &\quad + \gamma_4 \ln(so_{i,t}) + \gamma_5 \ln(tx_{i,t}) + \gamma_6 \ln(pk_{i,t}) + u_{i,0,T}, \end{aligned} \tag{14.7}$$

where local government spending on education and culture $(c_{i,t})$, social welfare $(s_{i,t})$, regional economy $(e_{i,t})$, and transportation and water resources $(so_{i,t})$, per-capita tax burden $(tx_{i,t})$, and per-capita private capital stocks $(pk_{i,t})$ are included as control variables.

Table 14.6 reports the results obtained from the estimation of Eqs. (14.6) and (14.7) for the period 1986–2014. We have applied both fixed and random effects and GLS (generalized least squares). Columns (1), (3), (5), and (7) of Table 14.6 refer to the equations with only one explanatory variable, namely, the logarithm of income per capita at the beginning of the period. Hence, they show the estimation results for absolute $\beta$convergence. The estimated coefficients of the initial values of per capita GRDP, $y_{i,0}$, lie between 0.073 and 0.044 and are statistically significant at the 1% level, which confirms that the $\beta$-convergence hypothesis regarding per-capita income holds among regions. Columns (2), (4), (6), and (8) add structural exogenous variables

**Table 14.6** Convergence of per-capita income across regions

| | Fixed effects | | Random effects | | Autocorrelation and heteroskedasticity | | Fixed effects, autocorrelation and heteroskedasticity | |
|---|---|---|---|---|---|---|---|---|
| | (1) | (2) | (3) | (4) | (5) | (6) | (7) | (8) |
| $\ln(y_{i,0})$ | −0.066*** | −0.148*** | −0.044*** | −0.100*** | −0.045*** | −0.086*** | −0.073*** | −0.165*** |
| | (−9.24) | (−6.55) | (−7.42) | (−6.37) | (−8.18) | (−6.38) | (−12.12) | (−7.49) |
| Education and culture | | 0.008 | | 0.005 | | .00 | | 0.008 |
| | | (0.88) | | (0.66) | | (0.03) | | (0.99) |
| Social welfare | | −0.005 | | −0.011* | | −0.009* | | −0.003 |
| | | (−0.70) | | (−1.77) | | (−1.73) | | (−0.45) |
| Regional economy | | −0.017*** | | −0.017*** | | −0.014*** | | −0.011*** |
| | | (−3.13) | | (−3.78) | | (−4.07) | | (−2.68) |
| Transportation and water resources | | 0.009 | | 0.010 | | 0.004 | | 0.005 |
| | | (1.02) | | (1.38) | | (0.71) | | (0.63) |
| Share of local tax | | −0.067*** | | −0.057*** | | −0.056*** | | −0.070*** |
| | | (−3.96) | | (−5.59) | | (−6.08) | | (−5.13) |
| Private capital stock | | 0.074*** | | 0.056*** | | 0.048*** | | 0.076*** |
| | | (4.68) | | (4.45) | | (4.31) | | (5.09) |
| Constant | 0.241*** | −0.058 | 0.173*** | −0.106*** | 0.178*** | −0.117*** | 0.278*** | 0.02 |
| | (11.10) | (−0.66) | (9.62) | (−2.63) | (10.63) | (−3.27) | (14.09) | (0.22) |
| $R^2$ | 0.171 | 0.243 | | | | | | |
| F or $\chi^2$ | 85.4*** | 18.8*** | 55.1*** | 128.1*** | 66.9*** | 165.1*** | 181.1*** | 225.8*** |

Note: *** is significant at 1% significance level, ** is at 5%, and * is at 10%

**Table 14.7** Convergence of per-capita income across regions for sub-period

| | Before 2000 | | After 2000 | |
|---|---|---|---|---|
| | GLS | | GLS | |
| | (1) | (2) | (3) | (4) |
| $\ln(y_{i,0})$ | −0.110*** | −0.161*** | −0.016*** | −0.076*** |
| | (−6.78) | (−5.40) | (−3.29) | (−5.61) |
| Education and culture | | 0.010 | | −0.011* |
| | | (0.78) | | (−1.95) |
| Social welfare | | −0.014 | | −0.017*** |
| | | (−1.07) | | (−4.03) |
| Regional economy | | −0.018*** | | −0.002 |
| | | (−3.38) | | (−0.55) |
| Transportation and water resources | | 0.014 | | −0.002 |
| | | (1.04) | | (−0.47) |
| Share of local tax | | −0.052*** | | −0.028*** |
| | | (−3.17) | | (−3.06) |
| Private capital stock | | 0.059*** | | 0.071*** |
| | | (3.30) | | (4.79) |
| Constant | 0.351*** | 0.06 | 0.080*** | −0.149*** |
| | (8.06) | (0.83) | (5.03) | (−3.71) |
| $\chi^2$ | 45.9*** | 87.6*** | 10.8*** | 87.9*** |

Note: *** is significant at 1% significance level, ** is at 5%, and * is at 10%

that can influence the region's growth in per-capita income; that is, they show the estimation results for conditional $\beta$-convergence. The estimated coefficients on $y_{i,0}$ lie between 0.165 and 0.086 and are statistically significant at the 1% level, providing evidence of convergence after controlling for variables that capture differences in government spending on major sectors including per-capita tax burden and per-capita private capital stocks. Additionally, among the estimated coefficients on the control variables, the estimates on social welfare are −0.011 for Column (4) and −0.009 for Column (6), and those on local economy fall between 0.017 and −0.011 for all specifications with statistical significance. It is also estimated that the local tax rate in each region has a negative impact on the region's economic growth rate, while private capital stock has a positive impact.

Table 14.7 shows the GLS estimates in the form of absolute and conditional $\beta$-convergence for 16 Korean provincial regions for two different periods: (1) the first sub-period, 1986–1999, and (3) the second subperiod, 2000–2014. The regression results confirm the convergence hypothesis for all sub-periods, with the estimated coefficients on $y_{i,0}$ being negative and statistically significant (at the 1% significance level), implying that poor regions grow faster in per-capita income than wealthy regions. In addition, the negative relation is stronger in terms of both absolute and conditional convergence for the first sub-period, 1986–1999, suggesting faster cross-region convergence in per-capita income during this period relative to the second period, 2000–2014. Moreover, the coefficient on local tax burden $tx_{i,t}$ is negative, and that on private capital stocks $pk_{i,t}$is positive (both are statistically significant), implying that local tax burden reduces the regional economic growth rate while private capital stock increases the growth rate.

The estimated coefficients of most conditional variables associated with government spending are negative and statistically insignificant, implying that regional government spending does not have a substantial effect on a region's economic growth rate. However, the negative estimates for the coefficients associated with both education and culture (−0.011) and social welfare (−0.017) for the second sub-period, 2000–2014, and the negative estimate for regional economy (−0.018) for the first sub-period, 1986–1999, are statistically significant at either the 5 or 1% level. These results indicate that government spending both on education and culture and on social welfare had a negative impact on the regional growth rate particularly in the second sub-period, while spending on regional economy did so in the first sub-period. Considering that government spending both on education and culture and on social welfare increased sharply in the second sub-period while that on regional economy increased in the first sub-period, the above estimation results imply that expanding government spending does not necessarily accelerate regional economic growth.

## 14.5 Conclusion

We examine the impacts of local government expenditures in four major sectors (i.e., education and culture, social welfare, regional economy, and transportation and water resources) on regional economic growth and per-capita income convergence by exploiting a rich dataset of sectoral regional government expenditures by 16 provinces in Korea during the 1986–2014 period. The dataset includes detailed data on the different components of local government expenditures as well as the private capital stock for 16 provinces in Korea. From the analysis, we have derived several major results.

Of the four sectors, although government expenditure both on education and culture and on transportation and water resources have positive impacts on regional economic growth, the effectiveness of government spending in these two sectors decreased sharply after 2000. On the other hand, when we examine the whole period (1986–2014), there is no concrete evidence to conclude that government spending on both social welfare and regional economy had positive impacts on regional economic growth. However, in contrast to the case of education and culture and the case of transportation and water resources, government expenditures on both social welfare and regional economy showed an improvement in terms of production effectiveness on regional economic growth after 2000.

We can confirm this finding by comparing the multiplier effects. The estimated multiplier is 3.2 for education and culture and 1.13 for transportation and water resources, which are significantly larger than one, implying that expenditures on education and culture and on transportation and water resources by local governments contributed to regional economic growth. However, the average level of the multiplier for social welfare expenditure is 0.83 for the country as a whole, suggesting that government spending on social welfare has been inefficient.

Our empirical analysis shows that the $\beta$-convergence hypothesis regarding per-capita income holds among regions: that is, poor regions grow faster in per-capita income than wealthy regions. In addition, the negative relation is stronger in terms of both absolute and conditional convergence for the first sub-period, 1986–1999, suggesting faster cross-region convergence in per-capita income during this period relative to the second period, 2000–2014. In addition, we found that government spending both on education and culture and on social welfare has a negative impact on the regional growth rate particularly in the second sub-period, while spending on regional economy did so in the first sub-period.

## References

Aschauer, D.A. 1989. Is public expenditure productive? *Journal of Monetary Economics* 23: 177–200.

Barro, R.J. 1990. Government spending in a simple model of economic growth. *Journal of Political Economy* 98: 103–125.

Barro, R.J., and X. Sala-i-Martin. 1991. Convergence across states and regions. *Brookings Papers on Economic Activities* 22 (1): 107–182.

Barro, R.J., and X. Sala-i-Martin. 1995. *Economic Growth*. New York: McGraw-Hill.

Baumol, W.J. 1986. Productivity growth, convergence and welfare: What the long run data show? *American Economic Review* 76: 1072–1085.

Brooks, C., and J. Manza. 2007. *Why Welfare States Persist*. Chicago: University of Chicago Press.

Bruckner, M., and A. Tuladhar. 2010. Public investment as a fiscal stimulus: Evidence from Japan's regional spending during the 1990s. *IMF Working Paper*, No. 110.

Choe, B., and K. Lee. 2014. Local fiscal multiplier and its implication to the restructuring of local expenditure (in Korean). *The Korean Journal of Local Finance* 19 (2): 25–57.

Fleisher, B.M., Y. Hu, H. Li, and S. Kim. 2011. Economic transition, higher education and worker productivity in China. *Journal of Development Economics* 94: 86–94.

Garcia-Milà, T., T.J. McGuire, and R.H. Porter. 1996. The effect of public capital in state-level production functions reconsidered. *Review of Economics and Statistics* 78 (1): 177–180.

Kim, S.S. 2009. The impacts of fiscal policy on economic growth: VAR approach (in Korean). *The Journal of Korean Public Policy* 11 (3): 255–280.

Lee, K., and B. Choe. 2015. Fiscal multiplier of local governments and the implication for local fiscal restructuring (in Korean). *The Korean Journal of Local Government Studies* 19 (2): 299–317.

Lichter, D.T., and R. Jayakody. 2002. Welfare reform: How do we measure success? *Annual Review of Sociology* 28: 117–141.

Lindbeck, A., P. Molander, T. Persson, O. Petersson, A. Sandmos, B. Swedenborg, and N. Thygesen. 1993. Options for economic and political reform in Sweden. *Economic Policy* 8 (17): 219–264.

Lucas, R.E. 1988. On the mechanics of economic development. *Journal of Monetary Economics* 22: 3–42.

Mankiw, N.G., D. Romer, and D. Weil. 1992. A contribution to the empirics of economic growth. *Quarterly Journal of Economics* 107: 407–437.

McCallum, J., and A. Blais. 1987. Government, special interest groups, and economic growth. *Public Choice* 54: 3–18.

McDonald, B.D., and D.R. Miller. 2010. Welfare programs and the state economy. *Journal of Policy Modeling* 32: 719–732.

Moon, S., K. Lee, and B. Choe. 2015. Spatial spillovers of SOC in Korea: The implication for the local fiscal restructuring (in Korean). *The Korea Spatial Planning Review* 84: 55–73.

Oh, B.K. 2006. An evaluation of local public expenditure by using panel data in Korea (in Korean). *The Korean Journal of Local Finance* 11 (2): 5–31.

Oh, B.K. 2014. A dynamic panel analysis on local public investment expenditure with various regional economic variables at South Korea (in Korean). *The Korean Journal of Local Government Studies* 18 (3): 143–164.

Oketch, M.O. 2006. Determinants of human capital formation and economic growth of African countries. *Economics of Education Review* 25: 554–564.

Persson, T., and G. Tabellini. 1994. Is inequality harmful for growth? *American Economic Review* 84 (3): 600–621.

Roh, K.H., C.S. Jung, and S.T. Kim. 1995. Regional economic growth and local public finance in Korea: A dynamic causality analysis (in Korean). *KyongJeHakYonGu* 43 (2): 37–64.

Sala-i-Martin, X. 1996. The classical approach to convergence analysis. *Economic Journal* 106 (437): 1019–1036.

Teixeira, A.A.C., and N. Fortuna. 2004. Human capital, innovation capability and economic growth in Portugal, 1960–2001. *Economic Journal* 3: 205–225.

Wolfe, B.L. 2002. Incentives, challenges, and dilemmas of TANF: A case study. *Journal of Policy Analysis and Management* 21 (4): 577–586.

# Chapter 15
# Remuneration Rule for Employee Inventions, Moral Hazard, and the Hold-Up Problem

**Keiki Kumagae**

## 15.1 Introduction

Under the patent Law of Japan, an inventor has a right to demand the remuneration as monetary compensation for the employee invention (Article 35).[1] If the inventor is dissatisfied with the amount of compensation they have paid, the inventor can file a lawsuit. When the inventor wins the lawsuit, the court can intervene in the level of the remuneration which has been agreed in advance and orders the employer to pay extra profit as a reasonable remuneration. In order to calculate this extra payment, the court takes the amount of profits that the employer will make from the successful invention and the contribution made by the employer and inventor into consideration.[2]

What impact does this intervene in the remuneration by the court have on employer and employee incentives to invent? This problem has been discussed in economics. Ishiguro (2005), Yasaki and Goto (2006) assume that the inventor can claim an extra monetary reward in a court after the outcome from the invention has realized and examine the effect that the right to claim has on the invention incentives of the employee and the employer. The court divides proportionally the outcome from the invention between the two players on the basis of employee's contribution to the success of the invention. They suggest that if the inventor's contribution is rated high by the court, the inventor exerts higher effort because he can get the ex post high remuneration, whereas the employer's investment is too small. Thus, there is

[1]The Japanese employee invention system guarantees the right to patent belongs to the inventor. Thus, when the right is devolved to the employee, the employer needs to pay 'reasonable remuneration'. Inoue (2015) explains the Japanese employee invention system in more detail.
[2]One of the most famous trial is the Nakamura *versus* Nichia Corp case. in this case, Nakamura went to court in order to claim 'reasonable remuneration for blue light-emitting diode technology. As a result, Nichia paid 840 million yen to Nakamura. Mochizuki (2004) gives a detailed description of this case.

K. Kumagae (✉)
Kyushu University, Fukuoka, Japan
e-mail: k.keiki8@gmail.com



M. Hosoe et al. (eds.), *Applied Analysis of Growth, Trade, and Public Policy*,
https://doi.org/10.1007/978-981-13-1876-4_15

a trade-off between the two party's incentive. The problem seems to lie in the fact that we cannot decide whether the intervention by a court is desirable from the view point the amount of incentive.

Yanagawa (2006), Schmitz (2012) study the incentive for research and development in the standard moral hazard framework. The principal needs to give the higher incentive to invent to the agent. Yanagawa (2006) shows that ex post court intervention cannot give a sufficient incentive for investment in R&D. Schmitz (2012) focuses on the hold-up problem in the R&D literature. In particular, when the inventor is protected by limited liability,[3] the inventor's investment for invention which is exerted before the principal offers the reward contracts may be under investment in spite of the strong bargaining power.

Although Yanagawa (2006) and Schmitz (2012) have studied the incentive problem in employee invention with moral hazard model, little attention has been given to the court intervention and the employer investment as an endogenous variable in their model. The present study discusses the effect that the intervention by a court has on the invention incentives of the employee and the employer in a general moral hazard framework. In particular, we put its focus on the existence of the trade-off relationships between two parties' incentive for investment in invention which have been proved by several studies.

The main result presented in this chapter are that when the inventor contribution is sufficiently large, the employee exerts the same effort as the first best levels, while the employer's investment may underinvestment in the case of the intervention by the court. This is because when the contribution is sufficiently large, the employee has strong incentive to take a court action. In the case, the employer pays larger remuneration to prevent a lawsuit and the employer's payoff is decreasing. These conclusions are different from previous studies which have claimed that there is a trade-off between employer's investment and employee's effort.

The organization of this chapter is following. Section 15.2 presents the model and first-best case. Section 15.3 discusses the case with no court intervention as a benchmark. Section 15.4 solves the level of the employer's investment in the case with court intervention and compare it with the investment levels of the first best case. Section 15.5 concludes this paper.

## 15.2 The Model

This model is based on the model presented by Schmitz (2012). We consider an employer and an employee(inventor) as two risk-neutral parties. Their reservation utilities are zero. At date 1, the employer has an project and gathers the information on the research theme by exerting effort $i \in [0, 1]$, which costs $\psi(i)$. We assume $\psi(0) = \psi(0) = 0$, $\psi(i) > 0$, $\psi''(i) > 0$, and $\psi'(i) = \infty$. At date 2, the employer

[3]Schmitz (2012) assumes that limited liability constraints means the rewards to the agent are non-negative.

succeeds in getting good-research-theme with probability $i$ or bad-research-theme with probability $1 - i$. At the same time, the employer can convey this research theme to the employee and makes a take-it-or-leave-it offer to the employee.

At date 3, the employee can exert unobservable effort $e \in \{e_l, e_h\}$, where $0 < e_l < e_h < 1$. $e_h$ is high effort with a personal cost $c > 0$ and denotes the probability that higher outcome $b_G > 0$ will be realized. $e_l$ is low effort with a personal cost zero and denotes the probability that lower outcome $b_l > 0$ will be realized, where $b_G > b_B > 0$. In order to focus the analysis on the most interesting case, we set the following assumption.

**Assumption 15.1** $(e_h - e_l)\, b_B > \frac{e_h}{e_h - e_l} c$

This assumption implies that increment of the surplus when the employee chooses higher effort under bad research theme ($(e_h - e_l)\, b_B$) is sufficiently larger than effort cost. Thus, whichever research theme, higher effort is always desirable for the employer.

At date 4, the employer pays transfer $t_1$ if higher outcome has realized or transfer $t_0$if lower outcome has realized. We assume the limited liability constraints $t_1,\ t_0 \geqslant 0$ because the employee does not have the initial assets.

At date 5, we assume the employee decides whether to file a lawsuit for the extra profit when the employee exerts high effort, $e_h$, and higher outcome has realized, $b_G$. One of the reasons is dissatisfaction with the employee. In particular, we consider the inventors are dissatisfied with treatment for successful inventions when they work hard.

We introduce the simple court intervention model in the same manner as Ishiguro (2005), Yasaki and Goto (2006). When the employee takes a court action, the court can intervene in the contract of remuneration for employee invention and divides proportionally the outcome from the invention between the two players on the basis of employee's contribution, $\lambda \in (0,\ 1)$, to the success of the invention. For simplicity, $\lambda$ is common knowledge given the sentences handed down in similar in the past. Without loss of generality, we assume that lawsuits costs are zero and the probability of winning lawsuit is one.

For simplicity, we assume interior solutions and set the following assumption.

**Assumption 15.2** $(1 - \lambda) b_G > b_B$

This assumption implies that the employer's profit divided by the court, $(1 - \lambda) b_G$, is sufficiently large than that under the bad research theme.

**First Best Benchmark**

We assume that $e$ is contractible to solve the first best $i^{FB}$. Assumption 15.1 ensures that the employer gives the employee incentive to exert high effort instead of low effort. At date 1, the employer decides $i$ to maximize the following joint profit:

$$i\,(e_h b_G - c) + (1 - i)\,(e_h b_B - c) - \psi(i) \qquad (15.1)$$

Following first-order condition must hold:

$$e_h b_G - e_h b_B - \psi^{'}(i) = 0.$$

Thus,[4]

$$\psi^{'}\left(i^{FB}\right) = e_h(b_G - b_B). \tag{15.2}$$

We can see that $i^{FB}$ is increasing when the increment of expected payoffs under good research theme is larger.

## 15.3 The Case with No Court Intervention

### *15.3.1 Optimal Contracts*

The employer makes the offer $(t_1 t_0)$ to the employee at date 2 based on the outcome $b = b_G$ or $b_B$. The employer solves the following problem:

$$\max_{t_1, t_0} e_h (b - t_1) - (1 - e_h) t_0$$

subject to,

$$e_h t_1 + (1 - e_h) t_0 - c \geqslant 0, \tag{IR}$$

$$e_h t_1 + (1 - e_h) t_0 - c \geqslant e_l t_1 + (1 - e_l) t_0, \tag{IC}$$

$$t_1, t_0 \geqslant 0. \tag{LL}$$

The employer's objective is to design the contract in order to maximize his expected payoff from this R&D project. (IR) is the individual rationality constraint of the employee. The left-hand side is the employee's expected payoff and the right-hand side is his reservation utility. (IC) is the incentive compatibility constraint to give the employee the incentive to exert high effort. This equation means that the employee's expected payoff under high effort is larger than that under low effort. The employer offers $(t_1, t_0)$ that satisfies (IC). (LL) implies limited liability constraint.[5]

We solve the problem in the same way as Shmitz (2012). It is easy to see that (IC) and $t_0 \geqslant 0$ binds and (IR) is not binding. It means the existence of limited liability leaves positive information rent to the employee.

Let $t_1^{NC}$, $t_0^{NC}$ denote the optimal transfers when the case with no court intervention and $W^{NC}$, $U^{NC}$ the employer's expected payoff and the employee's expected payoff respectively. We index the solution to above problem with superscript "NC" meanings No Court. We have the following Lemma 15.1.

---

[4] $i^{FB}$ is interior solution because of the convex function $\psi$.

[5] Schmitz (2012) focuses on the influence that limited liability has on the optimal contract.

**Lemma 15.1** *The optimal contracts and the players' expected payoffs in the case with no court intervention are following:*

$$t_1^{NC} = \frac{c}{e_h - e_l},\ t_0^{NC} = 0,\ W^{NC} = e_h \left[ b - \frac{c}{e_h - e_l} \right],\ U^{NC} = \frac{e_l c}{e_h - e_l}.$$

### *15.3.2 The Optimal Employee's Effort Level*

We get $i^{SB}$ as the second best solutions which maximize the expected payoff of the employer at date 1 through the first order approach. The expected payoff of the employer at date 1 is

$$ie_h \left( b_G - \frac{c}{e_h - e_l} \right) + (1 - i)\, e_h \left( b_B - \frac{c}{e_h - e_l} \right) - \psi(i)$$

Thus,

$$\psi'(i^{SB}) = e_h(b_G - b_B). \tag{15.3}$$

This implies second best effort level equals to the first best effort level ($i^{SB} = i^{FB}$) and the there is no hold-up problem. This is because, in this model, we assume that the employer has all bargaining power and can offer take-it-or-leave-it contract.

## 15.4 The Case with Court Intervention

In this section, we consider the case where the court intervention is possible under Article 35. When the inventor goes to court, the court orders the employee to pay the reasonable remuneration. It is calculated using the employer's contribution to success invention, $\lambda$, and the outcome from the invention, $b_G$. Furthermore, like Yasaki and Goto (2006), the employer pays the reward which is paid when the invention fails to the inventor in the court. Thus, the employee gets $\lambda b_G + t_0$ when he files a suit.

### *15.4.1 Optimal Contracts*

In this paper, like in the model setting in Yasaki and Goto (2006), we restrict the contracts to prevent the employee's court action[6]:

$$t_1 - c \geqslant \lambda b_G + t_0 - c. \tag{NCA}$$

[6]We can consider the case where to get tangled up in legal action by the inventor costs the employer much time, court costs and a high reputation.

In particular, the right-hand side is the payoff when the employee takes a court action. This equation means that if the employee's contribution, $\lambda$, gets bigger, the employee has strong incentive going to court. In this case, the employer must pay the higher reward to successful invention, $t_1$, in order to prevent the employee from filling a lawsuit.

We add the employer's problem in the last section to (NCA). The modified problem is, therefore,

$$\max_{t_1, t_0} e_h (b_G - t_1) - (1 - e_h) t_0$$

subject to,

$$e_h t_1 + (1 - e_h) t_0 - c \geqslant 0, \quad \text{(IR*)}$$
$$e_h t_1 + (1 - e_h) t_0 - c \geqslant e_l t_1 + (1 - e_l) t_0, \quad \text{(IC*)}$$
$$t_1 - c \geqslant \lambda b_G + t_0 - c, \quad \text{(NCA)}$$
$$t_1, t_0 \geqslant 0. \quad \text{(LL)}$$

It is easy to see that when (LL) and (IC*) (or (NCA)) is satisfied, (IR*) must satisfy. Furthermore, $t_0 \geqslant 0$ and (IC*) (or (NCA)) will satisfy $t_1 \geqslant 0$. In this case, we find that $t_0 \geqslant 0$ is binding.

Then, equation (IC*) can be written as

$$e_h t_1 + (1 - e_h) t_0 - c \geqslant e_l t_1 + (1 - e_l) t_0$$
$$\leftrightarrow t_1 \geqslant t_0 + \frac{c}{e_h - e_l}$$

Equation (NCA) can be written as

$$t_1 \geqslant t_0 + \lambda b_G$$

We substitute (IC*) and (NCA) for $t_0 = 0$ and get the following constraints. Therefore, the employer's problem is then:

$$e_h (b_G - t_1) - (1 - e_h) t_0$$

subject to,

$$t_1 \geqslant \frac{c}{e_h - e_l}, \quad \text{(IC*)}$$
$$t_1 \geqslant \lambda b_G \quad \text{(NCA)}$$

We can see that whether (IC*) or (NCA) is binding or not is dependent on the value of $\lambda$. We index the solution to this problem with superscript (A,B) meanings each case A or B. These conclusions are recorded in Lemma 15.2.

**Lemma 15.2** *The optimal contracts and the players' expected payoffs in the case with court intervention are following:*

*Case A* $\left(0 < \lambda < \frac{c}{b_G(e_h - e_l)}\right)$: $t_0 \geqslant 0$ *and* (IC*) *is bind.*

$$t_1^A = \frac{c}{e_h - e_l},\ t_0^A = 0,\ W^A = e_h\left[b_G - \frac{c}{e_h - e_l}\right],\ U^A = \frac{e_l c}{e_h - e_l}$$

*Case B* $\left(\frac{c}{b_G(e_h - e_l)} \leqslant \lambda < 1\right)$ : $t_0 \geqslant 0$ *and* (NCA) *is bind.*

$$t_1^B = \lambda b_G,\ t_0^B = 0,\ W^B = e_h(1 - \lambda)b_G,\ U^B = e_h \lambda b_G.$$

The intuition is simple. In case B where $\lambda$ is sufficiently large, (NCA) is binding because the extra profit from a lawsuit is bigger and the employee has strong incentive to take a court action. Then, the employer pays larger remuneration to prevent a lawsuit ($t_1^B \geqslant t_1^A$).[7] Thus, the employer's expected payoff, $W^B$, is a decreasing function of $\lambda$. This employee's contribution, $\lambda$, is interpreted as the bargaining power of the employee. Thus, the right to demand the remuneration as monetary compensation for the employee invention under the patent Law of Japan raises the reward for successful invention.

In case A where $\lambda$ is sufficiently small, (IC*) is binding instead of (NCA). Then, the optimal contracts are the same as the case with no court intervention because (NCA) does not have an effect on the optimal contract.

### 15.4.2 The Optimal Employee's Effort Level

Now we consider the optimal employee's information gathering effort at the date 1. Let $i^A$, $i^B$ denote the optimal effort levels in each case A or B.

*Case A:* $0 < \lambda < \frac{c}{b_G(e_h - e_l)}$

As previously mentioned, the optimal contracts are same as the case of no court intervention in this case A. Thus, the expected payoff of the employer at date 1 is

$$ie_h\left(b_G - \frac{c}{e_h - e_l}\right) + (1 - i)e_h\left(b_B - \frac{c}{e_h - e_l}\right) - \psi(i)$$

Hence, we get

$$i^A = i^{SB} = i^{FB}$$

[7]This results are shown by Yasaki and Goto (2006), Muramoto (2016).

*Case B:* $\frac{c}{b_G(e_h-e_l)} \leqslant \lambda < 1$

Note that the objective function under good research theme is $W^B$ in Lemma 15.2. The employer's expected payoff at date 1 is

$$ie_h W^B + (1-i)\,e_h\left(b_B - \frac{c}{e_h - e_l}\right) - \psi(i)$$

$$\leftrightarrow\; ie_h(1-\lambda)b_G + (1-i)\,e_h\left(b_B - \frac{c}{e_h - e_l}\right) - \psi(i).$$

Following first-order condition must hold:

$$e_h(1-\lambda)b_G - e_h\left(b_B - \frac{c}{e_h - e_l}\right) - \psi'(i) = 0.$$

Thus,[8]

$$\psi'\left(i^B\right) = e_h\left[(b_G - b_B) + \frac{c}{e_h - e_l} - \lambda b_G\right]$$

This first-order condition implies that the employee's investment level is the decreasing function of the contribution, $\lambda$. This is because $W^B$ is decreasing function of the contribution according to Lemma 15.2.

Next, we make a comparison between their efforts in the case where a court can intervene in the level of remuneration contracts and first best effort. For simple calculation, we can establish the following proposition.

**Proposition 15.1** *When the court intervene in the level of remuneration, only the employee's investment can be underinvestment (Case B).*

*Case A* $0 < \lambda < \frac{c}{b_G(e_h\ e_l)}$*: The employer's investment incentive is same as the level of first best,* $i^A = i^{FB}$.

*Case B* $\frac{c}{b_G(e_h-e_l)} \leqslant \lambda < 1$ *The employer's investment incentive is less than the level of first best,* $i^B \leqslant i^{FB}$.

The intuition is as follows. As described in Lemma 15.2, the contract in the case A is same as the case of no intervention by the court. Hence, the employer exerts the same levels of effort as first best case. On the other hand, in the case B, the higher remuneration decreases the employer's payoff under good research theme because (NCA) constraint is binding. Thus, the employer exerts less investment than the levels of first best. Japanese company managers often claim that the intervention by the court prevents the firm managers from investing sufficiently in R&D. This result

[8] Assumption 15.2 guarantees that the right-hand side is positive. Therefore, $i^B$ is an interior solution from the assumption of the cost function, $\psi$.

may support the claim. Note that the employer induces the employee to choose high effort because the employer wants to keep high expected payoff.

We can conclude that only the employer's effort levels may decrease compared to the first best levels. These conclusions are different from previous studies. This is because unlike Ishiguro (2005) and Yasaki and Goto (2006), we consider the intervention by the court with moral hazard where the employer gives the employer an incentive to exert effort in this paper.

## 15.5 Concluding Remarks

In this chapter, when the court intervenes in the contract in a firm under Article 35, we consider the effect that the intervention has on the invention incentives of the employee and the employer with moral hazard and incomplete contract model. As a result, when the contribution is sufficiently large, the employee exerts the same effort as the first best levels, while the employer's investment may underinvestment in the case of the intervention by the court. These conclusions are different from Ishiguro (2005), Yasaki and Goto (2006) which have claimed that there is a trade-off between employer's investment and employee's effort.

Some interesting avenues remain for future research. This model does not focus on how the court calculates employee's contribution. In this paper, we assume the employee's contribution is given for simplicity. However, in fact, the court calculates it taking the extent of their effort levels, the ability of the inventor and so on. Like Yasaki and Goto (2006), we will consider the extension model where the employee's contribution is endogenous variables. Therefore, in this model, Japanese employee invention rules may not be desirable in terms of the firm management's incentive in R&D.

Furthermore, inventors seem to have strong intrinsic motivation to invent surprising technology, new method helping society and so on. The employer must design the contract in light of these facts. Nagaoka et al. (2014) says that inventors' intrinsic motivation and extrinsic motivation are complementary each other and the firm management needs to take intrinsic motivation into consideration. In this paper, we only focus on the employee's extrinsic motivation as pecuniary reward. Like Kumagae (2017, 2018), we can introduce intrinsically motivated workers in this model. These tasks are left as subjects for future research.

## References

Inoue, Y. 2015. Heisei 27 nen Shokumu-hatsumei seido kaisei nituiteno iti kosatsu. *Tokkyo Kenkyu* 60: 18–27.

Ishiguro, S. 2005. Shokumu-Hatusmei no Keizaibunseki -Keiyakurironteki Sekkin. *Nihon Rodo Kenkyu Zasshi* 541: 24–33.

Kumagae, K. 2017. Joho shushu moderu niokeru Naihatutekidoki wo motu Rodosha heno Saiteki keiyaku. *Oyo Keizaigaku Kenkyu* 11: 35–54.
Kumagae, K. 2018. Optimal task design for intrinsically motivated workers with an incomplete contract. *Journal of National Development* 31 (1): 29–38.
Mochizuki, S. 2004. Aoiro Hakko Daiodo Tokkyo Jiken no iti kosatsu. *Patento* 57: 41–49.
Muramoto, A. 2016. Shokumuhatumei-Seido no Keizai bunseki -Kenkyu Kaihatsu Insenthibu to Taika -Seikyu-Sosho niyoru Keizai Sonshitu no Kantenkara(Economic analysis on employee invention system from the viewpoint of R & D incentive and welfare loss arising from lawsuit against for remuneration for invention (In Japan)). *TizaiKen Kiyo* 25: 1–7.
Nagaoka, S., Owan, H. and Onishi, K. 2014. Hatumeisha heno Insenthibu sekkei: Riron to Jissho, RIETI discussion paper series, 14-J-044, 1–58.
Schmitz, P.W. 2012. The hold-up problem, innovations, and limited liability. *Economics Letters* 117: 841–843.
Yanagawa, N. 2006. Ho to Kigyo-Kodo no Keizaibunseki, Nihon Keizai Shinbunsha.
Yasaki, Y., and A. Goto. 2006. Contribution-proportional remuneration rule for employee inventions and its effects on effort and investment incentives. *Economics of Innovation and New Technology* 15 (7): 665–678.

Printed by Printforce, the Netherlands